# Kids, Drugs,
and Crime

# Kids, Drugs, and Crime

Cheryl Carpenter
Syracuse University

Barry Glassner
University of Connecticut

Bruce D. Johnson
New York State Division of Substance Abuse Services
and Narcotic and Drug Research, Inc.

Julia Loughlin
Syracuse University

**Lexington Books**
*D.C. Heath and Company/Lexington, Massachusetts/Toronto*

This study was funded by a research agreement program (80-IJ-CX-0049-S2) to Narcotic and Drug Research, Inc., by the National Institute of Justice, U.S. Department of Justice, under the Omnibus Crime Control and Safe Streets Act of 1968, as amended.

Additional support was provided by the New York State Division of Substance Abuse Services, Narcotic and Drug Research, Inc., and Syracuse University through the Department of Sociology and Health Studies Program.

Points of view or opinions in this document do not represent the official position or policies of the U.S. government, the New York State Division of Substance Abuse Services, Narcotic and Drug Research, Inc., or Syracuse University.

*Library of Congress Cataloging-in-Publication Data*

Kids, drugs, and crime.

Bibliography: p.
Includes index.
1. Youth—United States—Drug use. 2. Drug abuse and crime—United States.
3. Juvenile delinquency—United States. I. Carpenter, Cheryl Jan.
HV5824.Y68K52    1988        364.3'6'0973        86-45634
ISBN 0-669-14098-8 (alk. paper)

Published simultaneously in Canada
Printed in the United States of America
Casebound International Standard Book Number: 0-669-14098-8
Library of Congress Catalog Card Number: 86-45634

The paper used in this publication meets the minimum requirements of American National Standard for Information Sciences—Permanence of Paper for Printed Library Materials, ANSI Z39.48-1984. ∞™

89 90 91 92 8 7 6 5 4 3

# Contents

Tables   vii

Acknowledgments   ix

1. Introduction   1

2. Research Methods and Respondent Characteristics   15

3. Adolescents' Perspectives on the Relationship between Drugs/Alcohol and Crime   27

4. Drug Selling and Dealing among Adolescents   39
   With Erica Wood

5. Theft and the Consumeristic Mentality   61

6. The Context of Violence   87

7. Delinquents' Perspectives on the Role of the Victim   103
   With Margret Ksander

8. Case Studies of Youths at Risk in Early Adolescence   119

9. Case Studies of Seriously Involved Youths   145
   With Margret Ksander and Mary F. Stuck

10. Experimentation versus Commitment   187
    With Margret Ksander and Bruce Berg

11. The Deterrent Effect of Adult versus Juvenile Jurisdiction   209
    With Margret Ksander and Bruce Berg

12. Summary and Conclusion   219

References   225

Index   237

About the Authors   245

# Tables

2–1. Comparison of Characteristics of Yule City and New York State Urban Areas   16

2–2. Drug Use Levels in Yule City Region and Statewide (Students Enrolled in Grades 7–12, Spring 1978)   18

2–3. Characteristics of the Yule City Samples   20

2–4. Percentage of Youths in Random, Purposive, and Detained Samples, by Crime Type and Drug User Type   22

2–5. Criminal Involvement by Drug Use and Age   23

2–6. Criminal Involvement by Sex and Ethnicity   23

5–1. Type of Theft by Sex and Drug User Types   84

6–1. Percentage of Subjects Reporting Experience of Violent Events, by Type of Drug Use   90

6–2. Percentage of Subjects Reporting Involvement in Violent Events, by Type of Drug Use   90

# Acknowledgments

The National Institute of Justice provided long-term funding for an Interdisciplinary Research Center for the Study of the Relations of Drugs and Alcohol to Crime. The continuing interest of the NIJ director, James Stewart, and project officer, Bernard Gropper, made completion of this research possible. Several persons at the New York State Division of Substance Abuse Services and Narcotic and Drug Research, Inc., were consistently supportive: Julio Martinez, Norwig Debye-Saxinger, David Diamond, Douglas S. Lipton, Hugh Schrader, Marion Ludlum, Valarie Murphy, Robert Bosman, and Eric Wish. Ann Brunswick, Patrick O'Malley, Robin Room, and Terry Williams served as members of the Interdisciplinary Research Center's advisory board.

Several individuals contributed to this study over the years. Guthrie Birkhead and Claire Rudolf supported this project from its initiation forward. Bruce Berg, Margret Ksander, and Mary Stuck were with the study from its earliest stages of research and analysis. Margret and Bruce were talented and sensitive field-workers and interviewers. Mary supervised the initial coding of the data with skill and patience. Margret, Bruce, and Mary, along with Erica Wood, have made significant contributions to this book as data analysts and writers. Nelson Pardee provided the computer-programming skills necessary for handling 20,000 pages of data without compromising the richness of the data. We are also grateful to Rosa Diaz and Celia Kamps for their assistance. Secretarial services were provided by Barbara Cico, Ruthe Kassel, Virginia Rampant, Nancy Meggett, Jacqueline Coward, Ana Santana, and Connie Ross. Without these people and their excellent work, this book would not have been possible. We are grateful for their help and support.

# 1
# Introduction

*Gallo*

*"I'm an average person. I like doing what I do. Getting stoned and working on cars. That's my life."*

Marijuana was an integral part of Gallo's day and his self-identity as a "cool drug-using hippie." He smoked three joints before leaving for school, another two on the way to school, and one in each break between classes. With a retinue of friends, he went home after school and used another dozen joints before bedtime. If he had money, he routinely consumed beer or his favorite wine (after which he was nicknamed). His weekends were devoted to "partying"; consuming extensive amounts of alcohol and marijuana were the main activities.

Gallo began dealing drugs after a carefully planned auto theft and burglary of an adult dealer netted him fifty pounds of marijuana. He was well known to local marijuana users as a consistent supplier. After school, other youths went to his house to purchase marijuana; if the weather was good, he hung out at the park selling marijuana. Gallo reports a particular drug sale episode where he shot a potential purchaser who tried to avoid paying for a kilogram of marijuana.

In addition to his extensive use of marijuana and alcohol, Gallo had tried almost every drug except heroin, but his consumption of such substances was limited. At an earlier age, Gallo had been a regular user of speed, but he didn't like the effects and stopped using it. He had also tried selling speed but found that it didn't pay.

Gallo always managed to keep his intensive drug use under control and to conceal his serious criminality from the law, although he had had brushes with the police. Such control and savvy were important aspects of the "cool" image that was so important to him. At age 17, Gallo had clear goals for his adult years. He planned to enter the military after graduating from high school, and to return after his term was up to open his own auto shop.

*Kevin*

*"I'll tell you, this is true, [I] had a lot of fun. I really did. I had a lot of fun, but it's not worth it in the long run, it isn't. You're just screwing yourself over, you go nowhere fast. Usually, you think you're going somewhere, but you don't know where, and you don't care."*

Kevin began committing delinquent acts in elementary school and started using marijuana at age 13; his involvement quickly became very extensive. He began consuming marijuana daily, started using psychedelic drugs, skipped school, and committed burglaries for which he had been arrested several times by the age of 14. He was sent to a youth camp and detention home, which, he says, did little to change his behavior. After his release, he drank and used marijuana daily and also took prescription drugs (barbiturates and Valium) and cocaine. He sold marijuana and cocaine regularly, and overdosed on pills and alcohol.

In retrospect, Kevin believes that he lost control of his drug use. He sees his drug use as directly related to an increase in the severity and frequency of his criminal behavior and to the deterioration of his familial relationships.

At age 20, Kevin entered a drug treatment program with the support of a girlfriend and his family and under criminal justice pressure. At the time of the interview, Kevin described himself as rehabilitated from both drug abuse and crime. Now he hoped to make a new life for himself, his girlfriend, and the child they were expecting.

*Norris*

*"What do they usually fight about? About me. Most, um, my mother thinks it's my father's fault, 'cause I got in trouble, and my father thinks it's her fault. So I get in trouble."*

Norris was 13 years old when interviewed at the local juvenile detention facility where he was serving 12 to 18 months for an auto theft and awaiting sentence for a second set of charges: car theft, burglary, and the use of an unauthorized ID.

Norris reported having a difficult relationship with his divorced parents; he had run away from home four times. He remembers elementary school as a time when he was "always getting into trouble" for being late and skipping school. He failed the seventh grade twice because he seldom went to class. His friends introduced him to marijuana at his twelfth birthday party, to prescription drugs shortly afterwards, and then to "mushrooms" on his thirteenth birthday. He also engaged in delinquencies (such as auto theft, theft, and property destruction) with his friends. He used marijuana and alcohol mainly at parties and when he was with friends. He was interested in using speed and also planned to try cocaine in the future. Before his arrest, Norris attempted to give up his crime and drug involvements by staying away from his heavily involved peers, but his new peer group was also involved in partying and other activities considered deviant.

When asked about the future, Norris said he saw himself as avoiding trouble and reaching a time when he would not have to steal for money. He felt, in fact, that he would "have to" give up such acts, for, as an adult, he would be held responsible for his actions.

*Elizabeth*

*"After I stole those records I didn't do it for a long time. Then my friends started doing it. Only little things mostly . . . just like necklaces. Little things. . . . Everybody does it."*

Elizabeth, a 13-year-old female, describes her childhood as one marked by frequent moves that meant leaving friends and changing schools. She was happy to be settled now with her widowed mother and her younger sister. Elizabeth describes her relationship with her mother as extremely close and positive, but she now preferred the company of friends and would disobey her mother in order to be with them. Elizabeth enjoyed school but liked being with friends more than going to class. Her first experiences with both cigarette smoking and drinking were with her friends, but she drank only once. She had no specific reasons for not drinking more and envisioned drinking in moderation when she or her friends were old enough to drink alcohol legally.

Although a few of Elizabeth's friends had used marijuana, she had not. Her reason for not trying marijuana was that she didn't like smoking but she did see marijuana smoking as an activity she would do with friends sometime in the future. She punctuated her statements about the future, however, with comments about people who were involved with marijuana and how she had "no desire to try it." She said she didn't like drug-using groups and, for that reason, kept her distance from them socially.

Members of Elizabeth's peer group, however, were involved in minor criminal activities. The females shoplifted, the males stole hubcaps and bicycles. Elizabeth admitted to committing several petty thefts, particularly shoplifting of minor items. She was once apprehended for shoplifting, which influenced her to stop for a while. She, however, did not see shoplifting as deviant, stating that everyone does it, nor did she view it as necessarily wrong. Elizabeth is vague about her future, but she does know that it will be filled with time spent among friends.

---

The four youths just introduced (whose case studies appear in chapters 8 and 9) spent their adolescent years in a typical middle-American city, which has been given the pseudonym of Yule City. Their community is socially and economically diverse, and the schools are well integrated. The local junior high school is considered one of the best in the state. The local high school is new and well stocked with equipment for band, athletics, science, and other subject areas and activities. Yet using drugs and engaging in delinquency are common among Yule City adolescents. Moreover, a number of studies have clearly demonstrated that these behaviors are common among adolescents in virtually every town, village, and city in the United States, among whites and blacks, among males and females, and among youths of all socioeconomic backgrounds. This book is about Gallo, Kevin, Norris, Elizabeth, and youths like them, and their drug use and criminal involvement. Like many others who study adolescents and delinquency, we began our study curious about how and why kids become involved in drug use and crime. We were particularly interested in investigating a line of questioning that had been present in the literature for several years: the question of the relationship between drug and alcohol use and crime.

Unlike many others who have investigated these questions, we undertook our study with the conviction that listening to adolescents is essential to the study of juvenile delinquency. By *listening* we mean more than the use of a technique. Listening is part and parcel of what Matza (1969) refers to as appreciation, what others have called *verstehen* (Truzzi, 1974), or what Becker (1966) most succinctly describes in the following quote as putting oneself in another's skin.

> By putting ourselves in Stanley's skin we can feel and become aware of the deep biases about such people that ordinarily permeate our thinking and the shape of the kinds of problems we investigate. By truly entering into Stanley's life, we can begin to see what we take for granted (and ought not to) in designing our research—what kinds of assumptions about delinquents, slums, and Poles are embedded in the way we set the questions we study. Stanley's story allows us if we want to take advantage to begin to ask questions about delinquency from the point of view of the delinquent. (Becker, Introduction to Shaw, 1930; 1966 edition:15)

Listening gives us a glimpse of adolescent behavior from the adolescents' point of view. In doing so, Becker (1966) points out, it enables us to ask important and often neglected questions about delinquents and delinquency. In addition, we believe that listening facilitates addressing questions that permeate the literature from a rarely, if ever, investigated "inside" view.

Our emphasis on listening and our way of defining it is intimately tied to our assumptions and goals regarding the study of social phenomena like kids, drugs, and crime. The theoretical position that, as Bogdan and Taylor (1975:1) put it, "guides our research and embodies our assumptions," is a product of a theoretical tradition loosely referred to as *interactionism* (Burgess, 1984).

Along with other interactionists, we believe that studying situations involving humans is radically different from studying nonhuman contexts. Therefore, it is imperative that we adjust our stance toward our human data as well as the modes by which we collect and analyze our data.

> The human scene exhibits special properties in addition to those which might be attributed to nonhuman contexts. These properties indicate a different order of thinking about [persons] and about studying [them]. (Schatzman and Strauss, 1973:2)

According to interactionists, human action is a product of how persons define their world. Humans have the ability to present themselves with definitions that become conditions for their actions (Schatzman and Strauss, 1973). Because people act on the basis of these definitions and interpretations, a necessary step in understanding human behavior is to have a sense of what these definitions—their perspectives—consist of (Blumer, 1969).

Perspectives are not products of individual psychology; they are social in origin, rooted in experience, the result of innumerable situations in which a social actor interacts with others. Social interaction necessarily involves entering one's biography into the interplay of context, nonverbal communication, and linguistic exchange with others doing the same (Schwartz and Jacobs, 1979).

Interactionists argue that experience is related to one's perspective. Thus, social actors may interpret the same object, event, or activity differently because each brings a unique biography to the situation. Common experience, however, may result in shared perspective. Bogdan and Taylor elaborate:

> Situations, or aspects of situations (the actor her- or himself, other actors), come to be defined in different ways by different participants for a number of reasons. One reason is that each actor brings with her or him a past and a certain way of interpreting what he or she sees. . . . Since actors in a similar position generally have opportunities to communicate with one another, they may develop shared definitions of a particular situation or a category of similar situations. Sometimes definitions and meanings are shared with new members by occupants of a position. Whatever the case, the phrase *shared perspective* refers to a definition of a situation which a number of actors hold. (Bogdan and Taylor, 1975:15)

Others who study kids, drugs, and crime hypothesize that certain attitudinal variables are somehow related to drug use and criminal involvement behavioral variables. Such studies consist of testing the hypothesized relationships. Rarely do such studies give us a sense of the fullness of one's point of view, how it is acquired, and how its connection may get played out in drug or crime episodes.

Although persons who work with or study youths may undertake a considerable amount of interaction with them, they are often isolated from how kids perceive the world around them and how youths' perceptions may influence their actions. Much of what has been done, though valuable for telling us some things, is limited in terms of what it can tell us about kids' day-to-day experience. Most studies begin with theories and employ data-gathering techniques such as experiments or surveys, which remove us from the experience and perception of kids. Such data are not designed to elaborate on how kids live their lives and confront choices about drug use and criminal involvement; we learn little about their experiences or what the drug/crime event involves. Policies are based on data so far removed from the experiences of those they wish to address, that they have little potential for effecting change.

> Although there are a great many studies of delinquency . . . very few tell us in detail what a juvenile delinquent does in his daily round of activity and what he thinks about himself, society, and his activities. . . . [O]ne consequence [of this deficiency] is the construction of faulty or inadequate theories. Just as

we need precise anatomical description of animals before we can begin to theorize and experiment with their physiological and biochemical function, just so we need precise and detailed descriptions of social anatomy before we know just what phenomena are present to theorize about. . . . (Becker, quoted in Matza, 1969:39)

If we are interested in prevention, we need to know how and why kids become involved in drug use and crime—or decide not to do so. We need to know which everyday situations and/or life circumstances are conducive to avoidance and which to involvement. Harvey Feldman, a seasoned ethnographer of drug users, made this point in an address to policymakers.

What we shall need is a kind of antenna that stretches into the streets and hang-outs of young people so that we can collect accurate information on how those drugs are being used, what adverse reactions they cause, and all the other pieces of information that are part and parcel of planning treatment, prevention, or education efforts *that are somehow connected to the realities of users themselves*. It strikes me that if we had identified the negative aspects of PCP as they were seen on the street early enough, our protective methods might have emphasized that "burning out"—the development of a spacey, hesitant, foggy, forgetful condition—was the feature of PCP that users found distressing and the violence that many experts associated with its use was *not* a key issue for PCP users on the streets. In fact, in our own ethnographic study, violence was an infrequent occurrence. Using violence as the touchstone for a preventive approach simply had no power of dissuasion among the street populations who used PCP. Each time those of us in policy making positions employ not simply fear tactics, but fear tactics that have a frail factual base, we lose credibility among the audience whose behavior we wish to influence. (Feldman, 1980:5; emphasis added)

Taking the perspectives of adolescents seriously may help us understand their behaviors. Adolescents know best what their lives are like. They are also observers of those around them. We treat them not as objects of inquiry but as expert informants (Spradley, 1979) about drug use, criminal involvement, and other aspects of adolescents' lives. This is the best information we can provide for persons who do not have direct access to the experiences of adolescents (Nash and Spradley, 1976).

Such an approach is also a more dynamic view of delinquency than other approaches that focus on the correlation of factors such as attitudes and behaviors. Our focus on perspectives directed our research away from factors to processes. Becker (1963:176) outlined one of the goals in studying perspectives as "the study of the processes by which perspectives are built up and maintained." The process by which perspectives are abandoned and replaced is also of great importance in the study of drug use and criminal involvement. Understanding this process helps us understand how youths move from involvement to noninvolvement or vice versa. It also helps us understand how and why youths' choices to engage in drug use/crime may vary by situation.

Listening is not completed by theory. It mandates an orientation toward collecting and analyzing data as well as toward the research–respondent relationship. We discuss our research methods at length in chapter 2. In the following section we will briefly outline our methodological approach.

## Design for Listening

Our strategies for listening include a year of fieldwork among youths living in an economically, socially, and racially mixed neighborhood. During this time field-workers became well acquainted with many youths, their schools, their hangouts, and their rounds of activities. It was through this fieldwork phase that youths were identified for subsequent interviews. After the youths (with their parents' or guardians' consent) agreed to participate in the interview phase of the study, they were interviewed by one of the field-workers. The interview guide was structured–open-ended (Denzin, 1978) with a life history format (Carey, 1968) and conducted in the language of the youths.

Structured–open-ended interviews consist of set questions and probes to guide the interview and to guarantee a measure of comparability of the data across respondents. The open-ended nature of the questions, however, provided an additional structure that invited the respondents to give answers in their own terms, unlimited by the interview or the interviewer. The open-endedness also allowed the interviewer to probe if the youth brought up or suggested something of interest or did not fully explain an action, event, or orientation. Through the use of the structured–open-ended interview format, we were able to ask the kinds of questions we sought to address about drug use and crime among adolescents. Informed by their fieldwork experiences, the field-workers were able to conduct the interviews in the youths' own terms and with high levels of rapport. Structuring the interviews in these ways placed the youths in the role of informants—persons who could inform the researcher about their life activities, interactions, behaviors, thoughts, and feelings.

In analyzing the interview data, we used a qualitative inductive approach (Bogdan and Biklen, 1982; Glaser and Strauss, 1967). This approach grounds analysis in the youth's experiences and perspectives. Very simply, for any given topic, we located all statements in the transcripts about the topic and sorted such statements according to emergent themes. Those themes then became the basis of the analytic narrative for a chapter. Analysis, here, is a form of presenting youths' perspectives in the richness and complexity of their own stories, in contrast to reducing their experiences and beliefs to variables or factors whose meanings are determined by hypotheses conceived separate from the data collected. This is not to say that the analyst's thinking never enters. As much as possible, the social scientists's modes of thinking enter primarily when the researcher seeks to tell the youths' stories to an audience with a different language and culture. Through the use of these strategies, we created the literal and conceptual space for "listening" to adolescents. Our direct presentation of extensive quotations allows readers, also, to "listen" to youths.

## Research Questions

Many questions about kids, drugs, and crime are suggested by the literature. Because these are the kinds of questions that concern parents, law enforcement personnel, and social workers, we decided to explore these questions directly.

We found that when answered from the perspectives of insiders—in this case, adolescents—the questions prevailing in the literature take on a new light. We also found that issues important to the kids we spoke to are sometimes quite different from adult and professional or researcher definitions of their situations. We believe it is imperative to a social science of adolescent behavior to give the young people a voice in the face of the proliferation of adult professionals' interpretations of their behavior.

The rest of this chapter outlines questions as presented by the prevailing literature and identifies the chapters where they are addressed.

### 1. *Does drug use lead to crime?*

Especially among high-risk youths (those who routinely commit crimes and use drugs), the links between drug use and criminal events have not been specified. Several studies of delinquents (Tinklenberg, 1973; Tinklenberg, Murphy, Murphy, and Pfefferbaum, 1981; Tinklenberg and Ochberg, 1981; Tinklenberg, Roth, Kipell, and Murphy, 1976) and incarcerated offenders (Bureau of Justice Statistics, 1983a, 1983b, 1983c, 1983d) show that many had been using drugs or alcohol prior to the crime that led to their detention or incarceration, but previous research has seldom investigated whether and how drugs or alcohol are involved in specific criminal events involving youths.

In U.S. society, a limited number of cultural beliefs are widespread as explanations for the links between drug use and crime. A majority of Americans (Abelson, Cohen, Schrayer, and Rappeport, 1973) believe that drug use and alcohol are important factors in crime because they lead to disinhibition (the loss of self-control) and the need for money. The drug–crime association is also ascribed to youths' prior criminal tendencies or to background factors (poverty, poor family relationships, bad associates, early deviance, and so on). Others, however, believe that drug use is not directly linked to crime. Criminals may make choices to commit crime regardless of their substance use.

Virtually all youths know these cultural beliefs about drug–crime links, but typically apply them to impersonal "others" who are believed both to use drugs and to commit crimes. Youths often have very different perspectives about the links between drugs and crime depending on whether the referent is themselves or someone else. They generally deny that *their* crime is due to their drug or alcohol use (Huizinga, 1986). Some youths may be using drugs and/or alcohol so routinely that virtually all their activities (including specific crimes) also involve prior drug/alcohol use.

Chapter 3 addresses youths' perspectives on their own and other's drug/alcohol use and criminality, both in general and in terms of specific events. Youths' statements of their intentions and alternative explanatory paradigms of behavior are central to establishing or refuting a link between adolescent drug/alcohol use and crime.

## 2. *Why do youths sell drugs, and how?*

One major form of crime, drug sales, is clearly and directly connected to drug use. Drug selling almost always occurs among persons who are regular users of a particular substance (Goode, 1970; Johnson, 1973; Single and Kandel, 1978). The best descriptions of drug selling were written more than ten years ago (Blum, 1972; Goode, 1970; Johnson, 1973; Waldorf, Murphy, Reinarman, and Joyce, 1977). Although more recent studies (Adler, 1985; Adler and Adler, 1982–1983; Clayton and Voss, 1981; Single and Kandel, 1978) statistically document the importance of drug selling, little new information has been provided about drug sales or youthful distribution networks in the intervening years.

In virtually every U.S. community, adolescents can obtain marijuana and many other drugs easily and cheaply. Drug sales are probably the most frequent crime committed by those who sell drugs (many sellers also engage in nondrug crimes as well). The dollar income from drug sales probably rivals or exceeds the value of merchandise stolen during property crimes.

We need careful delineation of youthful drug sales. Why do youths sell drugs? How do they obtain supplies and adjust for supply and demand factors? To whom do they sell? Do they make money from such sales? How concerned are they about police, school, parents, and other social control agents? The information presented in chapter 4 is among the first to address such important issues.

## 3. *How are thefts linked to drug use?*

If drug sales are directly linked to drug use, the general population (Abelson et al., 1973) clearly believes that drug users commit crimes, especially property crimes, in order to finance the purchase of drugs. Drug and alcohol users are believed to need the next dose so much that they are willing, if no legal income is available, to commit crimes that yield money or property that can be resold. This belief is based largely on generalizations about physical and psychological dependence involving heroin abuse or expensive drugs (see Ball, Rosen, Flueck, and Nurco, 1981; Ball, Shaffer, and Nurco, 1983; Collins et al., 1982a, 1982b; Crawford, Washington, and Senay, 1980; Goldstein, 1985; Inciardi, 1979, 1981, 1984; Johnson, Goldstein, et al., 1985; Nurco, Ball, Shaffer and Hanlon, 1985; Nurco, Cisin, and Balter, 1981a, 1981b, 1981c; Wish and Johnson, 1987).

Whether adolescents who both use drugs and commit crimes report such compulsions is much less clear. Many youths have denied (Huizinga, 1986; Johnson, Wish, and Huizinga, 1986) that their reason for committing crimes was to obtain money for drug purchases. If our subjects deny any such compulsion, why, then, do they commit property crimes? The analysis in chapter 5 connects most property crimes to youths' participation in the American culture of consumerism.

4. *How are assaultive crimes related to drug and alcohol use?*

As noted earlier, it is widely believed that disinhibition as a result of intoxication on drugs, especially alcohol, is associated with serious crimes against persons (mainly assault, rape, homicide, and robbery). Although there are a variety of presumed linkages (see G. Collins, 1982; J. Collins, 1981; Room and Collins, 1983), the fundamental cultural assumption is that the substance, rather than the person, is to blame for the crime or its severity. Disinhibition appears in legal statutes as "mitigating circumstances," whereby persons found guilty of crime may be given a less severe sentence if their alcohol or drug intoxication is an important factor in crime (Weissman, 1979).

In an extensive analysis of the alcohol literature (see Room and Collins, 1983), the general consensus of experts was that disinhibition is more a cultural explanation for, than a pharmacological property of, alcohol abuse and aggression. That is, disinhibition is a "rhetoric of explanation or justification" (Morgan, 1983) by which heavy drinkers shift responsibility for their assaultive actions, especially against family members, from themselves to the substance.

Qualitative research on alcohol and aggression (Burns, 1980; Levinson, 1983; MacAndrew and Edgerton, 1969) documents that youths frequently drink heavily and consume drugs in order to get high, "have a good time," "get rowdy," "be brave," "be macho," and so on. Burns's (1980) observations of a group of drinking males showed that aggressive behavior did not occur in heavy-drinking contexts where such behavior was disapproved. Rather, heavy-drinking youths, before engaging in threatening and aggressive acts, sought out social contexts in which both heavy drinking and aggression were informally tolerated.

As a relatively normal part of group behavior, youths engage in drug or alcohol use and do things they would not otherwise do—commit crimes, challenge others to fights, and so on. That is, motivations and preexisting normative expectations of youths with respect to aggression lead to a cycle of heavy drinking, and possibly drug use, in which youths also seek out social contexts where violent events are likely to occur. Thus, the consumption of alcohol and drugs is only one of several factors leading to and perhaps influencing this kind of delinquent event. Chapter 6 delineates several of these delinquent contexts and explores whether alcohol and drugs play an important role in youths' assaultive behavior. A closely related theme, discussed in chapter 7, is how substance-abusing delinquent youths characterize the victims of their crimes.

5. *How do risk factors influence precocious drug and alcohol use and delinquency?*

Quantitative research (Brunswick, 1979; Gold and Petronio, 1980; Jessor and Jessor, 1977; Kandel, 1978; Robins, 1966; Robins and Wish, 1977) identifies a wide variety of risk factors that are frequently associated with the initiation and continued use of drugs and alcohol and with involvement in delinquency: delinquent peers, alcoholic parents, poor relations with parent(s), poor school performance, low IQ, inadequate moral development, sex, ethnicity, and poor neighborhood, among others.

Precocity—in this context, initiation at a very early age to various deviant behaviors—has proved to be a relatively important risk factor for subsequent involvement in serious criminality, continued maintenance of deviant behavior, and antisocial behavior that continues into adulthood (Blumstein, Cohen, Roth, and Visher, 1986; Robins, 1966; Tracy, Wolfgang, and Figlio, 1985; Weiner, 1984; Wolfgang, Figlio, and Sellin, 1972). Youths who begin a particular delinquent behavior about the average age (or older) of their cohort are less likely than precocious youths to be as frequently involved in that behavior or to begin more serious delinquencies; the less precocious youths also tend to cease delinquent behavior (Tracy, Wolfgang, and Figlio, 1985; Weiner, 1984; Wolfgang, Figlio, and Sellin, 1972).

Age 13 is a critical age for determining precocity. It marks the beginning of the teenage years, the onset of puberty for many youths, and—for large numbers of youths—the initiation of a variety of delinquent and drug-using behaviors (Elliott and Huizinga, 1984). Age 13 is close to the modal age for initiating petty theft, petty assaults (fights), and alcohol use. But burglary, robbery, and use of drugs other than alcohol or marijuana are very rare at age 13; youths who do commit these crimes at age 13 are quite precocious in comparison with their counterparts who do not.

In chapter 8, two case studies compare 13-year-old youths (Norris and Elizabeth) who are at high and low risk, respectively, for serious delinquency and drug use in their teenage years. In this chapter, the youths' own accounts of how their lives have evolved reveal the interaction of some of the risk factors identified in the quantitative research.

6. *How do drugs, alcohol, and crime interrelate in the life processes of serious drug-abusing delinquents?*

Many factors have also been identified as crucial in the development of serious involvement in drugs, alcohol, and criminality (see, for example, Elliott, Huizinga, and Ageton, 1985; Jessor and Jessor, 1977; Johnston, O'Malley, and Eveland, 1976, 1978; Kandel, 1978). Among these factors are poor attachment to parents, deviant peers, poor school performance, defiance of authority, early onset of minor and major delinquencies as well as alcohol/drug use, and low socioeconomic status. Quantitative studies provide statistical evidence for how these factors interact among samples of youths, but they rarely provide information about the lives of individual youths who are committed to both heavy drug use and delinquent behavior. Nor is there much evidence to document the process by which youths tend to give up such behaviors in young adulthood (Kandel and Logan, 1983).

A major strength of qualitative research is that the life processes of individual subjects can be systematically explored and related to other behaviors. The case study method permits an exploration of how factors identified by quantitative studies may influence the processes of change in the focal behaviors of individual subjects. Moreover, case studies permit examination of the role of specific factors from the subjects' perspectives. Subjects can describe directly to the reader their intentions and their actual behaviors.

Chapter 9 presents case studies of two youths (Kevin and Gallo) who began drug use and delinquency at an early age, became daily users of drugs and alcohol, engaged in serious crimes on a routine basis, but began moving away from routine criminal behavior as they reached young adulthood. One (Kevin) also made a commitment to stop drug and alcohol use, whereas the other (Gallo) included "controlled" use in his plans for the future.

Chapter 10 builds on the case studies presented in chapters 8 and 9 to explore the dimensions of experimentation and commitment to drug/alcohol use and crime among the other youths in the study.

7. *Do criminal justice sanctions deter adolescent criminality and drug use?*

Quantitative research has generally documented a decline in delinquent and criminal behavior after age 16 among widely different populations of youths, including delinquents (Elliott and Huizinga, 1984; Gold and Petronio, 1980; Montmarquette and Nerlove, 1985; O'Malley, Bachman, and Johnston, 1977, 1984; Wolfgang, 1983). Such evidence, however, is unclear about why this decline in delinquency occurs. Are youths moving toward adult roles and hence giving up delinquency? Or does the threat of criminal justice sanctions have a deterrent effect? Or both?

Some evidence (Gold and Reimer, 1975; Gold and Williams, 1969) suggests that delinquency may *increase* after arrest and sanctioning. Yet in the case studies of Kevin and Gallo, both youths state explicitly that their concern about being incarcerated was one of several important reasons for limiting their current and future criminality.

It is less clear whether youths with no or little legal contact are also deterred by the threat of jail and criminal justice sanctions. Although general deterrence is an important legitimation for legal statutes, according to legal philosophy (J. Kaplan, 1973; Packard, 1968; Zimring and Hawkins, 1973), research evidence for deterrent effects among the general youth population is very slight. Gold and Reimer (1975) found that youths reported that exceeding the age of juvenile jurisdiction was an important reason for ceasing some delinquent behaviors, especially more serious crimes. Many youths in this study spontaneously mentioned concern about being treated as an adult by the courts (chapter 11) as a reason for reducing delinquent behaviors, as was their movement toward the assumption of adult roles.

Chapter 12 concludes with a summary of the findings.

# 2
# Research Methods and Respondent Characteristics

I n order to explore questions regarding the role of drug and alcohol use in adolescent crime, a community with demographic characteristics similar to those of the general U.S. population was selected for intensive study. Youths from two schools (junior and senior high) were chosen as research subjects, and both interviews and fieldwork were used to collect data.

## Selection of Research Site

The research for this study was conducted in New York State. In order to win the cooperation of appropriate officials in gaining access to research subjects, we promised to maintain the anonymity of the participating localities and all individuals involved in the study. The study community has been given a pseudonym, Yule City, which conveys its location in the snowbelt of the northeastern United States.

In selecting a research site, we sought an area that had demographic characteristics close to New York State and national means; several suburban and urban areas in New York had such characteristics. The selected community is sufficiently typical that market research firms routinely use it for test marketing their products and advertisements.

At the time Yule City was selected as the research site, the 1980 census had been conducted, but only 1970 census data were available. On the basis of the 1970 census data, Yule City is similar to other medium-sized cities in New York State and the United States generally in terms of age and ethnic distributions, socioeconomic structure, and income distribution (table 2–1). The city's crime rate and drug use patterns were virtually at the state average and very close to national figures (Federal Bureau of Investigation, 1982; Johnston, Bachman, and O'Malley, 1982).

The comparative data presented in table 2–1 for urban areas come from detailed census tabulations for all New York cities with populations of 100,000 or more or for Standard Metropolitan Statistical Areas (SMSAs) of 250,000

**Table 2–1**
**Comparison of Characteristics of Yule City and New York State Urban Areas**

| Characteristics | Yule City | State Urban Areas (Cities over 100,000 or SMSAs over 250,000) |
|---|---|---|
| Race (percentage) | | |
| White | 88 | 87 |
| Black | 11 | 12[a] |
| Hispanic | < 1 | (5) |
| Other | 1 | 1 |
| Percentage in school at ages | | |
| 7–13 | 96 | 97 |
| 14–15 | 97 | 97 |
| 16–17 | 89 | 91 |
| 18–19 | 65 | 68 |
| 20–21 | 46 | 43 |
| Percentage of high school–age students attending public school | 75 | 76 |
| Percentage completing high school | | |
| Among those 18–24 | 70 | 65 |
| Among those 25 and older | 52 | 52 |
| Median age of population | 28 years | 30 years |
| Among blacks | 19 years | 24 years |
| Median family income | $9,246 | $10,719 |
| Among blacks | $6,339 | $ 7,292 |
| Percentage of families below poverty level | 10 | 9 |
| Among blacks | 26 | 20 |
| Among youths aged 1–6 in 1970 and aged 12–17 in 1981: percentage black | 20 | 17 |

Source: 1970 census data.

[a]Demographic characteristics of persons of Hispanic background are influenced by the inclusion of New York City.

or more. The SMSAs include New York City, which has unique demographic features, but they also include eight other SMSAs, including the Yule City SMSA, that have more typical characteristics. Thus, in table 2–1 Yule City is included among the state's urban areas with which it is compared.

The racial composition of Yule City is virtually identical to the average for New York's urban areas, with the exception that the proportion of persons of Hispanic birth or parentage is much lower in Yule City. Generally, this is due to the large number of Hispanics who are concentrated in New York City and its region, but not elsewhere in the state.

Virtually all youths are enrolled in school until age 16, as mandated by law. In the 16–19 age range, Yule City youths are slightly less likely to be in school than their counterparts in the state as a whole, but those 20–21 years old are more likely to be in school. The proportion of high school–age youths attending public schools is equivalent to the state average. The proportion completing high school is slightly higher among those 18–24 years old in Yule City, but identical to the state figures among those over 25.

In 1970 Yule City had a slightly lower proportion of black citizens than the state's urban areas, and Yule City blacks were generally younger and poorer than New York State's blacks in urban areas. The entire population of Yule City was somewhat less well off (1 percent more below poverty level and $1,500 less in median income) than residents in the state's urban areas.

Among youths who were ages 1–6 in 1970 (and would be 12–17 at the end of 1981—midway in the data collection period), there was a somewhat higher proportion of blacks (20 percent) in Yule City than in the state's urban areas (17 percent). Overall, however, the statistical profile for Yule City is generally the same, plus or minus 3 percentage points, as that of the state's urban areas.

Since 1970 the New York State Division of Substance Abuse Services (and its predecessor agencies) has conducted several major statewide surveys of drug use; Yule City has been one of many localities sampled in all such surveys. In virtually every survey, the Yule City region (the SMSA and outlying rural areas) has had levels of use for each drug that are almost identical to the statewide average, plus or minus 4 percentage points.

Unpublished data from a 1978 survey by the Office of Drug Abuse Services show drug use levels for seventh- through twelfth-graders in Yule City were close to the statewide averages (table 2–2). Yule City youths were slightly (but not significantly) more likely than youths statewide to use inhalants, hallucinogens, hashish, stimulants, depressants, and tranquillizers, but less likely to use marijuana, cocaine, and heroin. Data from the Division of Substance Abuse Services (1984) and the Division of Alcoholism and Alcohol Abuse (1984) also show that Yule City remains very close to statewide averages. The New York data, in turn, are similar to data from the National Youth Survey (see Elliott, Ageton, Huizinga, Knowles, and Canter, 1983; Elliott and Huizinga, 1984) and other major surveys (Johnston, O'Malley, and Bachman, 1984; Miller et al., 1983).

Students from a junior and senior high school serving a quandrant of Yule City with a wide variety of socioeconomic characteristics were chosen for this study. The community in which the schools were located included middle-class, working-class, and low-income neighborhoods; there were both racially segregated and integrated neighborhoods in the community.

## Methods

School authorities in Yule City were informed of the intent of our study and methods of research and assured that both parental and youth consent would be

Table 2–2

**Drug Use Levels in Yule City[a] Region and Statewide (Students Enrolled in Grades 7–12, Spring 1978)**

*(percent)*

| Substance | Lifetime Use (Any Use) | | Recent Use (Past 6 Months) | | Current Use (Past 30 Days) | | Heavy Use (10+ Times in Past 30 days) | |
|---|---|---|---|---|---|---|---|---|
| | State-wide | Yule City | State-wide | Yule City | State-wide | Yule City | State-wide | Yule City |
| Marijuana | 54 | 50 | 46 | 43 | 37 | 33 | 17 | 16 |
| Hashish | 25 | 27 | 19 | 22 | 12 | 14 | 2 | 1 |
| Hallucinogens | 9 | 12 | 6 | 8 | 4 | 4 | * | * |
| Cocaine | 11 | 9 | 8 | 6 | 4 | 2 | * | * |
| Heroin | 3 | 2 | 2 | 2 | 1 | 1 | * | * |
| Methadone (illicit) | 2 | 3 | 2 | 2 | 1 | 1 | * | * |
| Inhalants | 16 | 18 | 8 | 9 | 5 | 4 | * | * |
| Stimulants | 15 | 18 | 11 | 12 | 7 | 7 | 1 | 1 |
| Depressants | 11 | 14 | 7 | 10 | 4 | 4 | * | * |
| Tranquillizers | 13 | 14 | 9 | 9 | 6 | 6 | 1 | 1 |
| Cough medicines with codeine | 11 | 12 | 7 | 6 | 4 | 4 | 1 | * |
| Other narcotics | 11 | 13 | 8 | 8 | 3 | 2 | * | 1 |

Source: Office of Drug Abuse Services, *Substance Use among New York State Public and Parochial School Students in Grades 7 through 12* (Albany, N.Y.: Office of Drug Abuse Services, 1978).
[a]Yule City refers to the entire SMSA of which Yule City is the central city.
* = < 0.05 percent.

obtained before youths were interviewed.[1] They cooperated by providing demographic information on the city's schools, access to schools so our staff could observe and talk with students, and lists of students for use in selecting the random sample. Law enforcement authorities were told of our purpose, methods, and consent procedures, and they assisted in the recruitment of officially known delinquents.

*Fieldwork and Sample Selection*

The fieldwork phase had three goals: (1) to identify relevant patterns of behavior, (2) to identify subsamples of respondents, and (3) to obtain information for use in developing the interview guide. The field-workers, a woman and a man, were senior graduate students in sociology. Each had primary responsibility for one of the schools, but both worked to become known and accepted at both schools.

During the first phase of the study, during January–August 1981, the field-workers got to know a large number of students by "hanging out" with them on neighborhood streets and in pizza parlors, parks, and other gathering places. A variety of topics were discussed in the field-workers' presence, including the use and availability of drugs and other illegal behaviors. The intensive interviews, to be discussed, were conducted during the period from June 1981 to June 1982. The field-workers met and interacted with more than 700 youths during this period.

The research plan was to focus mainly on youths who were seriously delinquent and routine drug users and to include a comparison group of less deviant youths. On the assumption that many delinquent drug users had no or little contact with police because of their illegal behaviors, whereas others had been arrested and punished by official sanctions, both officially known and unknown delinquent drug users were selected. Resources made it necessary to limit the study to 100 youths, who were carefully selected to represent a wide range of drug- and crime-related behavior, ranging from serious involvement to complete avoidance. Three subgroups of subjects were selected for inclusion in the study:

1. *Purposive Sample:* After 6–9 months of intensive observation and conversations with many youths in the community, the field-workers knew 100 or more youths whom they had observed using drugs routinely or believed to be active in several delinquent behaviors. Forty youths were asked to participate in the study (one youth refused and a replacement was selected), and the written consent of the youths and their parents was obtained. These youths were at liberty in the community and were not officially labeled as "delinquent" (although a few had reported a prior arrest). They represent youths who are part of the hidden crime problem.

2. *Random Sample:* To obtain a cross-section of relatively "normal" youths in the community, staff randomly selected 40 names from lists of youths enrolled in the two study schools. Parents and youths were sent a letter explaining the purpose of the study. The field-worker typically visited the home and obtained the written consent of both the parents and the youths. All 40 youths selected were subsequently interviewed.

3. *Detained Sample:* In order to study youths who were officially labeled as delinquent and residing in the local detention facility or group homes, staff provided social workers of the criminal justice agency with consent letters, which were transmitted to and signed by the youths' parents or guardians and their lawyers. Only after informed consent had been given by the guardian did the field-workers visit the youths in the facility and ask them to participate. All 20 youths approached by the staff agreed to be interviewed. Staff did not learn how many parents or other agents had failed to give their consent, for the youths involved could not be approached by the staff.

## Characteristics of Respondents

Table 2–3 shows that the complete sample included more ethnic minorities and more heavy drug users than would be expected in a national random sample.

Table 2–3
Characteristics of the Yule City Samples
*(number of subjects)*

| Characteristics | Random (N = 40) | Purposive (N = 40) | Detained (N = 20) | Total (N = 100) |
|---|---|---|---|---|
| Sex | | | | |
| Male | 20 | 26 | 18 | 64 |
| Female | 20 | 14 | 2 | 36 |
| Ethnicity | | | | |
| White | 25 | 33 | 15 | 73 |
| Minority | 15 | 7 | 5 | 27 |
| Age | | | | |
| 12–13 | 9 | 2 | 2 | 13 |
| 14–15 | 18 | 10 | 11 | 39 |
| 16–17 | 11 | 15 | 5 | 31 |
| 18–20 | 2 | 13 | 2 | 17 |
| Drug use type | | | | |
| Nonuser | 19 | 0 | 2 | 21 |
| Light user | 14 | 6 | 4 | 24 |
| Heavy user | 7 | 33 | 14 | 54 |
| Missing data | 0 | 1 | 0 | 1 |
| Crime type | | | | |
| No crime | 31 | 12 | 0 | 43 |
| Episodic | 3 | 5 | 0 | 8 |
| Serious | 6 | 22 | 20 | 48 |
| Missing data | 0 | 1 | 0 | 1 |

The Yule City random sample, however, is very close to national estimates. Fifteen percent (6/40) of the youths in the random sample were classified as seriously involved in crime (table 2–3), the same proportion (15 percent) that were index offenders among the nation's youths in 1979 (Elliott and Huizinga, 1984; Johnson, Wish, Huizinga, 1986), although the definitions and cutoff points differ. Eighteen percent (7/40) of the random sample were heavy drug users, compared with 12 percent of the nation's youths who used pills, hard drugs, marijuana, and alcohol (Elliott and Huizinga, 1984; Johnson, Wish, and Huizinga 1986) and 22 percent of New York State youths who used marijuana three times or more a week, plus other substances (Division of Substance Abuse Services, 1984).

Although the cutoff points employed in this study are different from those in other studies, and the sample size is far too small for generalization, the foregoing evidence suggests that the youths in the random sample are reasonably similar to their counterparts in other studies. Therefore, the findings based on the random sample that follows are probably close enough to typical patterns of adolescent behavior to provide a better understanding of the links of drugs and alcohol to crime and delinquency.

**Table 2–5**
**Criminal Involvement by Drug Use and Age**
*(number of subjects in each cell)*

| Crime Type | 12–13 | 14–15 | 16–17 | 18–20 | Total |
|---|---|---|---|---|---|
| | | | Age Group | | |
| | | | *Nonuse* | | |
| No crime | 8 | 10 | 1 | 0 | 19 |
| Episodic | 0 | 0 | 0 | 0 | 0 |
| Serious | 0 | 2 | 0 | 0 | 2 |
| | | | *Light Use* | | |
| No crime | 0 | 9 | 6 | 2 | 17 |
| Episodic | 1 | 0 | 0 | 1 | 2 |
| Serious | 2 | 2 | 1 | 0 | 5 |
| | | | *Heavy Use* | | |
| No crime | 2 | 3 | 1 | 1 | 7 |
| Episodic | 0 | 1 | 3 | 2 | 6 |
| Serious | 0 | 11 | 19 | 11 | 41 |
| Missing data | 0 | 1 | 0 | 0 | 1 |
| Total | 13 | 39 | 31 | 17 | 100 |

the detained sample. Whites constituted 63 percent of the random sample, 83 percent of the purposive sample, and 75 percent of the detained sample.

Table 2–6 shows that males were more apt than females to be classified as seriously delinquent.[2] Likewise, whites were more likely to be seriously delinquent than minority group members, mainly because such a large proportion of whites were recruited through the purposive and detained samples.

*The Interview Schedule*

The fieldwork provided extensive information on the subjects' concerns, typical activities, friendship networks, and preferred meeting places. Thus, the interview

**Table 2–6**
**Criminal Involvement by Sex and Ethnicity**
*(percent)*

| | Males (N = 64) | Females (N = 36) | White (N = 73) | Minority (N = 27) | Total (N = 100) |
|---|---|---|---|---|---|
| | *Sex* | | *Ethnicity* | | |
| None or minor delinquency | 30 | 47 | 29 | 56 | 36 |
| Serious delinquency | 70 | 50 | 70 | 44 | 63 |
| Missing data | 0 | 1 | 1 | 0 | 1 |
| Total | 100 | 100 | 100 | 100 | 100 |

schedule could be developed using the subjects' own terms, as these had come to be known through the field-workers' efforts (see Agar, 1986; Bogdan and Biklin, 1982; Cicourel, 1964; Schwartz and Jacobs, 1979; Spradley, 1979; Webb, Campbell, Schwartz, and Sechrest, 1966). The interview schedule consisted of 220 structured, open-ended questions and related probes. The questions were designed to elicit the subject's biography, with special focus on issues and events concerning peers, school, activities and interests, religion, and family background, as well as involvement with alcohol, crime, and drugs (Becker and Geer, 1960; Feldman, 1974; Frazier, 1978; Holsti, 1960; Richardson, 1965; Schatzman and Strauss, 1973).

Such an in-depth interview is the preferred format when the analyst seeks to understand the ways in which subjects themselves think and talk about the issues at hand. Many of the issues to be discussed were sensitive, so that close rapport between subjects and interviewers was essential. In order to provide the most comfortable setting for the subjects, all interviews were conducted by one of the field-workers, who had become a known and trusted feature of the subjects' world, in places within their own locale of activity. (The interviews with subjects who were in detention centers were not conducted under ideal conditions, but privacy was assured and the interviewers were skilled in establishing rapport.)

The 100 subjects were interviewed for 3 to 11 hours (mean time 5 hours). The interviews were conducted as conversations, and the longer interviews were completed in two sessions to avoid fatigue. Focal topics (drugs, alcohol, and crime) were raised in more than one way and at different times in the discussion. The interviews elicited a wealth of information about the subjects' activities and interests, why and how they became involved with focal activities, the meanings they assigned to criminal and drug-related behaviors, and the ways in which those meanings changed over time. Subjects were also asked to describe criminal events and episodes of drug/alcohol use.

*Accessing the Data*

The interviews were tape recorded and transcribed verbatim onto computer tape, with 90 to 300 single-spaced pages of text generated per subject. These transcripts are the basis for case studies of subjects who offer special insights into the focal issues and relationships (see chapters 8 and 9). Excerpts from the transcripts are also used throughout the report to illustrate the points being made.[3]

Using inductive analysis and the constant comparative method (Bogdan and Taylor, 1975; Glaser, 1975; Glaser and Strauss, 1967; Holsti, 1960; Kirk and Miller, 1986; Krippendorff, 1980; Spradley, 1979), a detailed systematic codebook (Johnson, 1981) was developed for cataloging the diverse contents of the transcripts. The codebook contained 45 major thematic topics, each of which was assigned a numeric code; each major topic also had up to 99 sub-topic codes. Thus, each code was a four-digit number, analogous to a noun and its modifiers. Much redundancy was built into the coding catalogue and coding process to compensate for inconsistencies in subjects' accounts and coder practices and for idiosyncrasies in analysts' retrieval practices. This improved the odds that relevant data could be retrieved.

Each of the 100 transcripts was coded and catalogued according to thematic topic. The codes were then entered into a computer program developed especially for the study. A computerized retrieval system was used to locate those pages, among the approximately 20,000 pages of transcripts, in which a given code or combination of codes appeared; the retrieval system could then print out the relevant pages for analysis. This particular retrieval process enabled us to maintain the integrity of the qualitative data by allowing us to read discussions in context and, at the same time, to access appropriate segments from the mass of data as needed.

## Advantages and Limitations of Methodology

This research and design has several important advantages in comparison with standard survey designs. First, the sample was selected to ensure the involvement of a sufficient number of youths who were involved in serious crime and heavy drug use. Substantial numbers of persons exhibiting relatively uncommon behavior are very costly to locate through random sampling procedures. Second, the interview schedule was flexible; it allowed areas of special interest that were relevant to the study's concerns to be explored at length with youths.

The methodology also entailed important limitations. First, it is not possible to estimate the percentage of respondents involved in focal behaviors. The questions were open ended, and thus respondents were not presented with forced-response categories by which they could be systematically compared and which might prompt their recall and responses. Rather, they responded in their own terms, which varied widely even for standard questions. Second, standard counts and statistical results are not warranted because of small sample size and the nonrepresentative nature of the sample.

We have described a strategy for listening to kids in order to understand their perspectives on alcohol, drug use, and crime. This strategy included both a set of questions about relevant topics and the selection of informants representing a variety of experiences. In the next chapters we hear the answers to these questions.

## Notes

1. Procedures for protecting the subjects of the study were developed and approved in cooperation with institutional review boards of the sponsoring agency. During

fieldwork, the researcher's role was explained to small groups of youths at a time, as were the steps taken to protect confidentiality, the purpose and funding of the study, and the benefits to be obtained. Youths were told that if they felt any discomfort or distress regarding an issue or a particular question, they should feel free not to answer. The identities of all subjects and places were changed in this report, all transcripts, and other records. All staff signed confidentiality agreements, and a Federal Certification of Confidentiality was obtained to protect the data from use in any manner by the legal system.

2. For these summary tables we have collapsed the nine categories of drug use and criminal involvement used in tables 2–4 and 2–5 into two categories. "None or minor delinquency" includes "no crime" and "no or light use of drugs," as well as "episodic crime and non-use of drugs." "Serious delinquency," therefore, includes all "serious crime," "all heavy use of drugs," and "episodic crime and light use."

3. A forthcoming book based on these same data (*Drugs in Adolescent Worlds*) provides more extended quotations about the drug use of these youths. Different groups of drug users are thus permitted to speak directly to the reader.

# 3
# Adolescents' Perspectives on the Relationship between Drugs/Alcohol and Crime

Quantitative research has systematically documented that users of drugs other than marijuana and alcohol are quite likely to engage in serious crime. Conversely, most persons who commit felony crimes (most of whom also commit many minor crimes) are among the most routine users of drugs and alcohol (Huizinga and Elliott, 1981; Johnson, Wish, and Huizinga, 1986; Johnston, O'Malley, and Eveland, 1976, 1978; Inciardi, 1980; Gandossy, Williams, Cohen, and Harwood, 1980). A relatively small proportion (probably 5 percent or less) of all youths appear to engage in a life-style that includes routine drug and alcohol use and frequent commission of crimes. Similar associations are evident among Yule City subjects (see table 2–4). This statistical association between drug use and crime, however, tells us nothing about the meaning of this relationship. The youths' own perspectives on drug–crime links offer some insight into this association.

The youths in this study have a rich repertoire of commonsense theories about the association between drugs and crime. Some were derived from broad cultural beliefs, but most were drawn from their own experiences and observations. This chapter examines adolescents' theories and how they differentiate along lines of youth experience and involvement in drug use and crime.

## The Respondents and Their Responses

The respondents in this section are 84 subjects who answered a direct question about the relationship between drugs/alcohol and crime. The interview schedule included the following basic question about this topic:

*Q:* We've talked about a lot of things having to do with your involvement in alcohol, drugs, and crime. Basically, we've dealt with each as a separate behavior. One of the main things we are trying to study is how these things are interrelated. That is, are these somehow related to each other? And if so, how?

In many instances, subjects had already addressed this topic at length earlier in the interview. These earlier discussions have been used to supplement the responses to the direct question.

In general, subjects' responses can be divided into three categories based on the extent of their involvement in drug/alcohol use and crime. First, those respondents with little personal involvement in, or knowledge of, the focal behaviors gave brief, conventional answers. They perceived crime as irrational, inexplicable behavior or saw drugs and alcohol as related to crime because of a need for money for drugs.

A second group was able to comment more thoughtfully on the relationship between drugs and crime. These were youths with more experience—those who had reported observing others using drugs, who knew about crimes in their neighborhoods, or who had experimented with alcohol and drugs and had been involved in minor criminal behavior. They estimated that a substantial proportion of crimes were committed by those using drugs or alcohol. They emphasized a broad range of "causes" of crime, including poverty, insanity, a desire for attention, and the rational choice of crime as a source of income.

The third group, those with extensive involvement in drugs/alcohol use and crime, offered several explanations of how drugs and alcohol may affect the criminal behavior of others, as well as several interpretations of why their own behavior was *not* affected by drugs or alcohol. Relevant sections of the interview transcripts are quoted hereafter to elaborate on these differing perspectives.

## Noninvolved Youths

About three-quarters of the random sample consisted of youths who engaged in no or very minor deliquent activity and who were non-users or only experimental users of alcohol or marijuana. Such youths typically had difficulty articulating what the relationship between drugs and crime might be, even after relatively extensive discussions of similar issues earlier in the interview. Typically, they would agree that there could be a relationship, because all were illegal activities, but they had trouble thinking of examples, other than violations of motor vehicle laws. A 15-year-old girl in the random sample who had experimented with alcohol and marijuana, but who reported no criminal involvement, explained:

Q: Do you think these issues are related—alcohol, drugs, and crime?
A: They could be.
Q: In what way?
A: I guess that, uh, if you drink alcohol, I guess it's an easy risk for crime, especially if you're driving, I guess. And the same thing for drugs, I guess.

Other relatively inexperienced respondents drew on the social stereotype of the drug addict's need for money to explain a relationship between substance abuse and crime. Addiction was also perceived as the cause of unpredictable, uncontrolled, "crazy" behavior. A 13-year-old boy in the random sample whose only experience of the focal behaviors was experimentation with alcohol described this model and referred to the media as confirmation.

*Q:* Do you think that getting into using drugs and drinking heavily will lead people to other kinds of illegal or criminal kinds of things, or do you think it's separate?

*A:* Yeah, I think, I think that it would probably be connected because, like, they, they've either done it because they don't like their life anymore and drugs has certain effects on them and it may persuade them, in a way, to do a type of crime like rob something, try to kill someone, and do all sorts of crazy things like that and try to kill themselves. And stuff like that. And I see movies, I saw a movie like that in school one time.

A similar response was given by a 17-year-old girl from the random sample. The respondent had been involved in minor theft in the past and had tried alcohol and marijuana:

*A:* The crime and the drugs. Let me see. Well, as you become addicted and you want to feel, need to get money, you might hold up a bank or something, hold up somebody, snatch gold, snatching purses, or mugging people 'cause you're angry at somebody but you can't hit that person. So, you might as well mug somebody. Or maybe it's some psychopath out there that's mad at his grandmother so he goes mugging little old ladies.

Other respondents who perceived addiction as an important cause of crime often mentioned insanity or mental instability as a related cause.

In sum, relatively inexperienced youths generally invoked conventional explanations for drug–crime links. But they did not compare these beliefs with their observations of others whom they knew or believed to be using drugs and/or to be involved in criminal activities.

## Relatively Experienced Youths

An important finding to emerge from secondary analyses of the National Youth Survey data is that virtually all youths, regardless of how heavily involved with drugs or delinquency, deny that their self-reported delinquent acts were committed in order to obtain money to purchase drugs (Johnson and Wish, 1986). This same denial was evident among the Yule City subjects, who observed that others—but not themselves or their peers—committed crimes to purchase drugs. They employed a variety of explanations to bridge this apparent discrepancy between their observations about others and their self-perceptions. Without invoking addiction as an explanation, relatively experienced youths spontaneously noted that many drug and alcohol users were involved in theft, and they mentioned incidents they had heard about or observed. For them, drugs and alcohol might be defined by those who used them as "necessities," much like clothing and records, and drug/alcohol users might steal for money to obtain any of these goods if they had no other source of money or if they were "someone who just steals."

A 19-year-old girl in the purposive sample, for instance, emphasized that she did not steal, although she had used cocaine and amphetamines, as well as alcohol and marijuana, and had been involved in vandalism and fighting. She contrasted her behavior with that of her friend, who stole not only for drugs but as a regular source of money and other goods:

*Q:* Is that true of most people you know that they steal so they can buy drugs?

*A:* Uh huh, Aster steal, 'cause she wants some money to get herb, or, to buy the baby some Pampers, or something . . . or she just want money to have in her pocket, just to be spending it.

The subjects were also explicit about other motives for theft. These imputed motives included: poor people's lack of alternatives, old people's (adults') need to "pay the rent," and kids' bids for attention (mentioned primarily by subjects with no actual personal criminal experience). Some relatively experienced youths also defined criminal activity, such as theft, as "fun" and "exciting"; this, and not gaining money for drugs, was their professed motive for stealing.

## Seriously Involved Youths

The seriously involved youths not only had had varied and continuing experience with the use of alcohol and drugs but also had been involved in the commission of serious crimes—that is, index crimes or persistent and systematic minor crime, such as property destruction and shoplifting. These youths used their own experience as a reference point: although they sometimes referred to more general social beliefs or their observations of others' behavior, for them the final authority was their own behavior. Few accepted a simple drugs-cause-crime explanation of anyone's behavior.

**Drugs lead directly to crime.** Only a few of the heavily involved youths asserted that there was a strong and important relationship between drug use and crime, both in general and their own behavior. Two were boys who had been in serious trouble and had reformed—that is, were no longer involved in drugs or crime and insisted that their lives had changed. One of the boys, a 16-year-old who was in detention and had been involved in assault, joyriding, and serious shop-lifting, affirmed:

*A:* Um, there's always a relationship between drugs and crime. 'Cause drugs distorts people values, their morals, their state of mind at the time, it always distorts that, you know, no matter what drug you do, I mean, a drug is a distor-tion, you know.

He modifies that position quickly, however:

*Q:* Do you think there are many kids who do crime who do not do any drugs or drinking?
*A:* Oh, I know there are a few, there are definitely a few people who do that. You know, it's just, you can't really, you can't blame it on one or the other, you know, you can't blame it on the drugs, you know, because I know a lot of people who do drugs and never think of rippin' anybody off, you know.

The other boy (Kevin in chapter 9), age 20, had completed a drug rehabilita-tion program. He asserted that both for him and for others the need for drugs led to theft:

*Q:* What makes the use of drugs different from just wanting clothes or wanting other kinds of possessions?
*A:* What make the difference?
*Q:* Hmm-mmm.
*A:* 'Cause there's a real psychological need, it's like I got to have this, or I won't be happy, all bummed out, and you know. So a lot of kids believe that the only way you can be happy is to be high. And things like that; they're looking for the instant payoff. It's not of no interest to them . . . what they're doing to their minds or their bodies, or to the people that love them.

A 15-year-old boy in the purposive sample who was involved in serious criminal behavior (including assault, joyriding, and shoplifting), as well as using various drugs, defined theft as an available means of obtaining money to buy what was "needed." Since drugs are relatively expensive and are not provided by parents, he argued, people may steal to obtain them; in fact, he thought he might do so if he moved on from the marijuana he could now afford to more expensive cocaine. The interviewer followed up on his statement that there was a connection between drugs and crime:

*Q:* Do you think the kids who get high, drink, are the same kids who are going to do crime?

*A:* Yup, yup, yup, yup.

*Q:* Why? What's the connection?

*A:* Because, because they, they'll be needing money if they wanna get high. Something like that, but, I guarantee most everybody get high still.

*Q:* Do you think any straight kids commit crimes?

*A:* Yeah, but not heavy crimes, not burglary; they do that light stuff, may steal a candy bar, or somethin', bubble gum, no serious money, they don't need money. What they gonna do with money? Their mom's gettin' 'em everything else, clothes, house; they ain't gonna buy no marijuana, if ya don't smoke, ya don't need it.

**Drugs and alcohol have psychological effects.** Both experienced and inexperienced subjects commented on this topic. They agreed that alcohol and marijuana (or "drugs" in general) affected responses in social settings, but they did not always agree about the likely direction. Several saw violence or aggression as more likely; others perceived some substances as having pacifying effects. The following comments were typical.

*A:* 'Cause, um, when you have alcohol, when you get drunk you might not know what you are doing and start beating up on somebody you know. Or with drugs, if you can't get the drugs you want then, you know, you might beat up somebody too, or you might try to hurt somebody because you can't have some more drugs or some more alcohol or something like that, you know, have physical contact because you don't get what you want, you know.

A 17-year-old from the purposive sample recognized that he was more aggressive and dangerous when he was stoned:

*A:* Yeah. My temper gets faster, you know, it's faster. 'Cause you fuck with me when I am stoned, and I'm liable to kill you or something. You know, I'm a little bit crazier when I don't have a clear head, you know. I'll just beat the shit out of you if I ain't got a clear head. If I'm stoned, I'll shoot you in a minute. You know, that's why I usually try not to carry my gun when I'm stoned. But if you fuck with me when I'm stoned, I'll shoot you.

An 18-year-old girl in the random sample who had been involved in minor crimes and polydrug use drew on her own observations in describing how "alcohol and drugs make you commit crimes":

*A:* Yeah, in some instances it has occurred, like these guys I know that used to be in gang fights up in my neighborhood, you know, they would get drunk, go stand by the corner store, buy quarts of beer and get drunk and then go fight.

Another 18-year-old girl with similar experience agreed that alcohol use was related to violence, but asserted that marijuana was not:

*A:* Herb don't make you do that, it just make you, be up in the morning for everything.

A 15-year-old boy from the random sample, on the other hand, seemed more willing to link drugs to crime than to view alcohol as criminogenic:

*A:* Um, oh, probably when they're drunk or stoned or something, from what I know they don't really know what they're doing. Well, they might commit a crime . . . or I thought—it seems to me that if someone is getting drunk they're doing it for fun unless they're a real heavy alcoholic, um, they wouldn't be thinking about doing any crimes or anything, just having a good time.

Without ever using the term, these respondents frequently referred to drugs and alcohol as *disinhibitors*. Room and Collins (1983:v) discuss disinhibition:

> Drunkenness not only makes one more clumsy, but also removes social constraints, making us, for instance, aggressive or affectionate, maudlin or mean, in a way that we would not be if we were sober. In recent years, evidence . . . suggests that the link between alcohol and disinhibition is a matter of cultural belief rather than of pharmacological action.

Although this model of disinhibition may be far more elaborate than described here, our youths were clearly drawing from several elements of this model to explain drug–crime linkages. Alcohol or drugs may impulsively bring about illegal acts that might not have occurred otherwise. An example is given by an 18-year-old boy in the purposive sample who had engaged in assault and minor shoplifting:

*A:* I think because—if you, when you start drinking or doing drugs, you know, you start losing, losing [sense] or, you know, losing touch with reality, and then you start—like you lose control. It ain't you. You the person you know. Some—something else takes over, and make you do that stuff. And, I don't know, it's just, you, you, your brains or your mind ain't, at its full, you know, you wouldn't do it, you ain't doing stuff, that you know, you do straight.

A 15-year-old boy from the random sample who had experimented only with alcohol commented more directly on the element of impulse:

*A:* 'Cause I think if people, you know, when they go off and smoke marijuana or something and get high. And someone all of a sudden says, hey man, let's go rob the liquor store or something. So the other people I think are just plain crazy.

A 15-year-old boy from the detained sample, who had experience with auto theft and other grand larceny, said:

*A:* I think that, ah, that if you take the drugs, that you might be pushed easily into doing something that you probably wouldn't do if you weren't on the drugs.
*Q:* What about with alcohol?
*A:* I think it's probably just about the same as drugs.

Most of the seriously involved youths were quite clear in denying, however, that such explanations invoking disinhibition applied to themselves. Though reporting crimes in which drugs and alcohol were used beforehand, during, or afterward, they denied that their drug or alcohol use had an important role in the occurrence or course of their crime. They always had their criminal behavior, as well as their drug and alcohol use, under control. Rather, they suggested a variety of other explanations for why their drug/alcohol use was essentially irrelevant to the conduct of their crimes. Discussion of several such explanations follows.

**Drugs and alcohol make life, including crime, more fun.** Drugs and alcohol are widely used to have fun, for socialization, and to combat boredom (Glassner and Loughlin, 1987). Seriously involved youths were frequently having "fun" while being high or drunk; criminal opportunities subsequently presented themselves or were sought out.

A 16-year-old detained youth who had used a variety of drugs and engaged in burglary and robbery said he was usually high during criminal events. When asked, "Why do you think people your age do crime?" he answered in terms of his own experience:

*A:* Ah, ah, a lot of us do it 'cause they need somethin' more, do it just to do it, man. Now me I used to do it just to do it, it was fun, you know. I ain't never really need nothin', man, I just do it for the hell of it, man, just bust out somethin' or rob somebody for their property, just to see the reactions on their faces in the mornin'. Somethin' like that, just be fun.

Another detained youth, 13 years old, who had used hallucinogens and amphetamines as well as alcohol and marijuana, reviewed with the interviewer the crimes they had discussed and the frequency with which drug use was associated with those criminal events. He was asked:

*Q:* Why do you commit crime?
*A:* For the money. And for the fun of it, sometimes.

*Q:* Uh-huh. Which is which, when do you do it for fun and when do you do it for money?

*A:* When I need the money I do it for money. When I just don't need any I just do it for the fun of it, see if I can break in and not get caught.

**My drug and alcohol use is incidental to my crime.** In several instances, seriously involved youths reported using drugs or alcohol shortly before or during criminal events. They would be drinking and getting high—their normal state during the day. For various reasons, an opportunity for crime would present itself, or the group would decide to do some crime. But they denied that the alcohol or drug use contributed in a significant way to the probability that they would commit a crime or to the severity of a crime. Rather, they saw their drug or alcohol use as incidental and not a cause of their crimes.

For example, a 16-year-old boy in the random sample who had been involved in burglary, assault, theft, and arson described a burglary:

*Q:* So you don't think that people break into houses to steal things, to get money to buy drugs?

*A:* Yeah, I know they do. But, if, I still think people would break into the house for that money, if even, if even, even, if it wasn't for drugs, for, you know.

Although this boy had used a variety of drugs and had been involved in a series of crimes, including burglary, grand larceny, and drug sales, he was unable to give an example of something he had done while under the influence of drugs that he would not have done "straight." He responded:

*A:* I . . . don't know if I did it because I was drunk, or I did it because I just wanted to do it. I don't know the reason why I did it.

**My motivation for crime did not include drug use.** In general, the youths involved in serious crime tended to agree that people may do things under the influence of drugs or alcohol that they would not otherwise do, and they identified minor events in which their own behavior was so influenced. They maintained, however, that their drug or alcohol use was not relevant to their decision to engage in criminal activity. They had other reasons for doing crimes. A 13-year-old boy in the detained sample, who had taken hallucinogens, amphetamines, alcohol, and marijuana, had been involved in auto theft, burglary, and shoplifting in addition to more minor offenses. He associated drugs and crime with impulsivity for others, but he denied that he engaged in behavior that might get him into trouble when he was high: "I just never want to get in trouble when we're high." A 16-year-old boy from the purposive sample who had been involved in grand larceny and major property destruction agreed. He rejected the notion of a general drug–crime relationship:

*Q:* Do you think that there's any relationship between people who do smoke reefer, or do drugs and do crime?

*A:* Naw, I don't think there is no "relishlationship."

*Q:* No? Why not, how come?

*A:* They jus' get high wit' one another 'n' leave again, they don't give a fuck about you.

*Q:* You don't think people that are doing crime are usually doing drugs too?

*A:* Nope.

**I choose to use drugs before some crimes; I avoid drugs before other crimes.** Seriously involved youths were very clear about making choices to use or not to use drugs or alcohol before committing some crimes they plan. They discussed the avoidance of drugs or alcohol prior to some crimes to ensure their safety and to improve their skill. At other times, they may consume sizable amounts of alcohol or drugs to achieve desired levels of courage or increase the fun of the crime. But there was no agreement on which substances to use or avoid.

A 15-year-old detained youth with experience in burglary explained why he would not engage in crime if he had been drinking:

*A:* How would you, you're laughin' when you're drunk so how would you walk in there, "Aaah, give me your money, or I'll blow your head off," you know; they'd just think of you're doin' a practical joke, that's all. And I'd go, they'd probably get smart, you know, "Get out of here," you know, and then you'd probably lose your temper still laughin' and start pullin' the trigger.

A 16-year-old boy from the random sample reviewed his involvement in stealing "fuzz busters," a daylight burglary, and a gang fight. Although he reported relatively high drug use, including alcohol, marijuana, amphetamines, and barbiturates in the month preceding the interview, he insisted that in each instance he was not using drugs. He observed, "You get high when it's time." But if you don't want to get caught engaging in crime, you avoid drugs: "You got to be mellow for that shit." (Also see lengthy section in chapter 9 where Gallo reports using or avoiding various substances before committing crimes.)

This choice of using drugs or alcohol before crime to achieve certain desired psychological effects (for example, to "get courage") is as close as seriously involved youths come to attributing their own behavior to disinhibition. In the process, however, they turn such disinhibition explanations inside out. Rather than consuming large amounts of alcohol or drugs and subsequently losing control of their behavior and doing crimes they would not otherwise commit, these youths begin with plans to commit a crime and only then seek to suppress their fears. They claim to control their consumption to a desired level so as to be better able to commit the crime effectively. Yet they also recognize that intoxicated states are not appropriate to every specific type of crime. This rhetoric of explanation, however, is a continued assumption of their ability to maintain their own self-control over the important physical and psychological effects of heavy drug and alcohol consumption.

## Summary and Conclusions

In this chapter we delineated how adolescents themselves view the relationship between drugs, alcohol, and crime. Substantial differences appear to exist between youths who are themselves involved in these activities and those who are not.

Noninvolved youths talked about the drug/alcohol–crime relationship in the most conventional or stereotypic terms—emphasizing the irrationality that results from drug use and the criminogenic aspects of drug addiction. These respondents did not offer lengthy or complicated responses.

More involved youths drew on their own experiences in order to make sense of the drug/alcohol–crime connection. For some, this was restricted simply to statements they had heard—that, for example, drug users steal, or that persons steal because they need something they could not otherwise acquire. These respondents disagreed about the influence of alcohol and drug use on crimes of violence (some described violence as more likely, others as less likely) where drugs or alcohol are involved. Quite consistently, however, the respondents viewed drug and alcohol use as resulting in *impulsive* behavior, including theft or vandalism, and thus as indirectly contributing to crime.

The most criminally involved subjects did not differ from the other respondents in these conclusions—they concur that drug use indirectly leads to crime under certain circumstances—but they often deny such a connection in *their own* cases, and few accept a simple drugs-cause-crime explanation of anyone's behavior. About themselves, they report behaving impulsively at times when under the influence of alcohol or drugs, but say they were never out of control. Rather, they maintain that they choose when and how to use alcohol and drugs; under some conditions these substances are ingested because they enhance the activity, at other times they are avoided because they interfere with skillful performance.

These different views on the relationship between drugs/alcohol and crime reflect varying experiences available to categories of adolescents and reveal the views of those most experienced in drug use and criminal involvement as being most different from adult understandings of delinquent behavior. In the next chapter we will also find a surprising difference between adult views of the role of dealers and the actual experiences of the respondents who buy and sell drugs.

# 4
# Drug Selling and Dealing among Adolescents

*With Erica Wood*

During a given year, it is estimated, 10 percent of all youths engage in illegal drug transactions (Huizinga, 1982, 1984; Johnson, 1973; Single and Kandel, 1978), and a few youths carry out many drug sales per year. Several general conclusions about drug selling are documented in the research literature, although they are not widely known to the public. First, the vast majority of drug sellers are drug users; non-drug-using dealers who sell marijuana or other illicit drugs to youthful consumers are atypical. Second, increasing levels of marijuana use are associated with drug selling and with initiation to the use of other substances (Blum, 1972; Goode, 1970, 1971, 1972; Clayton and Voss, 1981; Johnson, 1973; Single and Kandel, 1978). Third, the probability of selling drugs other than marijuana increases as the frequency of such drug use increases.

Adolescent drug dealing is highly concentrated. In a sample of the nation's youth (Elliott and Huizinga, 1984; Huizinga, 1984; Johnson, Wish, and Huizinga, 1986), less than 3 percent of the youths used cocaine (virtually all of these also used marijuana and pills). Almost 60 percent of these cocaine users sold illicit drugs, and one-quarter sold nonmarijuana substances. The cocaine users–dealers also sold marijuana (and other drugs) much more frequently than did their pill-using and marijuana-using counterparts; the former had an estimated average of 81 drug sales a year (Huizinga, 1984).

Such information about the social distribution and volume of dealing, however, reveals little about the drug dealers, their clients and patterns of drug selling, or the social structure of drug sales by adolescents to other youths. In a paper on a related topic, Single and Kandel (1978:127) remarked that "the subcultural model of drug escalation must be expanded to consider situational, social, and psychological factors."

Goode's (1970) description of marijuana selling and Waldorf et al.'s (1977) descriptions of cocaine dealing provide the best ethnographic accounts of drug dealing. These authors found little evidence of a non-using drug dealer who sells to youths for profit only. Even the high-level importers and wholesale distributors studied by Adler and Adler (1982, 1983; Adler, 1985) were heavy drug users.

The informal nature of interactions between drug distributors and their drug-using associates was also emphasized by the authors just cited (see also Blum, 1972; Carey, 1968). A user who buys, say, an ounce of marijuana, is expected to share it with friends or to sell them some at cost. A user also quickly discovers that selling marijuana (or other drugs used) is an easy way to obtain that drug "for free" (that is, with no cash outlay by the user–dealer). Many illegal drug transactions occur in a social context wherein the seller is expected to provide drugs for free or below retail cost, or where the buyer is expected to "turn on" with the dealer. Relationships between a retail dealer and higher level distributors, however, are more difficult to identify.

Important questions about drug selling among adolescents remain to be answered. From whom do youthful drug sellers obtain supplies, and in what quantities? What are the characteristics of their customers? Where, when, and how do drug sellers conduct sales? What precautions do sellers take to prevent arrest and victimization?

Among our respondents, virtually all sellers were users of a wide variety of substances. The level of their dealing varied significantly, from those who sold drugs a few times to those who engaged in a more structured activity. The respondents themselves differentiated between *selling* and *dealing*. Drugs were frequently "fronted" or given on "credit" by a higher level dealer to the retail dealer, who had to return an agreed amount of money. Many retail dealers sold drugs without significant cash profit in order to gain "free" drugs for themselves. The most heavily involved dealers, however, sold drugs for a distinct profit in either cash or future credit in drugs. Those buying large quantities of drugs (kilos of marijuana or hundreds of pills) for resale reported acquiring the drugs from older, established dealers, who generally came from outside their school community and often from outside their neighborhood. With a few exceptions, nearly all selling occurred within a loosely structured circle of friends, relatives, friends of friends, and acquaintances who were considered trustworthy. Dealers considered certain locations as safe and viable and others as hazardous for both seller and client. Although most dealers also engaged in nondrug crimes, they rarely reported committing such crimes while selling drugs.

The interviews with our respondents were designed to provide answers to the questions raised earlier. Specifically, respondents were asked how they obtained cannabis and noncannabis drugs, when they began buying drugs, from whom they bought drugs (close friends? acquaintances? street sellers?), and how frequently they had purchased drugs within the past thirty days. The 32 respondents who reported selling drugs at least once were asked the following questions: When did you first sell? Have you sold more than once or twice? What is the most you ever sold? How do you get drugs to sell? To whom have you sold? How do you go about selling? How much money comes from drug sales?

The analysis of the subjects' responses is presented in two sections. The first describes characteristics of the dealers: the extent of their dealing, their reported motives for dealing, their own drug use, and their association with crime-related activity. The second section describes the suppliers from whom adolescents get their drugs, the market for drugs, the buyers, how the deal is communicated, where transactions most frequently occur, and the risks involved in the transactions as perceived by the adolescent dealers.

## Characteristics of Adolescent Dealers

Those adolescents in our sample who sold drugs often had an observed or reputed involvement with drug use or other criminal activity. Of the 32 respondents who reported selling drugs at least once, 4 were from the random sample, 20 from the purposive sample, and 8 from the sample of detained youths. All of the detained sellers had been arrested on charges other than drug selling. Their drug-selling activity was largely unknown to police. All but 3 of the dealers were male and all but 3 were white.

### Sellers versus Dealers

Although these subjects all violated legal statutes against selling drugs, in their own minds they made important distinctions between "selling" and "dealing." A 17-year-old female from the purposive sample who actively used both cannabis and noncannabis drugs (amphetamines, cocaine, and barbiturates), and who also had a history of minor fraud, vandalism, shoplifting, and other petty larcenies, defined her behavior as occasional "selling," which she explicitly distinguished from "dealing."

> *Q:* Have you ever sold any other drugs, have you ever dealt marijuana or any of the other drugs?
> *A:* Yeah, a little bit, I can't afford to do it, anything big but . . .
> *Q:* What have you dealt?
> *A:* Well, I don't, I don't consider it dealing. I mean I'll sell, hits of speed to my friends and, an, uh, joints or nickel bags to my friends but that's not really dealing.

A 15-year-old male from the purposive sample with a history of using marijuana, LSD, amphetamines, and cocaine and of committing minor crimes made a similar distinction between dealing and selling:

> *Q:* Have you ever sold marijuana?
> *A:* Yah, I mean, I never deal, deal, like persons who deal, but I sold lots of times. I be out on the street and only got herb, and need some money, sell two joints, that's two dollars ya know.

Others buy and sell drugs in substantially larger quantities and do so on a frequent and predictable basis. A 15-year-old male in the sample of detained youths said his first supplier was a friend who used to steal pot from a brother. Later, after his dealing activity intensified and his contacts expanded, a new supplier would loan or "front" him several pounds of marijuana at a time:

*Q:* Ah, how do you usually buy it now, just in bags, or ounces, pounds?
*A:* Pounds, I don't buy it. He [fronts] it to me, then I get the money from the guys, then I give it to him. Then, he gives me so much money out of that, well, maybe $80 or $90. Takes me probably three months to sell it all. He gives me about two pounds, which is a lot.
*Q:* Well, how do, where do you keep it?
*A:* Right in my room, under my bed. There's a bag, about two bags the size of this. Did you ever hear of a kilo? Probably about this wide, and about this perfect square, like that, about this high, thick bag; if anybody ever calls me up and say they want something, I just, I'll take it out, stick in a baggie, how much they want.

The subjects appeared to perceive themselves as "dealing" only when they purchased in large amounts (either by weight or by dollar amount). In addition, "dealers" appear to be those who can obtain sizable amounts of drugs on credit; that is, they can repay the supplier after they have sold the drugs.

## Reasons for Dealing

Generally, the youths who sold drugs give two major reasons for their behavior—acquiring a supply of drugs for their own use and obtaining money. The two reasons were frequently mixed, however, and difficult to disentangle; the nondrug profits from drug sales were used to purchase other substances or a wide variety of minor consumable articles.

A number of respondents who described their dealing and selling activity as limited said they sold drugs to get quick cash or drugs. A 16-year-old male from the purposive sample said that he sold when he needed pocket money:

*A:* Or, Ashley want some speed, or, Ashley I want this, I want that. I's saying, what am I, a neighborhood drug store or something?
*Q:* Why do you suppose people think that?
*A:* I don't know, maybe it's just because, some, I usually have stuff. But I usually don't, I don't like . . . I deal only when I need money. Like much money. I'll sell a couple of hits of speed, or I'll just need pocket money, I'll sell speed.

Another male respondent, a 17-year-old from the purposive sample who sometimes sold joints of marijuana for beer or cigarette money, said he smoked away most of his profits, a problem facing adolescent dealers:

Q: When you sold, uh, the pot, do you usually just sell bags or did you sell joints, or . . .?
A: Never sold joints, never. I used to pinch and, like, if I needed a dollar, you know, if I needed to buy a pack of cigarettes, or I wanted to get some beer, I'd sell, you know, a couple of joints. But, my downfall is I smoked a lot of my profit.
Q: Hmmm.
A: Because the guy that we got it from doesn't even get high, and he was selling dope, and that's like, the best way to, sell dope.

A 14-year-old male in the detained sample described how he made a substantial cash outlay for marijuana but got little money for selling it because he smoked most of his stash:

Q: Ah, how much money did you make?
A: I paid $220 for it, and I didn't make that much back, 'cause I smoked it.

Most of the sellers–dealers appeared to use most of their profits to buy more drugs (either to use or to sell); any residual profit was disposable income. Only two of the dealers, both from the purposive sample, reported accumulating substantial amounts of cash from their selling activity. A 17-year-old male from the purposive sample described his profits from dealing, his savings, and his plans:

Q: How come you have the money?
A: Because it's in the bank.
Q: And that's left from what?
A: From, uh, two summers ago and last summer.
Q: So how much do you have in the bank right now?
A: Uh, about four thousand. I just leave [it] there for my car. Soon as I get my license, shit, I'm going to buy my car.

Another 17-year-old male from the purposive sample, who at one time was heavily involved in drug dealing, was saving his profits for college. He described his willingness to work hard and the apparent irony of "doing something illegal to make something good":

A: I love working, I've never not liked working, you know. I will do anything for, for money. You know, anything legal. You know I used to deal drugs, used to . . . I just stopped about a month ago.

*Q:* Why?

*A:* You know it's good money, it's like, I was doing something illegal to put money in the bank for college. I made, eleven hundred dollars, and put it in the bank. So that's like, you know, I was doing something illegal, to make something good. . . .

Some of those who sold drugs occasionally suggested that abstaining from use (which they preferred not to do) was the best way to maximize profits. However, the dealers who reported making the largest profit and even saving substantial sums did so by handling relatively large quantities of drugs, especially marijuana, which was the bulk of their business.

### Dealers as Users

As noted at the beginning of the chapter, most drug sellers routinely use drugs themselves. Moreover, once a drug user begins selling drugs, the extent and variety of his or her drug use may increase. A 20-year-old male from the purposive sample typifies the relationship between selling and using:

*Q:* But, did you use them [uppers] ever?

*A:* A couple of times. Not very much. Just tried them. Whenever something new came around I'd try it before I got it and sell it.

When dealing, respondents either consumed part of their dealing supply, obtained a commission in drugs rather than cash from their supplier, or both. One 17-year-old male from the purposive sample reported occasional use of cocaine, pills, and acid and daily use of marijuana. He described a typical pattern among adolescent dealers who keep their own supply ("head stash"):

*Q:* And how do you get that?

*A:* My head stash? Dealer. You know when I buy a quarter I get to keep an ounce out of the quarter and I can sell a quarter in a day. You know if I only smoke half an ounce a day I have that half ounce left, and I just keep on saving it. I had something like eight ounces one time. Eight ounces of my own head stash.

The most commonly used and sold substance is marijuana. Among youths who sold drugs, virtually all were near daily users of marijuana and sold it more routinely than any other substance. Most sellers also used other substances, but on a less regular basis. Those who sold nonmarijuana substances generally used by preference but sold according to what was popular in the market.

The same 17-year-old who reported using speed in an earlier excerpt was reluctant to deal speed in small quantities because it involved too much effort for too small a return:

*Q:* Did you deal other things besides marijuana?

*A:* No, except for speed, and that was when I was 15. I dealed a little bit of speed, and that was it.

*Q:* You didn't like dealing with speed?

*A:* No. Fifty cents a hit. Be realistic. People would come over to my house and ask for about five hits. Uh, don't laugh.

One 15-year-old male from the purposive sample said that although he used speed, he stopped selling it because he lost money:

*Q:* So that you could charge them almost anything and they'd buy it, just to—'cause they thought they were cool or something.

*A:* Yeah. But I didn't sell anything at school. I couldn't . . . nobody would buy it. Nobody was buying it. They didn't know what it was.

## Dealers' Histories of Involvement with Other Crime

All of our drug-selling youths also reported some level of involvement with nondrug crime. With only a few exceptions, however, they did not engage in nondrug crime while they were selling drugs. (Huizinga, 1982, 1984, 1986; Johnson, Wish, Huizinga, 1986; Johnson et al., 1984, report that almost all drug sellers commit some types of nondrug crime.)

When an illegal act (usually unreported) did occur in association with dealing, it generally involved stealing the drugs that were part of the potential deal. "Ripping off someone else's stash" occurred fairly frequently. The following quote from a 15-year-old male from the purposive sample is representative of this type of activity:

*Q:* How about that summer?

*A:* Nah, occasionally. During the tenth grade, which was kind of, me an Lane stole forty hits [of speed].

*Q:* Why do you say that's bad?

*A:* 'Cause I don't like to steal it. You know, it was kind of hard to pass it up.

*Q:* Tell me the story, how did you steal it? When was this?

*A:* See Lane, Lane bought some 'cause we wanted to buy a joint, or something to get high after school, and Lane had a dollar in his locker, so he bought two hits from this kid. And so I was going to buy two hits.

*Q:* Was this a kid that you knew?

*A:* Not really. But we seen him, Lane seen him and he asked if he wanted to buy two hits.

*Q:* And you bought them in school?

*A:* Yah, so he said, "It's in my locker," so we walked down to his locker, and he was opening up his locker and getting it, and me and Lane both had the same idea . . . we just watched, you know, looked at his combination. Then, like, it was late, so I gave him a dollar and we walked up the hall and ran and just went back to his locker.

*Q:* You took them all?

*A:* I didn't really want to take them all. Lane just pulled the bag and ran into the bathroom. Then we split 'em up, we were just, like, we were giving them away. This was when I knew Erin. I sold a bunch to her. Lane gave this girl like twelve hits, eleven, she took eleven.

In the one incident in which violent crime occurred in conjunction with a drug deal, Gallo (see chapter 9) reported shooting a man in the leg for trying to steal the marijuana before it was paid for. This 17-year-old dealer from the purposive sample had one of the most extensive histories of drug dealing in the study sample.

Gallo described his neighborhood as a "rowdy" place where a lot of young people lived and spent their time "getting stoned, breaking windows, slicing tires." Most of his friends also "got high." He reported that his parents were separated and that his relationship with his mother was stressful, to the extent that he felt she hated him. His involvement with crime ranged in intensity from writing graffiti to burglary, arson, serious assault, and the shooting he reported in his interview.

*Q:* Okay, so you were up in the park selling reefer?

*A:* Yeah, and this dude came over and he wanted four pounds.

*Q:* Did you, were you waiting for him, did you know him?

*A:* No, we didn't know he was coming, somebody told him where we were. And, uh, we were up in the round circle where it goes, like a little pool, one time, and there was little bushes all around it. And the dude came up and asked us for four pounds. And, uh, he checked it out and everything, and he liked it. And then he went to haul ass. And he got shot.

*Q:* You shot him in the leg?

*A:* Yeah. And that was it. He fell to the ground, and we grabbed the dope and hauled ass.

*Q:* And nothing ever happened? It never got reported?

*A:* Nope.

In general, a more representative trend from the sample would suggest that when crime-related activity does occur during a drug deal, it usually involves stealing the drugs or money associated with the drug transaction. (Theft of drugs and violence surrounding selling are discussed at greater length in chapters 5 and 6). Persons who sell drugs are also active in various types of nondrug crime, but generally at other times and places.

## The Structure of Drug Dealing

Drug dealing among our respondents does not appear to have had a predictable organizational structure, as suggested in some of the literature on street dealing. The population of adolescents in our sample represents the lower end of the hierarchy of drug distribution with respect to both the organization of those involved in making the sales and the quantity of drugs being sold. However, a distinct sense of the relationships between adolescent dealers and their suppliers emerges from the data, as does some definition of the drug market and the method and locus of the drug deals (see also Adler, 1985; Johnson, 1973; Waldorf et al., 1977).

In this section we look first at how the adolescent dealers describe their relationships with those people who supply them with drugs and how the connection is generally made in a drug deal. We also describe which markets exist for various drugs and why, the relationship between the adolescent dealer and his or her buyers, the methods of communication in a drug deal, acceptable locations for a deal, and perceptions of risk while dealing.

### The Suppliers

The analysis suggests that there were two types of sources for drugs in most of the drug deals described. Depending on the adolescent's level of involvement in selling, the source generally was either (1) an older, more established dealer outside the adolescent's school, social community, and neighborhood or (2) a friend in his or her network of friends who essentially acted as middleman in the deal and passed the drugs (with and without commission) to the adolescent to sell.

**Adult Suppliers.** Six youths who sold large quantities of drugs on a regular basis were about the only subjects who reported that some of their suppliers were older persons who sold to them. Those adults lived in Yule City but were generally outside the youths' school, social, and recreational circles. Such adults generally will not sell to youths, except to those (like themselves) who buy in large amounts for resale to other youths. The 17-year-old male (Gallo) from the purposive sample with highest level of dealing activity in the sample described some of his prime contacts:

*Q:* How do people know that they can come to you to do stuff like that?
*A:* 'Cause they know who there is. They know who's in business and who ain't. 'Cause they find me out from their friends. And you know a lot of people know me. And a lot of people know that, and I can get anything you want. All I do is go see if my brothers, so, see, Ditto, D.D., Henry. Them are my big-time dealers. Henry, Ichebod, and uh, Pepper are all the big-time dealers.

*Q:* Anyone from the college?

*A:* Yeah, I've got one dude in the university named Tyrone.

*Q:* And these are all older guys? About how old?

*A:* Yup . . . 29, 30, 32. D.D. is 35. Ditto is 32, uh, Henry's 34, Pepper is 29, Ichebod 28, Tyrone's, uh, 30, and Iven Clam is 30.

The same respondent explained that he was one of the few to have connections with big-time dealers. Generally, big-time dealers do not want to take the risk of trading with young people:

*Q:* Do you think it's easier for kids your age to get reefer or a lot easier for adults?

*A:* No, its easier for adults.

*Q:* How come?

*A:* 'Cause adults, you know, they, uh, they got the money, and little punks or, you know, something like that. Most big dealers, they don't like little punks coming in their house because it looks suspis, you know, sus . . .

*Q:* Suspicious?

*A:* Yeah. Suspicious.

One 16-year-old male from the random sample described his relationship with his supplier, the manager of a local chain restaurant, as part friendship, part business:

*Q:* Who are you thinking of?

*A:* Um, he's the manager of Jackson's on Rayno Road, his name's Tom . . . He's more of, like a friend than an acquaintance.

*Q:* And you said he's a dealer friend, is he someone you buy a lot of drugs from, or just some pot, or periodically, or what?

*A:* More, if I need a place to get, that's where I can get it, but like, I don't really, he's more into like pounds, quarter-pounds, hundred hits, a thousand hits, you know, things like that. And so, he's just an acquaintance. Like a lot, I go there with a lot of my friends that are buying different things.

*Q:* So what does he deal in, what kinds of drugs?

*A:* Everything. Just, you know, he deals drugs that I haven't heard of, that come in just [snap] and "Hey, it's in town, but it won't be back."

One 15-year-old male from the detained sample described his drug suppliers as older adults, associated with the Mafia, who dealt in large quantities:

*Q:* So, you really don't have to worry about things you are telling me. So, what are you saying, these older people, older friends are dealers.

*A:* Mafia.

*Q:* Are you serious about that? How did you get to know them?

*A:* There's a friend that I know, his uncle. They call themselves Mafia, but it's nothing like that, nothing like that. Like what you see on TV. It is the Mafia, but not like what you see on TV. . . .

*Q:* Well, what is it really like?

*A:* Just regular people. Except they deal a lot of stuff; they're into a lot of stuff.

*Q:* Like what? Drugs?

*A:* They are high-paid hit men and things like that. So, I usually get my stuff from them, they give it to me, and I sell it to people. They [front] it to me, then I sell it to kids, then I give them the money; I keep some for myself.

**Adolescent Suppliers.** A few of the respondents said that they would buy drugs from anyone who had a supply of the type of drug they needed, but most adolescent dealers preferred to trade either with the type of suppliers just mentioned or with friends. Although the largest dealers will sell drugs to people they do not know personally, buyers still either have to be recommended or must be in the right place (a particular park or bar) and look like "heads." Without a recommendation, buyers can obtain only small amounts and risk being sold inferior goods. In almost all cases, our respondents who sold small amounts of drugs, even regularly, obtained the drugs from other youths who dealt regularly. If irregular users obtained drugs from adults, the adults were relatives or employees; often, adult suppliers were unknowing contributors whose "stash" or prescription was stolen by a babysitter or younger sibling. Generally speaking, the data suggest that most adolescent drug distribution occurs between acquaintances and friends considered trustworthy and involves relatively small quantities of drugs and youths who have a limited involvement in dealing.

One of the three females in the study who reported dealing , a 15-year-old from the purposive sample, said she sold drugs for a friend just out of friendship:

*Q:* When you sell, do you usually sell what you have of your own, or do you make a deal with Andy and get it?

*A:* Sometimes I sell my own if I have it, and if I don't, I make the deal, and I go to Andy.

*Q:* About how many days in the last month have you sold?

*A:* In the last month? Let's see, seven or eight.

*Q:* How much money have you made?

*A:* I haven't made anything. Andy makes it.

*Q:* He doesn't give you any cut at all?

*A:* He gives me pot here and there when I need it.

*Q:* But nothing regularly when you make the deal, or get a head stash or anything?

*A:* Ah, ah, he offers, but, ah, naw.

*Q:* Why?

*A:* 'Cause we're friends. He's a good friend, he's my best friend's boyfriend. It's just doin' him a favor.

Another young woman, a 14-year-old from the purposive sample, described selling for a boyfriend:

*Q:* Okay. Have you ever sold any?

*A:* Uh-huh.

*Q:* When was that? When did you do that?

*A:* I did it for Harold. I was selling it for Harold.

*Q:* How come? How did you work that out?

*A:* He just asked me if I would sell it for him. I said all right. I sold it for him.

*Q:* I mean how come he asked you and then what did you do?

*A:* He just asked me if I wanted to deal because he had a lot to sell.

*Q:* Uh-huh.

*A:* And he asked me if I wanted to sell some. I said all right. I just called up some people and said, "Do you want to buy some pot?" and they said yeah. "Come on over and get it." They came over.

*Q:* Do you think you'll do that some more?

*A:* If he asked me to. I won't do it for anyone else.

*Q:* Um, did you get some money out of the deal or something?

*A:* Yeah.

*Q:* How much?

*A:* An ounce and some money, too.

Frequently, a friend will introduce an adolescent dealer to a source of supply. Gallo described this kind of introduction:

*Q:* How did you meet him? How did you get involved with him?

*A:* Because I know Otto's brother, and I just met him one day. 'Cause he wanted Otto to do some work, and he, Otto said—he asked Otto if, um, he wanted to bring a friend and Otto said yeah, Han, come on along, you know, and he got us blasted, and he said, "Yeah, I deal," he said. You know, that's how we hooked up. Then Otto's brother gave us the front money to get that going.

## The Drug Market: Supply and Demand

The interviews provide some insight into the interplay between supply and demand in the drug market among adolescents. Neither side of the equation is as clearly defined as are supply and demand in a more traditional market situation, but some specificity on both the demand and the supply side emerges from the analysis.

On the supply side, it is clear that some dealers specialize in certain types of drugs, whereas others deal whatever drug they can get. Frequently an adolescent dealer reported, for example, that he got marijuana and speed from one supplier and acid and cocaine from another. In a very general sense, it appears that cannabis drugs (marijuana and hashish) and noncannabis drugs tend to define two separate arenas of·the market and that nearly all suppliers–dealers and adolescent dealers have had some experience selling marijuana.

Gallo pointed to some supply specificity when he described his hashish connection:

*Q:* When you buy hash do you buy it from pretty much the same people you buy reefer from?
*A:* No, D.D., D.D. gets some good hash.
*Q:* How come? He gets hash but does he get reefer too?
*A:* Yeah. He gets reefer too, but he can get the best hash.
*Q:* How come?
*A:* 'Cause he's the best person to get it from. He gets it from his brother and his brother gets it from uh, uh, I forgot or some bullshit. He gets it from, straight from the border, so you know it's excellent hash.
*Q:* So he's the one you really get it from?
*A:* Yeah.
*Q:* Do you ever get it from anybody else?
*A:* No.

In the following interview passage, another 17-year-old male from the purposive sample, an active adolescent dealer, described a conversation he had with a young dealer friend in which they evaluated a supply-side decision:

*Q:* Well, how do you decide, or get involved in this dealing?
*A:* Because I said, Otto, you know, we need to make some money. What can we do, 'cause speed's ten times easier to deal than dope, a hundred times easier to deal than dope. Well, it's easier, and then it's not easier, because you can sell dope quicker, but speed's easier to deal, because you don't have to break up bags and stuff, you know, and it's not, you know, you don't have like big quantities. You just have a little bag, you know, dope's in more demand than speed. So we just . . .
*Q:* Is it as easy to get speed from a dealer, is there as much speed around as there is dope?
*A:* Um, no, there isn't, but I know where to get it. You know, I can get a whole bunch of different kinds, but we just decided, we said, Otto, I said, Otto, 'cause Otto's about the only person I would trust dealin' with 'cause you know,

if one of us ever got caught, you know, we would not [turn] each other in. But, um, you know, we said, I said Otto let's do somethin' to make some money. I started dealin' something. You know, we thought of dope, and dope is a pain in the butt, you know, we'd be goin' to school, too, you know, I could take speed to school and stuff and sell it. But, um, you know, so we decided that we weren't gonna do any of it, well, we had, if we wanted to do speed, we'd get it from somewhere else. So you know, we didn't do any speed when we were dealin'. We got a thousand hits, we sold those, and got another thousand, and when they ran out, we quit.

Occasionally, an adolescent dealer will curtail or limit his selling activity for other than economic reasons. The same dealer just quoted explained why he wouldn't sell acid:

*Q:* Do you ever sell [acid]?
*A:* Um, no, never sold [trips]. I wouldn't do that.
*Q:* Why?
*A:* Because like I said, it affects everyone different. And I wouldn't want to be responsible if somebody got stupid and took like two hits and just tripped their brains out.
*Q:* So when you sell drugs you really feel responsible for how the people use them?
*A:* Well, dope, dope I know doesn't affect people like that. Speed doesn't either, 'cause you know, if someone takes speed and they get sick, they know not to buy it, and if they're buyin' speed they're stupid, but, um, I wouldn't sell trips 'cause it affects everyone different.

Demand in the drug market is less clearly defined than supply. Traditionally, demand sparks supply; here, however, because of the illegality of the market, what is accessible often seems to create the demand. There is little question from the analysis that the most frequently used drug is marijuana. Marijuana, the data suggest, is by far the most easily and consistently accessible drug, followed by speed and hashish. Rush (an over-the-counter type of inhalant), cocaine, acid, and prescription-type drugs (such as Valium or codeine) are less frequently sold and used relative to the demand for marijuana and then speed and hashish.

It is difficult to establish the determinants of the demand for drugs among adolescents. The data, however, indicate that some aspects of the following may be involved: (1) expected sensation from and impact of the drug (marijuana makes you mellow; speed makes you fly), (2) peer pressure and current fashion (the people who use drugs and the drugs they use are emulated by others), (3) available supply, and (4) cost. As the following discussion indicates, other factors, such as the season of the year, time away from school, and nature of the buyers, also influence the dealing behavior of youths.

## Methods of Dealing: Buyers, Communications, and Locale

Adolescent dealers in the sample generally sold drugs to their friends and to friends of friends who were known to be trustworthy. A 17-year-old adolescent from the purposive sample who was heavily involved in dealing described his relationship to the majority of his buyers:

*Q:* Who do you usually sell to when you sell or deal?
*A:* Carolyn, uh, and just friends.
*Q:* You never sell to just acquaintances, people you kind of know from school or . . .?
*A:* Yeah, I sell to other people, too, but not as much as I do my friends.
*Q:* Do you ever sell to somebody you don't know at all to just, you know, who wants to buy?
*A:* No.

At times, the buyers were members of the respondent's family. The same interview continues:

*Q:* Do you ever sell to adults?
*A:* Yeah, Yvonne.
*Q:* How old is she again?
*A:* She's, uh, 19, 20, something like that.
*Q:* How about older adults though?
*A:* Yeah, my brother. Once in a while I have to get them some reefer. They can't find none so I have to get him some.

One 15-year-old female from the purposive sample indicated that selling drugs to family members was acceptably safe, but selling to friends at school was risky:

*Q:* What kind of people come to you?
*A:* My sister, my friends, my aunts, cousins.
*Q:* How about people at school?
*A:* I wouldn't be caught doing that stuff in school, I don't do it in school. They know I get high but they don't know I sell for people.

At times the criteria for safe buyers extend from friends to people who have an acceptable appearance, who look "cool" or look "like heads." A 16-year-old from the detained sample said he sold mostly to friends but also to kids who looked cool:

*Q:* So you never just went out and tried to start selling it?
*A:* No.

*Q:* Who would you sell it to? Just close friends?

*A:* Um, sometimes, like a kid that seemed real cool with me, you know, and he seemed like that—I was that type of person who, like I could get some pot for him—weed, we'd call it. And, he just asked me if I could get him a half-ounce after school and I said, yeah, so, you know. You just come out over my house, you know, I told him, wait at my house, I run down the street, get it for him and I go over to [the] house or something like that, and just tell him to wait at the school or something. . . . After a while I just had him come over [where] he could get it himself.

*Q:* How can you tell a person who looks like they can buy pot for you?

*A:* Oh, I never dress up to go to school in my life. I mean, I mean, when I went to take pictures, sometimes I went to school in shorts and stuff—and I just never comb my hair or nothing. I comb my hair but it doesn't, I mean, like some kids are in the bathroom all day, you know.

Another respondent, also a 16-year-old from the detained sample, said he sold to heads:

*Q:* So, you just sold to everybody, not just friends, not just people you knew?

*A:* I sold, not to everybody, you know, but people—I don't know. Heads.

Just as buyers were consistently friends, acquaintances, and even family of adolescent dealers, the method of communication in a drug transaction was consistently found to be verbal. The data reveal that, without exception, communications were verbal, never written, and made mostly in person, frequently at social gatherings and many times over the telephone. A 16-year-old male described a drug transaction this way:

*Q:* Okay, so like tell me, this afternoon if you went home and called your dealer, and he said he had an ounce for you to sell, then who would you, how would you go about it . . . ?

*A:* I'd call up Ned, who was wanting, looking to buy, and he'd probably buy the whole ounce.

*Q:* Okay, if he didn't want it, who would you call?

*A:* Probably Hale Armitage.

*Q:* All right. Anybody else who you just normally think of?

*A:* No.

*Q:* Just those two, any girls?

*A:* Yeah. No, no girls.

*Q:* Okay, and then what do you do after you've made that contact? Do you go over to Hale's house or what?

*A:* Um, no, I just call him up and he comes over and picks it up.

Gallo complained that his house had become such a locus for drug sales and socializing that his "house" got him high:

*Q:* So that's how you spend your afternoons?

*A:* No, no, let me finish, um, then, uh, after that, about 1:00, like, kids might skip school, to go to, 'ford [Oxford High School], you know, go find somebody that might skip school and come over to my house. We'll just hang around, 'cause they think I have drugs or something. And then, about 2:00, Every School gets out. And then people I know from Every School come over to my house, and by this time there's about ten people in my house, and I don't like that. And this happens like every day, and I, I get so frustrated. Au'uh . . .

*Q:* Well, why don't you like it?

*A:* Because I don't like people hanging around my house. You know. Just, you know, I don't mind one or two people but I don't like millions of people in my house. And uh, some then, everybody leaves.

*Q:* Why don't you tell them that?

*A:* Oh, I have, you know, I kick them out, when I get mad, just say "everybody leave." And then, uh, then about 5:30 my mother comes home and, blah . . .blah . . .I shoot the crap with her for a little bit, then I go out, eat dinner, and then go out and do whatever. You know, it varies from now and then, you know, different times.

*Q:* Yeah.

*A:* But, like I said, my house gets me high, you know, people come over and say, oh let's do this, you know, just 'cause they want to hang out somewhere, and, you know, not staying in [the public and stuff].

*Q:* Uh-huh.

*A:* And I mind but, then again I don't. You know, because I'm getting, you now, I'm getting high for free. But, I don't like it to be like that though. You know. I don't like my house to get me high, you know. I like friends to come over and get me high, you know. It's, it's, it's strange.

The data indicate that some specific locations are favored as acceptable and safe places for drug transactions. The most frequently used location appears to be the homes of the adolescent dealers or the homes of their friends. Other favored locations include a city park well frequented by adolescents, the city swimming pool, and to a lesser extent the city skating rink. Some sites are not considered safe, especially drug selling "in the open" on the street. One of the most active dealers in the sample, a 17-year-old from the purposive sample, described some precautions he took when dealing:

*Q:* Any other things like that, that you do to avoid getting into trouble?

*A:* Uh, you know, stay off the, no, just go by people on the street like I said. Don't go that way or anything. I just don't look for trouble, like going through parks and shit anymore. I don't go for that. After I got jumped by those six kids, I don't go for shit like that. I used to try to do that to avoid people, you know? Just try going through them bushes and shit, you know, just to avoid it. One time I made it through with a quarter pound and slid up through them bushes. But the time I went through that, I only had that ten dollars, I didn't make it. You know, is that type of thing, I try avoiding everything I can. I don't like dealing on the street, 'cause you can get ripped off on the street. Unless you, you carry, whatever, but that is what I try to do. I try avoiding it.

Another 17-year-old male, also from the purposive sample, described his use of location:

*Q:* Well, what really made you decide to start dealing?
*A:* Because we needed the money. And it's good money. Good business. Very good business. So . . .
*Q:* Well, how would you work it?
*A:* Um, we'd get two pounds of dope, break it down, into ounces. Break it down into half-ounces. Nothing smaller than that. We'd go out to Reid's Pond every single day. We weren't, we weren't going out there to deal dope, we'd go out there to swim, 'cause it's a great place to hang out. We'd go there, and uh, we'd just ask around. Anybody want any dope, someone, we sold a quarter-pound one day, at Reid's Pond. And that's, you know, two or three pounds, you know, that's only like four quarter-pounds. We did it every . . .sold a quarter-pound a day.

The intensity of dealing is frequently episodic and also appears to vary considerably with the season, the available supply, and to some extent the adolescent's time away from school. Summer, according to several of the respondents, is the prime time for dealing. A 17-year-old male from the purposive sample said that he both sold and smoked marijuana less frequently during the winter. After the end of the ninth grade, however, his activity in both respects increased.

*Q:* After ninth grade. Now, isn't that the summer you met Ollie?
*A:* Yeah. We just—I don't know, I'd say [smoked] maybe four times a week.
*Q:* So it did go up a little bit?
*A:* Yeah.
*Q:* Okay, why?
*A:* Because, like, I said to get an ounce from Ira, everyday, and me and Ollie would go out and, to Reid Pond, and sell it.
*Q:* Uh-huh.

*A:* And, we'd just, either we'd sell it for forty-five cents and make five, or else we'd just take some out and sell it for forty cents. And we usually just took a little out, a couple of joints. And just got high. . . .

The data also indicate that adolescent dealers are not significantly concerned about the risk in dealing drugs with respect to legal or parental authority. One 16-year-old male from the purposive sample described his father's attitude toward his drug dealing:

*Q:* Does your father know when you're buying your own or selling it or do you try and hide it?
*A:* I don't have to. He doesn't ask. He doesn't look.

Although a number of the adolescent dealers reported that they had come close to being arrested for drug use and selling, few expressed concern about getting "busted." A 16-year-old male from the random sample who was an active dealer explained that even though the local police were aware of his dealing activities (he was on their list), he and his dealer friends were selling drugs in too small quantities to be of major concern to authorities:

*Q:* How come he got involved in that?
*A:* I don't know. I'm, he got to know this guy in it, and then, I asked him, you know, I said, what's the deal? And he said, he's seen me on the dealer's list. So I asked the guy, the undercover, I know the undercover, kind of, he showed me the list and I was smack dab on there. But they don't usually arrest us dudes, we're too small. You know, they only arrest people with twenty pounds and shit. All the pounds. If you arrest the . . .
*Q:* What?
*A:* If you arrest the small guy you don't get the big guy. You know, it ain't worth it.

Another respondent, an 18-year-old male from the purposive sample, curbed his selling activity according to his perception of the priorities and interests of local authorities:

*Q:* What have you dealt?
*A:* Reefer and speed. Some acid.
*Q:* Oh, acid?
*A:* I don't like dealing that because you got to, go with friends completely, you can't go meeting no new people or nothing, you know?
*Q:* Hmmm.
*A:* That's the way I feel. Yule is a bitch on chemicals, if you get busted.

## Summary and Conclusions

As in national studies (Elliott, Dunford, and Huizinga, 1983; Elliott and Huizinga, 1984; Elliott et al., 1985; Huizinga, 1984; Johnson, Wish, and Huizinga, 1986), about 10 percent of the randomly selected Yule City youths reported selling drugs. Overall, 32 of our 100 subjects did so, but we deliberately overselected sellers. The 32 youths revealed considerably diverse drug-selling patterns. Six subjects (one from the random group) were intensively involved in dealing; they had adult suppliers, purchased large quantities at a time, or obtained drugs on credit. These 6 sold to or supplied associates with drugs for subsequent resale and also made many direct sales to the ultimate consumer. Only 2 of the 6 reported saving large amounts of cash for nondrug purposes.

Among the remaining dealers, selling generally appeared to be an episodic, quasi-social activity that was done for or with friends. A primary motive for such subjects was to obtain "free drugs" (that is, without cash payment). Even those who reported wanting money frequently noted that they "smoked up the profits." Cash income generated by their drug sales was small ("pocket money") and may have been used to purchase other illegal substances.

Also consistent with national data (Clayton and Voss, 1981; Elliott, Dunford, and Huizinga, 1983; Elliott and Huizinga, 1984; Huizinga, 1984; Johnson, 1973; Johnson, Wish, and Huizinga, 1986) showing that drug selling increases directly with the extent of use, the Yule City drug sellers were typically daily or near daily marijuana users who also used other substances (speed, pills, cocaine, and heroin) on a less regular basis. Although all these drug sellers also reported committing nondrug crimes, they tended to avoid committing other crimes while selling drugs (with the exception of "ripping off" drug dealers).

If the behavior of these Yule City youths is reasonably typical of American youth, several major conclusions can be drawn from the analysis in this chapter. First, although sellers report two major motives—to gain drugs or money—few report substantial cash earnings or savings from sales. Most engage in sales primarily to obtain the drugs they use—at little or no cost. That is, near daily marijuana consumers constitute much of the "demand" for marijuana and other drugs, but many such users also "supply" those drugs to themselves and other, less frequent drug users. By engaging in this illegal activity, drug users–sellers maintain their high level of consumption with little or no cash outlay.

Second, much selling activity is highly private. Almost all sellers have friends, family, and acquaintances as their main customers. The transactions are typically made in the homes of sellers and customers. The dollar amounts in a given drug sale are rarely significant. Our respondents defined such activities as "selling," not "dealing." Selling may be seen as doing a favor for friends or lovers, as well as a means of obtaining "free drugs." Further, selling within their private social circles protects them from arrest and the loss of drugs or money.

Third, a few sellers do appear to become "dealers." Dealers are seen as those who can obtain large amounts (by weight or cash) of drugs on "credit" from (mainly adult) suppliers. Dealers appear most likely to sell drugs at public locations (parks, schools, street) where other drug-using youths hang out; to sell to persons who are personally unknown to them ("friends of friends," "heads"); to use their close friends to help them sell; to engage in daily or near daily selling and in multiple transactions per day; and to sell in large amounts (quarter-ounces of marijuana, hundreds of pills or hits).

Fourth, few sellers, including the dealers, appear concerned about parental or police pressure against their selling. Although they are aware of the risk of arrest, their selling activity is managed so that even the most active "dealers" appear to be small-time sellers. As a result, they are rarely arrested for drug sales; none of our eight self-reported dealers held in detention was arrested for drug sales, nor did any have a prior arrest for drug sales. Similar findings are reported by Dunford and Elliott (1982).

# 5
# Theft and the Consumeristic Mentality

I n chapter 3 we examined theft primarily in terms of its relationship with alcohol and drug use among youths. The findings outlined in that chapter suggest that, according to the youths, the relationship between drugs/ alcohol and theft has two major aspects: (1) drugs and alcohol are valued commodities sought by adolescents, and (2) theft provides a way for them to acquire either drugs and alcohol or the means to purchase those goods. Drugs and alcohol, however, are only two among many goods that Yule City youths described as goods they "need" or "want."

The youths' descriptions of drugs and other goods they steal and their reasons for doing so run somewhat parallel to the definition of *consumer goods:* "goods that directly satisfy human wants" (*Webster's New Collegiate Dictionary,* 1981 edition). The attitude the youths take toward such goods is also in line with what *Webster's* defines as a *consumer:* "one that utilizes economic goods."

In this chapter we look at the youths' descriptions of specific instances of theft events and their discussions of theft in general and suggest how young people legitimate their thefts by references that have parallels in a consumeristic mentality.[1] Specifically, we look at (1) youths' descriptions of theft events in which they were involved as actors or witnesses; (2) their explanations for their involvement in specific theft events; (3) their general theories about theft— that is, why persons (including themselves) steal; and (4) how their involvement varies with their sex and level of drug use.

Theft activities by youths in the Yule City sample ranged from shoplifting food items, makeup, and clothes to stealing a car and burglarizing houses. Within this range are included many other theft activities, such as stealing from parked cars and from parents, employers, and peers.

Shoplifting and petty theft were by far the most common theft activities and the ones in which most youths engaged early in their theft careers (Klemke, 1978). Burglaries of houses, stores, and cars were also reported by those most seriously involved in criminal activities. Theft of vehicles such as bicycles or cars—either temporarily (for practical use or for a joyride) or to keep or sell— were also described by many of the youths.

## The Consumeristic Mentality

The main characteristic of the consumeristic mentality, as expressed by the youths in our sample, is "wanting" or "needing" valued goods and services.

The main impetus the adolescents cited for their thefts (and the thefts of others) was the desire to acquire what they wanted or needed. Money is the main means of exchange by which they can legally acquire goods and services, and lack of money for items they wanted or needed was cited by the majority of youths as the reason behind their thefts (general and specific). Not only was theft undertaken to enable a youth to achieve the status of consumer (whether legitimate or not), but the activity of theft as well as the role of the youth in the theft can be seen as analogous to the legitimate activities of everyday consumers. The components of this consumeristic mentality and its role in theft events are described next.

### Theft to Acquire Consumer Goods

Yule City youths who had been involved in theft described their theft activities as ways to acquire "consumer goods" in the sense defined earlier. Added to the definition, however, is their concept of human "need." A 14-year-old male heavy user from the detained sample who had been involved in major crime, including auto theft and burglary, explained:

Q: So when you've shoplifted, it's always been for a reason?
A: Yeah. I needed it or I wanted it.
Q: Couldn't you have bought it? If you wanted it?
A: No. No.
Q: How come?
A: 'Cause I didn't have the money.

A 16-year-old male heavy user from the detained sample who had been involved in serious crime, including auto theft:

Q: Well, why do you think kids take things, you say you don't know why you do, why do you think other kids might?
A: Something to do maybe, they ain't got the money for it so they steal it.
Q: You think that's usually it?
A: Yup.
Q: Think it's 'cause they need it? Is that usually why you . . . ?
A: They usually stealin' it for money for something else.
Q: Um. . . .
A: I don't know, it's something bigger than you. This kid did it, he did it for this other kid; this kid was about six foot tall and asked him to go steal something and he got caught.

*Q:* How come the bigger kid wouldn't do it himself?

*A:* I don't know, 'cause he was scared or something.

*Q:* Um, what . . . under what circumstances would you take things? When would you?

*A:* When I don't have anything, no money, I'll take something.

A 14-year-old male heavy user from the detained sample who had been involved in serious crime, including burglary and mugging:

*A:* I guess, I just went out and did it 'cause I wanted to do it. . . .

*Q:* Uh-huh.

*A:* Stealing and so on and the money, ya know. I mean like my parents, my mother give me money, ya know money that she works every week for, ya know, and I mean, she's now paying for the house, and the new walls that she just put in, and stuff like that, and stuff for the house. She ain't got that much to give me, ya know, she give me, ya know, ten bucks a week, something like that, ya know. Ya know an that, that don't, take you no place. Ya know, so I feel I need more money, so I go out and steal it.

The same youth explained the importance and necessity of money for people who steal in general and for himself in the specific incident of his running away:

*Q:* How about crime, how come you do crime?

*A:* For money.

*Q:* How come people your age usually do crime?

*A:* Money.

*Q:* So what are the other reasons [besides drugs and alcohol] why people do it then? What are some of the other factors that enter into why people do crime then?

*A:* To get money for drugs, or get money, or get valuables, or, get something like that.

*Q:* Let's take a look at some of your stuff and see about that. If we look at some of the theft stuff, let's check it out. When you were doing the house burglary?

*A:* For money to get to Louisiana.

The theme continues, although in reverse, when the youths talk about refraining from theft. A 16-year-old male who was a light user and who had engaged in serious crime, including burglary:

*Q:* So since Hootertown, you haven't really been doing any of this stuff.

*A:* Right.

*Q:* How come, tell me a little about why you stopped.

*A:* 'Cause I don't have time for that no more. I don't need to steal no more, man, I don't think about it no more. Wha's somt'm I needed? I don't need nothin' desperately. People need somt'm desperately steal it.

*Q:* Is that why you were stealing stuff before?

*A:* [Yawning] Yeah. Money, I needed a lot of money.

*Q:* What did you need money for?

*A:* Just needed it.

*Q:* Nothing in particular?

*A:* No.

*Q:* You don't think you need a lot of money now, though?

*A:* [In a low voice] No, not now.

*Q:* How come, what's different about now?

*A:* I don't need no money now, what I need money for? I don't need no job. Yeah, I need a job, but you know, but what I need to carry money aroun', I don't need the money everyday. 'Cause I know I'll spen' it like crazy.

What and where youths steal and how they go about it are consumeristic in that the activity of stealing and the roles they play within that activity are analogous to the activities of and the role of a "consumer."

## *The Thief as Consumer*

Four broad forms of theft can be viewed as somewhat analogous to the motivations of a "consumer": (1) theft as shopping for goods, (2) theft of cash, (3) theft as work, and (4) theft as sport. All these activities are ultimately organized around the acquisition of consumer goods. Next we consider each of these in detail through the accounts of the subjects.

**Theft as Shopping for Goods.** Many of the theft events reported by our subjects can be viewed as "shopping" for desired goods, but money as the medium of exchange is replaced by what the youths perceive as skill and prowess in taking things without paying for them and without getting caught. This skill— what some of the youths referred to as being "slick enough not to get caught"— often consists, as we shall point out later, of recognizing or creating opportunities for taking things and "pulling it off" with little consequence beyond the successful acquisition of the valued item.

Many aspects of consumers' shopping behavior seem to be reflected in the youths' theft activities. Like most legitimate consumers,[2] the youths engaged in routine, planned, and unplanned acquisition, albeit all through theft. As with regular consumers, they were not limited to one type of shopping as individuals, nor was a single shopping trip limited to one of these types. As in regular shopping, the type of shopping event was dependent on the context of the shopping trip, planned and unplanned. The youths' goal, as for all buyers in shopping, was the direct acquisition of valued goods.

**Routine Theft.** For youths who steal, as well as everyday legitimate consumers, much of their activity is routine in nature. They discover they "need" or "want" something, go to a place where there is access to it,[3] and acquire it as quickly as possible. The legitimate consumer buys it; the thief takes it. The goal of the routine purchase is usually acquisition of such everyday items as food, cigarettes, or gas. Access to such items is typically very clear and certain. For the thief, knowing where to get such items quickly and believing that they can be stolen with ease (opportunity) is what makes this type of theft "routine."

A 16-year-old male heavy user from the detained sample, who had been involved in serious crime, including drug sales and joyriding:

Q: And where were you?
A: We were, uh, up in the attic, smokin' and drinkin', and stuff. So, come downstairs, we're all wasted, went outside, went down to house, got more wasted, got more drunk, then they stayed there, and I said I was gonna get some more beer: went to get more beer, brought it back up: I stole it and I got away with it, so I thought I was gonna, brought it back and said, ya, wait a minute, I'll go and get some more. . . .

A 15-year-old female light user from the detained sample was involved in minor crime, including shoplifting:

Q: Have you ever taken, um, or stolen things from a store, ya know, shoplifting?
A: Um, candy, and M&Ms, and that stuff. I walk around the store eating.
Q: So you just take a bag and open them up and eat them?
A: Yep. I just . . . yeah, I just take a bag off the shelf and I walk around the store and eat the whole bag. I eat apples and stuff. I did that before.
Q: Is that stealing?
A: Yeah, it's stealing. But at least you can't get caught.
Q: How come you do it?
A: I don't know. I, I just . . . I did it before, I, I stole M&Ms, and I stole an apple, and I was just walking around the store eating it.

An 18-year-old male heavy user from the purposive sample who had been involved in serious crime, including burglary and auto theft:

Q: Anything else? Have you ever taken anything else, of someone else's?
A: Gas, that's about it.
Q: What do you mean gas?
A: Some nights we'll go out and—we used to do it all the time, ah, 'cause my friend, ya know, he, he wasn't working but he had his car so it was the more gas he got, the more you went out, ya know, the later, the later he'd drive till, ya know, go home—if he had—go out and gotten a lot of gas, ya know,

you'd come home at six o'clock if you didn't. But he got caught and ah, ya know, he went through court a long time, and he finally got all the charges dropped, I don't know how—I didn't ask him, ya know. But lately I've only done it like once in the past month and, ah, it was just that he ran out of gas and we just went and siphoned it.

A 15-year-old male heavy user from the purposive sample who was involved in minor crime, including drug sales and graffiti:

Q: Do you know anybody who's gotten caught?
A: Yeah, he got caught finally. He was in Hillery Stores and they had cops all over the place. 'Cause people were stealing stuff out of their store. And they were wondering who was doing it. And he was—he—all he went in there for, he went in there to steal a candy bar, and he walks back out and this guy with a three-piece suit walks out behind him and said "hey didn't you just steal a Snickers that doesn't belong to you?"

**Planned Theft.** When legitimate consumers want or need a particular item or set of items, they often plan the purchase. This may include saving money, budgeting, watching for sales, or simply planning a specific time for the purchase. Some of the theft events described by the youths were planned in this manner. Money, however, did not play a role in the plan, except that lack of money was said to necessitate the plan. Instead, the plan included locating and going where access and opportunity for the desired items were known to exist and carrying out the theft.

Planned acquisition is different from other types of theft in that *specific* goods are the goal of the theft. The items are typically not everyday or small items (access and opportunity combined), so a certain amount of planning is required. Planned thefts follow a sequence in which the youths decide they want or need a particular item and then seek access–opportunity to acquire that item. Once access and opportunity are discovered, they commit the theft. An 18-year-old male heavy user from the purposive sample who had been involved in serious crime, including burglary and auto theft, explained how he went after a bicycle:

Q: Tell me about it.
A: All right. The first time I, was the time I took—I took two at once. Um, I was planning on it. Because summer school came up and for the first week we got a ride with my friend's mother, it was the three of us, Ned, Ivan, and myself, and they had bikes and that was the first week, ya know, we had to start riding bikes to school and I didn't really feel like walking to Oshkosh from my house. So I was gonna take the bike and the night I was gonna take it, they had it out—they had it on, on a bike rack with another bike on their car, so, ya know, I went, I went out about twelve o'clock and I had some bolt cutters

and I, I didn't have them with me, I mean, my friend had them and, ah, I was trying to get it and I had it about halfway and then I just set my alarm and woke up around three o'clock in the morning and just went out and got, got the two bikes, and I took the nicest bike of the ones and I just combined the parts, ya know, whatever was nicest and I just put it together and rode it to school, and rode it a couple—ah, a year and a half, two years.

Most often the youths were aware of access to a particular item they wanted and planned the theft accordingly. A 15-year-old female heavy user from the purposive sample who had been involved in drug selling described her friend's reasons for stealing shoes:

Q: Did Ethel ever get caught [shoplifting]?
A: Um-um, she does it all the time.
Q: Really?
A: Yeah.
Q: Real expensive stuff?
A: No. Just shoes. And little things.
Q: She likes shoes a lot?
A: Uh-huh. She gets a new pair, every time she thinks she needs a pair.
Q: And where does she usually get them?
A: Izzy's.
Q: How much do you think the shoes were worth, that you stole?
A: The ones we took? They were including tax and everything, about twenty dollars.

A 14-year-old male heavy user from the detained sample who had been involved in serious crime, including burglary:

A: I had a race car set and my, and the race car, ah, the race cars broke, my brother Bobby broke them. . . .
Q: Uh-huh.
A: So I went down and I stole some other ones from Armstrong's, or not Arms, Oliver's.

The following subject described his reason for breaking into a school and taking scales. He was a 17-year-old male heavy user from the purposive sample who had been involved in such crimes as burglary and major property destruction:

Q: How come you took the scales?
A: Um, I don't know. 'Cause I wanted them I guess.
Q: What for? What are you doing with them now?

*A:* Um, well, weigh pot, or whatever. Let my brother use them. 'Cause he always has something to weigh.

A 17-year-old male heavy user from the purposive sample who had been involved in serious crime, including burglary and auto theft:

*Q:* Did you ever plan out jobs? You know, like pick a house and really set it up? Tell me about it.

*A:* This one right next to [East's] house, his father's house. We planned that out like for about three days. Me and East had a, and East, we were only, thought we were going to go in there for reefer, 'cause this guy deal . . . dealt, quarter-pound. And East grabbed that, and I went into this one bedroom and there was a strong box sittin' there right? I busted it open, there was like a [billfold] of twenties; $400 in twenties. That was the only one we planned.

*Q:* What were you planning, what happened when you planned it, were you watching the house, watching when they left, or what?

*A:* Yeah, 'cause he had his dogs and, East knows the dogs and, what time he gets home from work, and his wife and all that stuff.

*Q:* Did you get busted on that one?

*A:* No.

**Unplanned Theft.** Unplanned theft is most akin to the consumer activity of browsing. In this type of theft, wanting or needing an item is not what prompts the theft (as it does in the planned or routine theft). The youth is browsing, discovers an item or an opportunity to take an item, and takes it on impulse.

Unplanned thefts take two forms. They can be differentiated by pointing out whether sudden recognition of a want–need for an item or access–opportunity to take the item prompts the event.

In one form of unplanned theft, the youths described themselves as seeing an item, suddenly wanting it or realizing they "need" it, not having (or wanting to spend) the money to acquire the item, and thus recognizing the opportunity for theft of the item and taking it. This is parallel to browsing, seeing something one likes, and buying it.

A 15-year-old female heavy user from the purposive sample who had been involved in drug sales and shoplifting explained a shoplifting event in which she stole some locks for her locker and bicycle:

*Q:* Did you go there, purposely to [steal the locks]?

*A:* Uh-uh. We were just browsing.

*Q:* Uh-huh.

*A:* We went out to buy a few things, records mostly, and while we were out there in the store . . .

*Q:* And that's the only thing you took?

*A:* Yep.

*Q:* Could you have taken other things?

*A:* Yah. Places are easy to rip off.

A 15-year-old male heavy user from the purposive sample who had been involved in serious crime, including drug sales and shoplifting:

*Q:* But that didn't occur to you at the time? Well, other than that day, did you go to other malls and take things pretty regularly? Is that sort of the normal thing to do?

*A:* No, just like, you know, every once in a while, I saw something that I wanted or something. But not really a lot.

A 16-year-old male heavy user from the random sample who had been involved in shoplifting:

*Q:* Tell me about what happened?

*A:* No, well, I used to take, they used to have everything all set up in the aisles, like their candies and things like that. I used to take them. And just, ya know, once in a while I'd find something in a store, something I might end up taking.

A 15-year-old female heavy user from the purposive sample who had been involved in shoplifting:

*Q:* So it was just a few times you did it?

*A:* No, well I was doing it, here and there, not big things ya know, like wow, I love that eyeshadow, ha, ha, ha, I don't do that any more though, I learned my lesson. Even after I was still stealing things though, it was like a little bit at a time.

A 15-year-old female heavy user who had been involved in shoplifting:

*Q:* Okay. But you've never taken anything from a store, or from . . . ?

*A:* A couple of times I went to the store, and I got a pack of earrings, me and my sister, we used to get earrings from the store.

*Q:* When would you do that? When's the last time you did it?

*A:* We went, we went to the store, and um, we asked our mother to buy us something. Buy us some earrings, but she said she didn't have enough money. So we used to get them, and put them on, and wear them. In the store, walk out with them.

A 16-year-old male light user from the purposive sample who had been involved in serious crime, including burglary:

*Q:* We were just talking about shoplifting and you were tellin' me that you had done that.

*A:* Shright!

*Q:* So just tell me a little about what happened.

*A:* I just steal something. Just easy, just stick sometem in you coat or pocket, an that's how you shoplift. I thought that's all you did.

*Q:* Is it generally something worth less than five dollars, or more, or what?

*A:* It don't make no difference, you like and you want it, you take it.

An 18-year-old male heavy user from the purposive sample who had been involved in serious crime, including drug sales and burglary:

*Q:* How did you start doing that [shoplifting], how did that happen?

*A:* Jes seen something I wanted, jes took it, didn't have any money.

*Q:* Did you ever see anybody else shoplifting, I mean, how did you get the idea to do it?

*A:* Jes take it, steal it. I don't think I got the idea from someone, jes took it.

*Q:* Did most of your friends take stuff like that too?

*A:* At that age?

*Q:* Did you ever go out to the store with the idea that you were going to steal something?

*A:* No.

*Q:* The idea just came once you were out?

*A:* Ya.

*Q:* Those times, were you usually alone or with other people.

*A:* Mm, with my mother, father, shopping.

The other form of unplanned theft can be compared to the "on sale" mentality. Here, the youths discover access–opportunity to an item, decide they can't pass up the opportunity, and take the item. The opportunity is of the utmost importance in providing an impetus for the theft. A 16-year-old male heavy user from the detained sample who had been involved in serious crime, including burglary and petty larceny:

*Q:* Do you ever take things off a car?

*A:* One time, oh yeah, I stole a, a AM-FM cassette deck out of a car once.

*Q:* Uh-huh. When was that?

*A:* Ah, last summer.

*Q:* Uh-huh.

*A:* Put it in my car, in my mother's car.

*Q:* Did your mom know it was stolen?

*A:* Huh?

*Q:* Did you mom know it was stolen?

*A:* I told her I bought it. She at first, she suspected. I told her I bought it off someone for twenty dollars, they needed to sell it, they needed the money, and I bought it. I think she believed me.

*Q:* Well, what were you thinking when you did that? I mean . . .

*A:* I don't know, it just looked nice, man. 'Cause my mother just had a plain AM radio and hated it. Ya know, like FM, cassettes, and all that. AM just put disco and shit.

*Q:* Do you usually do these things by yourself?

*A:* I did that one by myself, yeah.

*Q:* Any other things?

*A:* That was it.

A 16-year-old male heavy user from the detained sample who had been involved in serious crime, including auto theft:

*Q:* Okay. What's the most expensive thing you ever. . . .

*A:* A TV. . . .

*Q:* Yeah? How'd you do that?

*A:* It was at nighttime. Just—I don't know, the door was open, I think. It was like a garage door. (Right there in the back.) I pushed it open. It was all, all kinds of stuff in there, TVs. Everything. All kinds of stereos and stuff like that.

*Q:* Like uh—

*A:* A little warehouse.

A 14-year-old male heavy user from the detained sample who had been involved in serious crime, including mugging and burglary:

*Q:* Uh-huh. So you've done shoplifting.

*A:* Yeah.

*Q:* Tell me about that, when was the most recent time you took something from a store, you shoplifted?

*A:* Jesus, I can't even think about it. Some . . . I think it was little or something like that. Me and Ollie Oswald went in, there was a whole bunch of us there, but we went over to the sport section. We were looking at the knife cases and one of them was broken on the side, you could pull it open, so, and I had . . . I pulled it open about this far and I told Ollie to stick his hand there and, don't fit, pull it open a little more, and I went like this and it went [crack] . . . 'cause I broke the door off, it went, pushed it back up. Came back maybe about two minutes later. There was nobody there fixing it. Opened it up, reached in and grabbed a handful of boxes, and there was all kinds of little knives and, took about five little tiny pocket knives, about this long.

A 16-year-old male heavy user from the detained sample who had been involved in serious theft, including grand larceny:

*A:* It was me and Ivan . . . me and Ivan were riding double on a bike going down to an apartment by, uh, Olive's Market, to see this chick named Evilin, and Evilin wasn't home, and the people upstairs were real noisy and in the hallway there was three bikes. Three ten-speeds and a girl's three-speed, so I just tiptoed, took one of the ten-speed's out, brought it to the door.

**Theft of Cash.** Some youths at particular times prefer to avoid theft-as-work (discussed next) and theft-as-shopping. They prefer to steal money directly and are not interested in the business of reselling goods or in the direct acquisition of goods. Here the youths' "need" is for money. Youths either look for access–opportunity for stealing cash (planned theft), or the access emerges and they act on it (unplanned theft). The intent is simply to acquire cash with which to purchase valued items. Theft of cash cuts across all levels of theft involvement, but most of the incidents recounted involved relatively little money.

Planned thefts of cash are planned to the extent that (1) money for consumer items (in general or specifically) is viewed as wanted or needed, (2) some sort of access to money is known or assumed, (3) an opportunity for taking money is sought, and (4) the youth acts on the opportunity when it is found.

A 15-year-old female light user from the purposive sample who had not been involved in crime:

*Q:* Have you ever taken money, or other things from your parents, or other family members, or friends, without their permission?
*A:* Yeah.
*Q:* What have you done?
*A:* Um, like maybe a couple of dollars from my mother.
*Q:* Tell me about that, when was the most recent time you did that?
*A:* Um, two or three weeks ago, I would say.
*Q:* Tell me the details of what happened.
*A:* Um, going out one night, you know, I needed some extra money.
*Q:* Uh-huh.
*A:* And just—went and got, maybe two or three dollars.
*Q:* Where?
*A:* From her purse.

An 18-year-old male heavy user from the purposive sample who had been involved in crime, such as burglary and serious assault:

*Q:* Have you ever taken money and other things from your parents or from family members without their permission?
*A:* Oh yeah. When you live in a big family, things like that always happen.
*Q:* Like what would you take?
*A:* Take money.

*Q:* Nothing like taking change or taking bills or. . . .

*A:* Oh yeah. On occasion like when I was on a streak there somewhere in there. Used to take twenty-dollar bills now and then.

*Q:* From whom?

*A:* My mother and father or my mother mostly.

*Q:* Did you ever get caught?

*A:* No. Not really. It was kind of obvious after awhile.

*Q:* Did your parents ever point their finger and say, "Hey, you've been taking money.

*A:* Well they couldn't actually point their finger, I mean there's so many of us, which way do you go? They had an idea it was me especially after I got busted. It kind of boosted them up a little. That wasn't a big thing, that was just once in a while.

*Q:* Uh-huh. What did you do with it when you took the twenty dollars.

*A:* Well, I'd take it for a reason.

*Q:* Like what, for instance?

*A:* Ah, no reason at all. I would just go out and buy something or do something, just have a good time.

A 14-year-old female heavy user from the purposive sample who had been involved in shoplifting and drug sales:

*Q:* When you started smoking were you ever worried or scared about getting caught?

*A:* Uh-huh, yeah. Not last year. Like when I was little, third through sixth grade. If my mother had found out she would have killed me. I stole like thirty-six dollars from my mother when I was little for cigarettes. Between third and sixth grade.

*Q:* How would you get it from her?

*A:* She had a whole big jar of silver dollars and I just kept taking them.

A 17-year-old male heavy user from the purposive sample who had been involved in drug sales and burglary discussed his involvement in house burglaries for cash:

*Q:* How much money did you usually average?

*A:* Back then, anywhere from $100 to $250.

*Q:* Did you just take money or did you take anything else?

*A:* Just money.

*Q:* Uh-huh. What about if there was jewelry or anything like that?

*A:* I wouldn't take it.

*Q:* How come?

*A:* Too easy to get busted with . . . merchandise.

*Q:* What about if you didn't find any money?

*A:* I'd leave.

*Q:* That's it, you wouldn't mess anything up, or . . . ?

*A:* No.

*Q:* What would you do with the money once you got it?

*A:* What did I do, or what . . . ?

*Q:* What did you do?

*A:* Bought things for myself, usually went for drugs.

Unplanned thefts of cash are parallel in nature to unplanned thefts of material goods. The youth sees a situation as an opportunity for theft of cash and acts on it. Typically, the money was used to buy consumer goods.

A 15-year-old male heavy user from the purposive sample who had been involved in shoplifting and drug sales:

*Q:* How often would you smoke then, during this whole time?

*A:* Oh, just off and on, about every weekend. But, it, ah, near the end I was smoking about two joints every two weeks, about every two days.

*Q:* So you just kept increasing over this time, getting more and more?

*A:* Yeah, that's when I started stealing money, which made me feel low.

*Q:* Okay, what's the most [drugs] you ever got up to?

*A:* Most I ever got up to. About half a nickel [$5 bag], somethin'.

*Q:* Half a nickel, that was right around country fair time?

*A:* Yeah.

*Q:* Before? Okay, uh, who did you steal from, how'd you get it?

*A:* Uh, if I went over someone's house, and, uh, their father's wallet was just laying there, I'd swipe a couple of bucks, or, uh, I would find money lying around, I just swiped it.

*Q:* You mean money lying around your house?

*A:* Yeah, even though I knew it was my parents' money, I was lying that I never seen it. Uh, [most of my money was] disappearing myself.

*Q:* Well where'd you buy [pot]?

*A:* I'd buy it off Rose.

An 18-year-old male heavy user from the random sample who had been involved in serious crime, including major property destruction and grand larceny, recalled an unplanned event when he was very young:

*A:* Naw, really one day, right, these dudes snatched this old lady's pocketbook. Me and my friends is young, so we seen them, we, hey, hey what you doing' . . . we was running after 'em, right? So I seen this dude running and all of a sudden and they keep getting up so the, uh, I went down there, seen all that money, so I put the money under a rock and gave the old lady back the pocketbook. No, I told my friend to give it to her 'cause . . . so he gave it to her and she said, oh, my money, my money. God damn money, it was about $200, so we—all my friends went and got our bicycles and rolled out to Armstrong Shop and I told that lady, I said give us seven pizzas. Not knowing this dumb lady was gonna go in there and get seven big pizzas.

*Q:* You meant seven slices.

*A:* Meant seven slices, so she go in there, I seen this lady walk out, man, and she got about four big pizzas, the other lady coming out with three more, so everybody ate a big pizza and I give them all $5, came home, gave my brother $100, and just split the rest up on candy every day.

*Q:* How old were you?

*A:* Nine. About nine, yeah.

**Theft as Work.** When theft is treated as work, the main goal of the youths who are involved (as for legitimate workers) is to acquire money—the legitimate means of exchange for the goods and services they want or need.

Theft as work or as a business further reflects a consumeristic ethos in the sense that to be in the business of theft for profit is to have knowledge of commodities valued by other consumers, as well as where there is access and opportunity for acquiring the items and where they can be resold. Theft as business is usually planned and there is little uncertainty involved in the venture. The actors know what they are going to steal, how they are going to go about it, and where their profit will come from. Youths partake in such theft on a somewhat regular basis as an activity for money-making.

An 18-year-old male heavy user from the purposive sample who had been involved in serious crime, including burglary and serious assault:

*A:* Cars, cars were just a joyride, bicycles, we used to, was a big business once upon a time; when I was 13 to 15, we used to take bicycles, was a big thing. We used to steal lots of bikes and make our own out of them, from the bikes we had, and sell the rest.

A 14-year-old male heavy user from the detained sample who had been involved in serious crime, including burglary and auto theft:

*Q:* Okay, tell me about that first time, how did it happen?

*A:* Well he was makin' all kinds of money, he was goin' to school with all kinds of money, and, I wondered how he got it, so he told me, and I started doing it with him.

*Q:* Well, what do you mean, he told you, tell me the details.

*A:* He told me how he made the money, like stealing, and I started stealing with him. Ya, me and Eddie and Lennie were doing jobs.

*Q:* Every day?

*A:* Yeah, every other day; whenever we needed money.
*Q:* Okay, so four, or five times a week?
*A:* Yeah.
*Q:* And, always houses then?
*A:* Yup, houses or, if we seen a good building or a bar.
*Q:* Well, what, what's a good building or bar, how can you tell?
*A:* If they don't have alarms or somethin' we'd do it.

A 20-year-old male heavy user from the random sample who had been in-volved in major crime, including serious assault and burglary:

*Q:* What happened, can you tell me the story?
*A:* There were some people, who wanted to go out and make some money so we could go to a concert.
*Q:* But, you remember how it happened, can you tell me a story?
*A:* Well, there was like five of us, and somebody said this old lady had coins, and I think he was telling me, hey, I know where you can sell all the stuff we get, and we can get some good money. And there was a concert coming up, I forget what it was . . . yeah, know what concert it was, and I remember it was like, all right, we'll go and get a bag of pot, and get some acid. And we was all psyched and we went and robbed the house, and got all these old coins.

Divisions of labor are developed when theft is conducted as business. An 18-year-old male user from the random sample who had been involved in serious crime, including major property destruction and grand larceny:

*Q:* Have you ever sold, um, stolen merchandise?
*A:* Uh-huh.
*Q:* Where'd you get it to sell it?
*A:* This dude dat come by . . . he used to steal bikes all the time. I used to buy 'em for ten and sell them for twenty-five.

A 19-year-old female heavy user from the purposive sample who had been involved in juvenile wrongs, such as fighting and graffiti:

*Q:* Uh, you ever, well, you've never—do you ever sell stuff for her? Sell, sell the stuff that she steals, for her?
*A:* Yeah.
*Q:* Well, how do you do that?
*A:* She give it to me to sell for her. She says can you sell that? I said, yeah, I'm going to sell it for a higher price. Sell it three dollars extra.
*Q:* And keep the money, huh?
*A:* Yeah.

A 15-year-old male heavy user from the purposive sample who had been involved in serious theft, including major shoplifting and auto theft:

*Q:* You ever sold stolen stuff to a fence or somebody who, ya know, makes a livin' selling stuff?
*A:* Have I ever sold something to them that they be selling?
*Q:* Yup.
*A:* Yup. I got this dude, if I get anything, anything, he'd buy anything.
*Q:* What have you ever sold him?
*A:* Sold him, some, what, ah, oh, ya, some watermelons.
*Q:* How'd you get watermelon?
*A:* Over at Upton School, they got some watermelons in, 'frigerator, they got quarts of orange juice, we jus' play basketball for a while, see if there's anybody around, jes' get some juice, we seen a whole bunch of watermelon.
*Q:* How'd you get it?
*A:* It was already open. Seen a whole bunch of watermelon, I seen him, I said, go park around there. He park around back, we jes load in, we got at least eight watermelons and we jes' sold 'em all.

A 15-year-old female heavy user from the purposive sample described how theft-as-work paid for her services:

*Q:* Did you ever go with her when she was stealing?
*A:* I went with her one day, 'cause I had babysitted for her. And she said she didn't have any money. She said after she steals some stuff and sells it, she was going to give me some money. And, you know, she said, um, do I rather get some money or, rather for her to steal me something. I said I'd rather for her to steal me something. So, she had took me out to, um, she took me to this, I think it was Look-and-See.
*Q:* Uh huh.
*A:* She took me out there, it used to be something else, but it, but it's Look-and-See now, she stole, uh, a red and white terrycloth, um, short set for me. And she stole some white socks. She stole a lot of those terrycloths. She stole one for me, one for her.

Some youths reported taking orders for items. A 17-year-old male heavy user from the detained sample who had been involved in serious crime, including grand larceny and serious assault:

*Q:* Anything else you've ever taken?
*A:* Mm, nothin' I can think of.
*Q:* You were saying something about, taking things off cars.
*A:* Yah, if we need a part go steal it.

*Q:* Who's "we" again?

*A:* Whoever I was with, [if] they needed a part, and they were gonna pay me for it, ya know.

*Q:* Would you do stuff like, on consignment, like, someone says, gee, I need a cam shaft or something, say, "I'll get it."

*A:* Sometimes, not, not like a cam shaft, I wouldn't sit there and overhaul the engine, but, you know, alternators, tires, sometimes.

*Q:* But, you'd do it on request, sorta, like someone asks you to and you'd run out and get one?

*A:* Sometimes, if I needed the money I would.

*Q:* What would you charge for something?

*A:* Depends on what it was.

*Q:* What about an alternator?

*A:* An alternator? Twenty bucks. 'Cause that's, that's reasonable, ya know, for them, 'cause I'm takin' the chance. But, I don't do it, I don't steal nothin' anymore, ever.

A 16-year-old male heavy user from the detained sample who had been involved in serious crime, including major property destruction and burglary:

*Q:* But that's the only time you've ever done that? How about take things from stores, or . . .

*A:* Um, let's see, I stole a stereo once. Me and Irving Richards and, um, Neil Rogers were driving around in a car, we were up at Raven getting drunk and we needed money for—he needed money for something and he asked me if I [had] twenty-five dollars, and helped him rip off this stereo from this apartment out in Indianhead. Is it easy? Yeah. So we went to the apartment and took the MasterCard, opened up the door. . . .

*Q:* Uh huh.

*A:* Went straight to the living room, grabbed the stereo, I grabbed the speakers, one of those great big speakers and tape deck. Hopped in the car, took off, that was it.

*Q:* Was it during the daytime?

*A:* No, it was during the night.

*Q:* Did he know the people in the apartment or something?

*A:* Uh huh. It was—he knew them, but he wasn't too fond of 'em.

*Q:* I guess not. Uh, then what did you do with the stereo.

*A:* He sold it for $200 and some. Gave me a third.

Sometimes resale of stolen items is not the original intent of theft. Resale can emerge much in the same way that theft emerges from an "opportunity" or a sudden "need." A 16-year-old male heavy user from the random sample who had been involved in drug sales and auto theft:

*Q:* Uh-huh. How about [buying alcohol] for friends?

*A:* No, stole a few times.

*Q:* From where?

*A:* One on East Street, man. They got the Bacardi right up in front. Get—can't resist it, you know, he's walking there and there's no one there, and he says, pick it up and walk out. It's easy, or you just ask them for a box. He trust me like a mother, man. If I want to rip him off I can rip him off anytime. 'Cause I use to, I always get boxes there. From my work. And he just says, right here, you know, and he goes in the back anyway, put one in the box and walk out.

*Q:* Have you ever done that?

*A:* Once. I can't do it too [much].

*Q:* Why?

*A:* I don't know, guy's an [honest] guy, he's nice enough to trust me and shit. I don't want to rip him off. Even though he's rich as hell.

*Q:* When was the last time you did do that?

*A:* That was last year. When I first started working there.

*Q:* Uh-huh. What'd you do with the bottle?

*A:* Took it in [to] work and set it up on the shelf. And then brought it home with me. They don't usually care what I do. My boss would probably laugh if he seen me rip it off, I think.

*Q:* What'd you do with it eventually, did you give it away, or did you drink it, or what?

*A:* I sold it. I needed the money, so I sold it.

A 14-year-old male heavy user from the detained sample who had been involved in serious crime, including drug sales, mugging, and burglary:

*Q:* Did you always steal money or did you steal things like stereos and . . .

*A:* I stole stereos, all kinds of stuff.

*Q:* What did you do with them?

*A:* Sell them. Sometimes keep 'em, it depends—on what's happening. Ya know, it depend on if I need money—I mean I had money every day, ya know, I have a couple hundred every day, ya know, that ain't no problem.

Other times, an opportunity to steal something presents itself, but the decision to steal the item is rooted in its perceived resale value. This type of behavior is illustrated by a 15-year-old male nonuser from the detained sample who had been involved in serious crime, including burglary and auto theft:

*Q:* What else, have you ever taken anything else?

*A:* Um, a diamond ring, that's it.

*Q:* When was that? Tell me about it.

*A:* End of July. Um, I [went] into my friend's house and I went up to use his bathroom and it was setting in, in, on top of the cabinet, and so I took it, I looked at it and it said it was real gold on it, so I took it, put it in my pocket.

*Q:* Was it a man's ring or a woman's ring?

*A:* A man's.

*Q:* What'd you do with it?

*A:* I kept it.

*Q:* So what became of it?

*A:* I had sold—I kept it for about a month and then I sold it.

*Q:* Uh-huh. Who did you sell it to?

*A:* This place downtown, and I don't know the name of it. But it's downtown.

*Q:* But was it a pawnbroker, or was it a fence or what?

*A:* Yeah, a pawnshop.

*Q:* How much did you get for it?

*A:* $250.

*Q:* And what happened to that money?

*A:* I put some away and I bought new clothes.

*Q:* How'd you explain to your, um, mom where you got $250?

*A:* I was working at the time and I told her I bought it with the money I got from work.

Some theft events described by the youths take on the nature of a business venture. These events are like other theft-as-business events, but the access to valuable items is much less certain. Some amount of access is assumed, but it is much less certain in the high-risk thefts. The youths either seek or recognize an opportunity for theft, but the items available within that opportunity are known only by assumption; hence the entrepreneurial risk involved. The youths balance the risk of getting caught (and everything that accompanies that) against the hope that they will obtain either money, items of value that satisfy personal wants or needs, or valuable items for resale.

A 17-year-old male heavy user from the purposive sample who had been involved in serious crime including burglary and major shoplifting:

*Q:* And did those other guys do that?

*A:* Um, I don't think they broke, ever broke in any stores. But um, you know.

*Q:* They did break into houses.

*A:* Yeah.

*Q:* What kinds of stuff would they take from houses?

*A:* Anything they could get, guns, anything.

*Q:* Uh-huh. Your brother did that? Did he bring stuff to your house?

*A:* Nope. . . . Never brought anything to my house.

*Q:* What did they do with it?
*A:* Put it, stashed it somewhere.
*Q:* Did they sell it, pawn it?
*A:* Yeah. They sold it all the time.
*Q:* Um. So he must have had a lot of money.
*A:* Yeah, he always had bucks, always. Richest 15-year-old kid I ever knew.

Sometimes the venture does not pay off, as in the case of the following youth who broke into a house, found nothing, and got caught. The youth was an 18-year-old male heavy user from the purposive sample who had been involved in shoplifting, petty theft, and burglary:

*Q:* Uh-huh.
*A:* We uh, didn't steal nothing from there, we didn't find nothing, we didn't break nothing. She said $27 was missing. And the side screen door was broken. That's what—that's what I figured just, people are going to lie like that. You know, say my house got robbed, I'll say $500 was stolen. You know, and maybe I'll get the money back. I mean, I never had it, you know. 'Cause we never took no money from her. And she said $27 was stolen. So it's [like] I robbed another house, and then they say that much money was gone, and I can't pay for that.

**Theft as Sport.** The consumeristic mentality is also portrayed by another type of theft activity, although in a slightly different way from those just described. In this type of theft, it is not so much the item that is of value but the daring, challenge, and risk involved in the act of taking an item and the way one feels about oneself as a result of having done so. The view of theft as sport coincides with youths' perceptions of crime as fun, which was reported in chapter 3.

Theft as sport was a way for the adolescents to relieve boredom and also, at times, a way to enhance self-esteem. An 18-year-old male heavy user from the purposive sample who had been involved in serious crimes, including grand larceny and serious assault:

*Q:* Anything else?
*A:* Oh, the Marble State Carnival, we went up and stole some sweatbands and stuff. And Appleton Farms, once we stole footballs and stuff, sweatbands, and stuff, it wasn't nothin' we planned, it was, you know, we were just havin' a little fun.

An 18-year-old male heavy user from the purposive sample who had been involved in shoplifting, petty theft, and burglary:

*A:* I was just—as I got, um, I got challenged, it's, something to do. I'm sly. Like the first house, a lady was in the front porch.

*Q:* She was there when you went in?

*A:* I went through the whole house. And she never knew it. Till my—someone came up to the side door to see what we was up to. There's three of us again. Came, [he] came up, see what was up to, and the guy next door seen him, and he came over and asked him what he was doing. So what's—me and the other kid were stuck in the house, listening in on what they were saying. Why are you here—the guy asked the lady if, um, he knew—she knew him. She said no and, he, soon as he let him go, he took off. And just, the other kid took off, and I just went out the front door and ran. Two people [slyer] than me.

A 16-year-old male heavy user from the random sample who had been involved in serious crime, including drug sales and auto theft:

*A:* We used to always have this skateboard competition, we used to see who could steal the most skateboards in a week. Me and Rob, Rob used to get like thirty skateboards.

*Q:* When was this?

*A:* When we used to do [our paper route], we used to go . . . . We used to pick them up, put them in our bag.

*Q:* When was that? How old were you?

*A:* Whenever I did the route, man. Let's see, I was 13, I think; 12 or 13. Used to be excellent. Best time of my whole life.

*Q:* What'd you do with them once you took them?

*A:* I don't know, we'd keep them, sell them to friends, or whatever.

*Q:* Uh-huh.

*A:* Or just take the wheels off, get rid of them. We'd just take any skateboard we could get our hands on. We used to be walking up—I'd be walking up the street, and he'd be walking down the street, we used to have four bags, that we carry, like this, two is [here], one in the back, and one in the back, like that. Used to have all them bags full of skateboards.

An 18-year-old female heavy user from the purposive sample who had been involved in shoplifting:

*A:* I wasn't really that scared to do it. I've lifted stuff off the counters with the cash register right in front of me. Um, I lifted four dollars worth of stuff out of a store with a state trooper standing right behind me. A lot of it I think was "ha, ha, look what I'm getting away with."

An 18-year-old female light user from the purposive sample who had been involved in shoplifting:

*Q:* About how many of these friends engage in any other forms of illegal behavior, you know, like shoplifting or breaking things or fighting?

*A:* Um, we've all shoplifted. Um, I'm sure I don't know about the guys much. I'm sure, yeah, I'm sure. I don't know about Andy though. But we've all shoplifted in our time.

*Q:* How did that come about? Could you tell me about that?

*A:* That was when that was the big thrill, you know, when I was in . . . I remember one time a group of us were at Highbridge, you know, and I went stealing testers of perfume. Wow, big thing, you know.

Joyriding often tends to be a product of access and relief of boredom. A 15-year-old male non-user from the purposive sample who had been involved in serious crimes, such as burglary, described his involvement in the theft of a motorcycle:

*A:* Nighttime and we didn't want to go home, so we said let's stay out all night and we were trying to think of something to do, and we had known— known where this motorcycle was and we were gonna take it and we were gonna go to Virginia and ride around and come back the next day. So we took the motorcycle—first we took the bus to where the motorcycle was. It was on the south side and then we took it and got on it and we rode around town—we went to the reservoir, and it got a flat—we had a flat tire, so we hid the motorcycle and this lady seen us hiding it and then she called the cops the next day and they picked us up.

## Differences in Types of Thefts by Gender and Drug Use

Although many of the youths who engaged in theft reported theft events across many or all of the aforementioned categories, some differences are apparent among particular groups of youths (table 5–1). Most striking, yet not surprising, are the differences that emerge according to sex. Females who reported involvement in theft typically had been involved in what we have described as "shopping" (or "browsing") events. Males, though also involved in theft-as-shopping events, were overwhelmingly more involved than females in the work (business and entrepreneurship) category of theft.

For example, 60 youths reported engaging in minor shoplifting events, and 59 reported engaging in petty theft. These were typically theft-as-shopping or theft-of-cash types of activities. Forty percent of the youths who reported shoplifting were females, and 60 percent were males. Females accounted for 31 percent of the 59 youths who reported petty theft. Burglary and grand larceny, the theft activities that are typically of a high-risk or entrepreneurial nature, were committed almost entirely by the males in the sample. Males committed 100 percent of the 29 burglaries reported and 92 percent of the grand larcenies reported (see table 5–1). (Similar sex-related differences are reported in Inciardi, 1981; Sanchez and Johnson, 1986.)

A 13-year-old female light user from the random sample who had been involved in shoplifting explained the lesser involvement of females in theft:

*Q:* Have you ever been with them [male friends] when they are doing anything [crime]?
*A:* No. Because they only do it with a bunch of guys. They wouldn't take a couple of girls with them.

As for drug use, heavy drug users most often reported engaging in all of the aforementioned types of theft events (see table 5–1). Although non-users and light users reported some involvement in theft (largely in theft-as-shopping and theft-of-cash activities), the percentage of those involved was much smaller than the percentage of heavy users who reported such thefts.

Of the 60 youths who reported involvement in minor shoplifting (theft-as-shopping), 7 percent were non-users, and 15 percent were light users, and 78 percent were heavy users. The percentages for petty theft were almost identical: non-users made up 2 percent and light users 15 percent of the 59 youths reporting involvement.

Heavy users also made up the largest percentage of those reporting involvement in high-risk theft activities. Twenty-nine youths reported involvement in burglary (typically a high-risk theft event); 83 percent (24) of those youths were heavy users. All but one of the 24 youths who reported grand larceny (also a typically high-risk event) were heavy users (see table 5–1).

## Table 5–1
## Type of Theft by Sex and Drug User Types

|  | Shoplifting | | Petty Theft | | Burglary | | Grand Larceny | |
|---|---|---|---|---|---|---|---|---|
|  | Percent | N | Percent | N | Percent | N | Percent | N |
| **Sex** |  |  |  |  |  |  |  |  |
| Males | 60 | 40 | 69 | 40 | 100 | 29 | 92 | 22 |
| Females | 40 | 20 | 31 | 19 | 0 | 0 | 8 | 2 |
| Total | 100 | 60 | 100 | 59 | 100 | 29 | 100 | 24 |
| **Drug user type** |  |  |  |  |  |  |  |  |
| Nonusers | 7 | 4 | 2 | 6 | 3 | 1 | 0 | 0 |
| Light users | 15 | 9 | 15 | 9 | 14 | 4 | 4 | 1 |
| Heavy users | 78 | 47 | 83 | 44 | 83 | 24 | 96 | 23 |
| Total | 100 | 60 | 100 | 59 | 100 | 29 | 100 | 24 |

# Summary

We have described how theft among youths is partly a product of a consumeristic mentality. In doing this, we looked at theft as the direct acquisition of goods valued by the youths, as a means of obtaining goods for resale, and as a direct source of cash. Theft events varied from the carefully planned to the fortuitous, and from businesslike activities to sport.

Theft for direct acquisition was a more common theft activity among the Yule City youths than was theft for resale. This type of theft was engaged in by youths at all levels of theft involvement, from the very minor to the very serious. Theft for resale was typically limited to those who engaged in more serious and frequent thefts,[4] as well as other criminal activities. Within this group of youths, both types of theft were common and were often engaged in simultaneously in one event.[5] Both males and females engaged in theft for purposes of direct acquisition, but only males in this sample stole for purpose of resale.

# Notes

1. We use the notion of the consumeristic mentality and various parallels between theft and consumer behavior as analytic tools. We do not argue that youths employ these terms to describe their behaviors.

2. We use the term *legitimate* in this context with caution. When we say *legitimate* here, we mean in terms of the legal mode of acquisition of consumer goods. This is not to say that the youths do not view their thefts as a legitimate means of satisfying their wants and needs. In fact, they describe extensively how their theft activities are legitimate by their definition.

3. The concepts of access and opportunity play a large role in this analysis. *Access* is defined herein as knowledge of the presence of an item in a certain place. As used here it is probably more appropriate to refer to it as *potential* access—meaning the item is there but its full access to the actor is not designated by its mere presence. *Opportunity* characterizes the situation in which the item is fully accessible. Accessibility, then, means (as defined by the actor) the item is there; opportunity means the situation as defined designates it as there for the taking—with little chance of negative consequences. To view something as an opportunity includes viewing it as a low risk in terms of getting caught.

4. We measure seriousness of theft involvement in terms of frequency and type of theft.

5. This is clearly the case in high-risk theft-as-work, where the choice to steal for direct acquisition or resale emerges once the event is undertaken.

# 6
# The Context of Violence

M ost studies of violence tend to concentrate on the "violent few" (Hamparian, Schuster, Dinitz, and Conrad, 1978), "violent delinquents" (Strasburg, 1978), or youths with serious arrest histories (King, 1975; Melvinhill, Tummit, and Curtis, 1969; Wolfgang, Figlio, and Sellin, 1972), as derived from official records and information on their personality characteristics, socioeconomic background, and subcultural patterns. Studies of delinquent behavior among adolescents in the general population typically address questions of violent behavior, but the proportion of youths reporting felony violence is quite rare (Elliott, Dunford, and Huizinga, 1983; Glaser, 1975; Gold, 1970; Gold and Reimer, 1975; Polk, Frease, and Richmond, 1974). Such studies generally neglect the drug use patterns of respondents as a possible correlate of violence, even though an extensive literature exists on the purported role of alcohol in disinhibiting moral restraints (G. Collins, 1982; J. Collins, 1981; Pernanen, 1976, 1981; Room and Collins, 1983).

Recent reports from the National Youth Survey (see citations by Elliott, Huizinga, and Dunford) as well as secondary analyses of those data (Huizinga, 1982, 1986; Johnson, Wish, and Huizinga, 1986; Johnson et al., 1984), demonstrate important associations between drug use and criminality and provide a background against which to assess the findings that will be presented here.

Dunford and Elliott (1982) reported that multiple index offenders (youths self-reporting three or more index offenses) committed five felony assaults (aggravated assaults, gang fights, and sexual assault) during a year, compared with 0.5 felony assaults among infrequent index offenders (youths who committed one or two index offenses per year).

The multiple index offenders also committed 50 minor assaults (hitting students, teachers, parents) compared with 18 among infrequent index offenders and 3 among minor offenders (no index offenses, only minor delinquencies). In short, research shows that assaults (and most other types of crime) are committed at high rates only among multiple index offenders. Elliott and Huizinga (1984) and Johnson, Wish, and Huizinga (1986) reported that half of the multiple index offenders were pill and cocaine–heroin users, 30 percent were marijuana and alcohol users, 7 percent were alcohol-only users, and 13 percent were non–drug users. The multiple index offenders using pills–cocaine constituted under 3 percent of the sample in the National Youth Survey, but they committed over half of the felony assaults, felony thefts, robberies, and drug sales reported by the sample.

Minor assaults were not so highly concentrated in the national sample: 18 percent of all youths in the sample were non–drug users, but they contributed 31 percent of the minor assaults (Johnson, Wish, and Huizinga, 1986). Many non-drug-using youths who would otherwise have been nondelinquents were classified as minor offenders because they responded positively to the item "hit students."

In short, information from a nationally representative sample of American youths permits specification of the types of youths who commit felony and minor assault and the rates at which they commit those crimes. These analyses show that felony assault (and other felony crime) is highly concentrated among a few youths who commit several index offenses and many minor delinquencies per year *and* who are also routine drug users. Youths who are less seriously delinquent or who limit their drug use to alcohol or marijuana commit felony violence much less frequently. Such findings and the survey techniques employed, however, provide almost no information about the nature of these felony or minor assaults (what happened?), the social context in which they occurred (where, when, and who?), or youths' perspectives regarding situations (why?) in which violence may occur or be an appropriate response.

Prior research on the social context of violence (A. Campbell, 1981; Erickson and Empey, 1963; Kitsuse and Cicourel, 1963; Marsh, 1978) has relied heavily on participant observation and in-depth interviews to examine what goes on between youths during violent episodes. Their analyses suggest that what is often viewed as violence between youths is better understood as ritualized aggression. The rituals entail obedience to tacit and informal rules accepted by members of the group and often involve "testing" of one another via insult to a participant or significant associates. The ritual is continued by responding with further insults to the honor of the other party. In such contexts, potential violence may result in a fight, but rarely causes serious injury. If one of the participants has previously been using drugs or alcohol, disinhibition theory (Room and Collins, 1983) suggests that a fight may be more likely.

The issues of honor and interpersonal aggression in general have been discussed by J. Campbell (1964), Lofland (1969), and Toch (1969). Protection of honor has also been discussed more specifically in terms of youth gang violence (Erlanger, 1979; Horowitz and Schwartz, 1974; Short and Strodtbeck, 1965; Yablonsky, 1959). Other researchers (Berkowitz, 1978; Farrington, Berkowitz, and West, 1982; Rawlings, 1973) argue that when one aspect of the context of violence is changed—for example, in an individual as opposed to a group fight—the provocation to fight is different. One-on-one fights are more often instigated in defense of honor (Berkowitz, 1978; Farrington, Berkowitz, and West, 1982), whereas persons engage in group fights in order to aid friends already involved in the fight, to ward off an attacker (Farrington, Berkowitz, and West, 1982), or because they are "expected" to perform in such a way (Rawlings, 1973).

Despite explication of these themes, relatively little is known about the social context in which violence occurs among normal (not officially identified as violent) youths. That is, given that violence occurs or is expected to occur, are there typical locations where it occurs or subgroups of youths who are involved? Are there tacit rules governing violence? Do violent events among these youths involve defense of "honor" or property?

These questions are addressed in this chapter. The information for the analyses was obtained through interview questions that asked about events in which the respondent was a participant in or victim of violence. Specific queries, such as, "Sometimes a person may be held up, hurt, or beaten by someone else, even family and friends. Have such things happened to you?" were followed by probes, such as, "Can you recall the most recent time this happened?" and "When did such things first happen to you?" In addition, a series of direct questions were asked regarding violence. These ranged from "Have you been involved in physical fights where someone was hurt?" to "Have you been involved in a gang fight?" All the responses to questions about violence were used for this analysis. The transcripts were searched for reports of violence or avoidance of violence, and all reported incidents were listed. The incidents were then sorted according to the social context and nature of the violence.

Our focus in this chapter is more on events than on the persons involved in the events. Our goal is to understand how the repondents view violence and violent events. The quotations used in the chapter represent typical responses (and typical events), rather than the most interesting events or must lucid accounts.

## Characteristics of Subjects Most Involved in Violence

Some of the youths in our sample had been involved in or knew about violence organized around illegal activities. These included bullying students at school for money, mugging, and protecting oneself and one's property during a drug sale. The most common type of violence reported by the subjects, however, was fighting. Such fighting ranged from one-on-one taunting fights to gang fights and racial/ethnic battles. Before describing the specific contexts in which violence occurred, we will characterize the subjects who appeared to be most involved in violence.

Table 6–1
Percentage of Subjects Reporting Experience of Violent Events, by Type of Drug Use

| | Drug User Type | | |
|---|---|---|---|
| Percentage of Group for Whom: | Nonuser (N = 21) | Light User (N = 24) | Heavy User (N = 54) |
| Family/friend was victim | 24 | 17 | 22 |
| Subject was victim | 10 | 29 | 43 |
| Subject was perpetrator of serious assault | 0 | 0 | 22 |

The youths who were most involved in drug use more often reported involvement in violence than did those less involved or uninvolved in drug use. This is suggested by several indicators; not only did higher percentages of heavy drug users report engaging in violence, compared with the other respondents, but they were also more often victims (table 6–1). This may be partially due to our respondent selection process. Heavy drug users made up only 16 percent of the group of 43 subjects who were not involved in other crimes, but they represented 54 percent of the total sample and 85 percent of the 48 subjects defined as seriously involved in crime.

The information in table 6–2 reveals several interesting findings about the distribution of violence by level of drug use.[1] For instance, almost all of the (rare) family violence was reported by the heavy drug users. In addition, three times as many heavy drug users as non-users carried weapons.[2]

These data must be read with great caution, because we intentionally oversampled for youths who were involved in drug use and crime. Nevertheless, they do suggest that it is the heavy drug users who tend to become involved in violence—a finding similar to that of Dunford and Elliott (1982); Elliott and Huizinga (1984); and Johnson, Wish, and Huizinga (1986).

Table 6–2
Percentage of Subjects Reporting Involvement in Violent Events, by Type of Drug Use

| | Drug User Type | | |
|---|---|---|---|
| Percentage of Group for Whom: | Nonuser (N = 21) | Light User (N = 24) | Heavy User (N = 54) |
| Domestic violence occurred | 0 | 4 | 24 |
| Fighting occurred | 43 | 71 | 86 |
| Weapon was involved | 0 | 17 | 33 |
| Subject was perpetrator of: | | | |
| Domestic violence | 0 | 0 | 3 |
| Fighting | 43 | 71 | 86 |
| Carrying a weapon | 0 | 8 | 26 |

With this pattern in mind, we look at how youths understand the violence to which they are exposed or in which they participate. In which contexts does it occur, and why? Again, our focus is the social settings in which violence occurs, as they are perceived by the youths themselves.

## How and Why Violence Occurs

In Yule City, as among the nation's youth, much youthful violence consists of fights that do not result in serious harm. In these fights, youths test one another or endeavor to protect their own honor or that of persons important to them. Serious violence appears to occur in four main social contexts: in the distribution of drugs, in gang conflicts, in ethnic group/racial battles, and as revenge for offenses committed against oneself. Violence is seen as a means of protecting one's property, "testing" others, protecting one's own or another's "honor," and protecting against homosexual approach.

Although these contexts and rationales are not a typology of violent events, they do provide an organizational structure for reporting our results. The categories, it should be noted, are not mutually exclusive. Gang and ethnic violence are similar and may overlap. Likewise, protecting one's property may underlie drug distribution violence or a less serious fight between two youths. We discuss the contexts and rationales next in terms of their seriousness and the nature of the youths' involvement. First, we discuss serious violence committed by the subjects, then potentially violent contexts, and finally minor violence.

### Serious Violence Committed by Subjects

**Drug Distribution Violence.** Four subjects, all heavy drug users who were seriously involved in crime, reported participating in this type of violence. The violence was associated with protection of the drugs.

Recall the discussion in chapter 4 of violence by and against drug sellers and dealers. One major drug seller, Gallo (also see chapter 9), a 17-year-old male from the purposive sample, was a daily user of marijuana and extensively involved in both minor and major crimes. He and a friend, while engaged in a drug sale, ended up shooting the potential buyer (a stranger) in the leg. The buyer had grabbed the four pounds of marijuana (estimated value: $1,200) and begun to run with it. After shooting the buyer, Gallo and his friend took the marijuana and left in their car.

**Gang Violence.** In Yule City there were both formal gangs—those with names and leaders—and informal gangs—groups of youths who engaged in ganglike activities but who did not consider themselves a gang and did not remain consistently together. Fourteen youths reported taking part in gang violence. Of these, 2 were light drug users and 12 were heavy users; 10 were seriously involved in crime, 1 was episodically involved, and 3 were uninvolved. Gang fights are often said to begin as battles between two persons, typically over the same sorts of issues that are noted here as the contexts for individual fights ("testing" and "honor").

An 18-year-old male from the purposive sample was a daily user of both alcohol and marijuana and also used hallucinogens, prescription drugs, inhalants, cocaine, and heroin. The subject had been involved in minor crimes, including vandalism, shoplifting, petty larceny, and minor fraud, and major crimes, including burglary, serious assault, auto theft, and grand larceny. He offered an example of how a gang fight begins:

*Q:* As far as a gang fight . . . out-and-out fight?
*A:* . . . One at Eddie's house. Our first party when we had a party at his house, and he was from Hayes High, and the Hayes friends came. I don't know what happened but downstairs somebody hit somebody and they took it outside and there was an all-out fucking war. It must have lasted for quite a while. Every time we ran into each other it went on.

**Ethnic Antagonism.** Six respondents discussed incidents of racial/ethnic violence. Of the six, one was a light user of drugs and five were heavy users. Five were seriously involved in crime and one was not involved in crime. These events are similar to those involving gangs: those heavily involved in drug use and crime appear more likely to participate, although other youths also take part; large groups of youths take part in the violence; and often the subjects see themselves as protecting their own territory. A significant aspect of the context in which this sort of violence occurs, however, is antagonism between racial or ethnic groups.

A 14-year-old male heavy drug user (including hallucinogens, cocaine, and prescription drugs) from the detained sample, who was involved in assault, shoplifting, drug selling, and robbery, talked about a fight in which he and "a few friends" were involved. While at a park, he reported, some black youths were "picking on" his sisters, and he got his friends to fight with them. One of his friends required stitches at a local hospital.

*A:* Yeah, there's a lot of fights around there. Ya know it's all the time blacks and whites going at it all the time.
*Q:* Really? Are there black gangs and white gangs or . . .
*A:* You see a lot of white kids walking down the street and a lot of black kids, ya know, a lot of black kids, man. They think they're bad, ya know, so we got to show 'em they don't run the neighborhood, man.
*Q:* . . . Well, how does it work, how does it happen? That the fights start?

*A:* You know, I mean you got people that are shoving my little sisters around, ya know what I mean, there's kids that, you know, my sisters' ages, ya know, 8 and 10, ya know, but I mean there's a lot of black kids start shit man, ya know, and I don't like that. So I just go over to my friends' house, ya know, get a couple people and shit, ya know, and a fight goes on, ya know, 'cause everybody's hanging around at the park, ya know, and I don't like that man, park's for everybody. It's not just for blacks.

**Revenge.** The subjects who engaged in violence typically described their violent acts as particularly justifiable when they were seeking revenge for perceived wrongs against themselves or close associates. Frequently, the revenge was directed against persons who were accused of having stolen from the subject. (As noted previously, those adolescents who were themselves involved in crime much more often reported that they had been victims of violence than did other subjects in the sample.)

Six subjects reported committing violence directly for revenge. Of these, one was a light drug user and five were heavy drug users. Five were seriously involved in crimes, and one was not involved in crime.

A 16-year-old male who used marijuana, alcohol, and hashish daily, and cocaine, PCP, inhalants, and other drugs on occasion, was involved in such crimes as burglary, shoplifting, and auto theft. He told of an incident in which another youth owed him $40 but had refused to pay:

*A:* He didn't pay me so, I, I finally caught him at school, and he was always avoiding me. We weren't on school grounds, so I beat the shit out of him, beat his ass for forty-five minutes.
*Q:* How come no one stopped you?
*A:* 'Cause I beat the shit out of them, too. I was mad.
*Q:* What was that about?
*A:* I gave him forty bucks, and he never paid me back. So I wanted my forty bucks, I wanted to let him know I wanted it . . . I was punching his head in the ground, man, there was bloodshed all over.

In all of the foregoing instances of serious violence (as well as other events not described because of space limitations), three central themes may be inferred. First, the respondent claimed a major role in creating a potentially violent situation, placing himself in it, and participating in the event. The drug dealer was selling large quantities of marijuana in a public place, carried a gun to protect against ripoffs, and used the gun to shoot a buyer who attempted to take marijuana without paying for it. When members of another gang came to a party, the respondent joined his friends in the gang fight. Ethnic conflict began when the respondent rounded up his white friends to fight the blacks in retaliation for their alleged treatment of his sister. The subject who was owed

$40 sought out and beat up his victim. Thus, youths who report involvement in serious violence appear to play a major role in creating that violent context.

Second, the actual details of these events are not clearly described by these youths. The subjects may exaggerate the violence they might or actually do commit in order to emphasize their eagerness to fight or their prowess in actual violent events. In both the gang fight and the ethnic fight, it is unclear what injuries actually occurred in the fight, or whether most youths walked away relatively unhurt. In the revenge situation, the respondent stressed his physical domination when he reported assaulting the victim for forty-five minutes, punching his head on the ground, and causing "bloodshed."

Third, the descriptions of violence reflect little if any concern for the physical injury or harm inflicted; the perpetrators display little empathy for the victims. The drug dealer shot his buyer/victim in the leg "and that was it. He fell to the ground and we grabbed the dope" and ran away. In the gang fight and the fight in the park, no information about injuries to victims was given. The subject who obtained revenge was proud of the "bloodshed" inflicted on his victim.

## Potentially Violent Contexts

Our subjects suggested two additional contexts in which serious violence would occur if the situation called for such a response: protection of one's possessions and protection against homosexual approach. (In this section, we do not report numbers of subjects who discussed these matters. There were sometimes no direct questions about these matters, and because these are hypothetical occurrences, such numbers would not be meaningful.)

**Protection of Property.** Subjects' discussions of hypothetical cases of protecting their property were usually stated in somewhat grandiose terms. Consider the comments of a 16-year-old male from the detained sample. The subject was a daily user of alcohol and marijuana until the time of his detention. He had tried cocaine and had used hallucinogens, prescription drugs, and inhalants. He had been involved in shoplifting, vandalism, petty larceny, drug selling, burglary, joyriding, auto theft, and major property destruction. He discussed what would happen if he caught someone "messin' around" his house or his parents' house:

*Q:* Has any of your own property ever been damaged or destroyed by somebody else?

*A:* Nope. They know better, ha, nobody messes around my house.

*Q:* So it's never happened to your parents' house, your family's house, anything like that?

*A:* Nope. If I ever caught anybody rippin' my house off, or doin' anything, I'd probably shoot 'em. Wouldn't even ask who it is, ha.

*Q:* Well, you keep saying about shooting, do you have a gun, have you ever shot anybody?

*A:* Nope, but I would if anybody come messin' around my house, or my parents'. I wouldn't think twice, I'd just shoot it. That's their problem.

**Protection against Homosexual Approach.** Especially among male subjects, quick and violent responses were offered when the youths were asked if they had ever been sexually approached by persons of the same sex. A 14-year-old male from the detained sample was a daily user of alcohol, marijuana, and hashish. He had also used hallucinogens, prescription drugs, inhalants, and cocaine and had been involved in vandalism, petty larceny, minor fraud, drug selling, burglary, joyriding, auto theft, and grand larceny. He gives an answer typical of the male subjects' responses to this question.

*Q:* Sometimes older men try and get younger, ah, boys to do stuff with them. Has anybody ever tried that with you?

*A:* No.

*Q:* What would you do?

*A:* I'd probably stab 'em, kill 'em.

Again, the hypothetical violence is described with great bravado.

### Minor Violence to Test or Protect

As is well known in the literature on adolescence, youths spend considerable time taunting one another and checking the limits of their peers' tolerance for bothersome behavior. This was true particularly of our males.

**Testing and Protecting One's Honor.** The subjects generally referred to these activities with the slang expressions "messin' with me," "talking shit," or "punkin." Many youths, especially those most involved in drug use and other crime, saw it as important to respond forcefully to provocation in order to establish boundaries, prevent further problems, or sustain one's image. Often what was at stake was their honor—they felt they had been demeaned through name calling or other forms of provocation.

Forty-one subjects reported having been involved in violence associated with either testing one another or protecting their honor. Of the 41, 3 were non-users, 12 were light, and 26 were heavy drug users; 16 were not involved in crime, 3 were episodically involved, and 22 were seriously involved.

As an example of testing behavior, consider a 17-year-old female from the random sample. She had tried alcohol and marijuana but was a non-user of alcohol and drugs and had engaged in petty larceny in the past. She talked about a time she was "pushed too far." She and her cousin had heard that a youth named Dee wanted to fight the cousin. Dee had made insulting comments to the subject's cousin, who ignored them. Later the subject steered her cousin away from situations involving Dee. Then one morning Dee confronted the subject in a library. The subject argued but soon walked away. Later she went into the hall, where she met Dee and Dee's friend and an argument ensued. Later in the day Dee and her friend confronted the subject and said, "I heard you want to fight me." One of them reportedly hit the subject, at which point a fight began. The subject was asked more generally about her fights:

*Q:* Have you ever gotten into any kind of trouble at school?
*A:* I had a fight in tenth grade. I only had two fights in my lifetime, and that's because people provoke me, you know, I just go on about my business, like if somebody come up in my face, "He said, she said," I walk away. But, it's just if you push me too far, then I'm just gonna have to hit you.

An example of being tested and needing to protect one's honor is given by a 16-year-old male from the purposive sample. He had been a daily user of alcohol; was now a daily user of marijuana; and had also used hallucinogens, amphetamines, and cocaine. He had been involved in minor crimes, including vandalism and shoplifting, as well as major crimes such as burglary. He explained an incident in a town where he lived previously.

*A:* I've had a fight, yeah . . . eighth grade . . . the beginning of eighth grade. Some kids were trying to punch and I got in a fight and I walked away with . . . I think it was a scratch on my arm. And the other kid, he walked away with a black eye, a big lip, and everything.
*Q:* And why were you fighting?
*A:* They were trying to punk, because I was like the new kid.
*Q:* What does that mean? Everybody uses the term, I don't know what it means.
*A:* Well, no one knows you . . . they don't know if you're tough, they don't know if you're a wimp or anything, so they test you. It ended up I was best friends afterwards.

**Protecting Someone Else's Honor.** In many cases, fighting was said to occur in the context of defending someone else's honor. The subjects reported that they had fought or would fight to defend the honor of their parents, siblings, girlfriends, or other friends. Thirty subjects reported engaging in violence associated with protecting someone else's honor. Of the 30, 3 were non-users, 7 were light, and 20 were heavy drug users. Nine were not involved in crime, 2 were episodically involved, and 19 were seriously involved.

An example comes from an 18 year-old male from the random sample who was a daily user of alcohol and marijuana and had tried prescription drugs and cocaine. He had been involved in the whole range of minor and major crimes reported by others in the sample.

*Q:* Have you ever had to use your knives?

*A:* Ah, almost. I had to make this dude really think I gonna get crazy 'cause I was walking home with my lady one night, and ah, you know . . . this dude kept calling my lady, so I seen him and I stopped and I said, "You don't mess . . . why do you go around keep calling my lady all the time," ya know. Said I don't appreciate that. So then, um, I was walking home and he left on the bike . . . I walk home and he rides up on the bike, so he jump off the bike, "I'm gonna bust ya." I said we can fight. So we was fighting and I was beating him up, right, and his friends, like jump off the bikes, starting to come get me. I pull out my knife, said I kill all you motherfuckers and they all . . . they all ran.

## Role of Disinhibition

Our discussions in this chapter have concerned many youths who were heavy drug users but who did not mention drug or alcohol use at the time of the violent events being described. A substantial body of literature suggests that the use of alcohol and certain other drugs results in disinhibition, including less self-restraint on one's impulses toward violent acts and, in particular, toward fights (G. Collins, 1982; J. Collins, 1981; Lindelius and Salvin, 1975; Room and Collins, 1983). In chapter 3 we reported that heavy drug users frequently accept the view that drug or alcohol use leads to crime for others, but insist that it seldom does so for them. The analysis in this chapter confirms this finding. In talking about the contexts of violent events, the more heavily involved youths almost never mentioned drug or alcohol use, or intoxication, as provoking their own acts of violence, although they did make this connection regarding others. In this section we explore youths' perceptions regarding the phenomenon of disinhibition.

Some of the youths argued that those persons who cannot handle drugs become violent, but they excluded themselves from this category. A 15-year-old female heavy drug user from the purposive sample who was involved in shoplifting and trading stolen goods provides an example:

*Q:* So you think there's a real difference between those other people and yourself?

*A:* But, yeah, I think so.

*Q:* How would you explain the difference?

*A:* 'Cause, you know, when they get high, they act, they act, um, more like a violent type, and uh, when I'm high I act more, like I'm friendlier, and a quiet person, you know.

A 19-year-old female heavy drug user from the purposive sample who was involved in juvenile wrongs:

*Q:* Okay, when you think of drinking in general, do you think there's anything wrong with it?

*A:* If you in control, then it's not. But if you get high, start acting like you wanna fight, some wrong, you can't control it.

*Q:* Do you think you can control it?

*A:* Mm, not when I'm drunk, though, 'cause I know I get loud.

*Q:* . . . do you get in fights?

*A:* No, I don't have fights when I'm drunk, I jes talk too much, too loud.

*Q:* . . . so do you think there's any connection? Between people drinking and getting into trouble and stuff?

*A:* I see young kids, they drink, they like to fight.

*Q:* But they like to fight when they don't drink, too, do you think so?

*A:* Worse when they drink. Try to kill each other.

This is not to suggest, however, that the subjects who were heavily involved in violence viewed *all* of their violent acts as unrelated to drug or alcohol use. Some did identify a few specific events in which disinhibition was an important factor. An example is offered by a 14-year-old male from the detained sample who was an occasional user of alcohol, marijuana, and speed. He had tried other drugs as well and had been involved in vandalism, shoplifting, petty larceny, minor fraud, burglary, mugging, and joyriding. He talked of an informal "gang fight" in which his friends opposed a group of black youths one evening at a shopping center. According to the subject, black youths started the fight; after the whites responded, the blacks came back with "a whole bunch of friends." Each side found more of their friends and a major fight ensued, which was broken up by the police. He reported that the whites "came out on top." Later in the interview he was asked about violence while intoxicated and referred back to this episode, although he had not mentioned alcohol when first talking about the event:

*Q:* Can you think of a specific time when you were either high or drunk that you did something which you probably wouldn't have done if you were straight?

*A:* Yeah. The, that time that I got in that so-called gang war. I was drunk. The kid hit me over the back with a stick, and I turned around and nailed him real hard in the face.

*Q:* Do you think you would've been involved in a gang war if you hadn't been drunk?

*A:* No, I probably would've left real quick if I found out there was going to be a gang war. And I wasn't drunk.

The disinhibition hypothesis is one that adolescents themselves use to explain their own and others' violent behaviors, but they see disinhibition as only one of several important factors and as important only in limited situations and instances. Although the heavy drug users were the most involved in violence, most violent events reported by these subjects occurred while the subjects were not using drugs or alcohol (see Johnson et al., 1984).

## Summary and Conclusions

The findings presented in this chapter suggest how youths themselves view violent events and the ways they develop. Yule City youths were neither equally involved in nor equally exposed to violence. Those more involved in drug use and other crime were more involved in violence than were non-users, light users, or those not involved in criminal behavior. This accords with the findings of national studies, as reported earlier. Also in line with those studies, we found that heavier drug users and more crime-involved subjects were not only more often perpetrators, but also more often victims of violence than were other youths.

By far the most common form of violence reported was fighting. A great deal of the fighting occurred in the context of youths' testing one another's limits for being taunted or otherwise provoked, or of youths' attempting to protect their own or a friend's or relative's honor. Others who have studied fighting by youths individually or as members of groups have noted similar testing activities (A. Campbell, 1981; Marsh, 1978) and themes of protecting honor (Lofland, 1969; Toch, 1969).

Our subjects indicated, however, that the more serious incidents of violence occurred in four circumstances: in the distribution of drugs, in battles among gangs, in instances of racial or ethnic antagonism, and in acts of revenge. We found that in each context considerably higher numbers of heavy drug users than light users or non-users were involved and that it was the more criminally active subjects who reported involvement in violence.

The contexts of violence discussed in this chapter share a common characteristic—*protectionism*. Youths say they fight in order to protect honor, possessions, and territory. The issue of protectionism elevated to the group level is a dominant one in the literature on youth gangs and violence (Erlanger, 1979; Horowitz and Schwartz, 1974; Short and Strodtbeck, 1965). The distinction between contexts of serious and minor violence, however, have remained unexplored up to this point. Perhaps this is due to the either-or emphasis in the literature: studies focus either on seriously involved youths or on what have been termed minor violent episodes. Farrington, Berkowitz, and West (1982) have begun to address these issues by looking at the distinction between group and individual violence as an important contextual factor related to provocation. They also suggest a relationship between these contextual properties and the severity of the violence.

Although much has been written on the relationship of alcohol and drugs to violence, few studies have investigated drugs/alcohol as features that change the context of a situation. Exceptions to this are studies of disinhibition as a product of situational contingencies (MacAndrew and Edgerton, 1969). Youths' beliefs about disinhibition have been neglected thus far in the literature (see chapter 3).

Our respondents' reports of their violent activity also suggest three themes that have been previously noted. First, youths report a major role in creating a potentially violent context and in participating in it. Second, youths reporting violent events provide limited descriptions of the actual violence and appear to exaggerate the harm that they may inflict in hypothetical situations or to emphasize their eagerness for or prowess in fighting. Third, their descriptions reflect little awareness of the physical injury or harm suffered by the victim in their violent events; they display little or no empathy for the victim's suffering. This is consistent with the denial of injury reported by Sykes and Matza (1957) and with emergent findings that aggressive and violent youths tend to underreport the seriousness of their violence (ADAMHA/OJJDP, 1984). That is, youths who actually engage in fighting appear to inflate their self-image as tough and eager to fight when provoked, but to deflate or deny the actual harm to victims that they impose. Thus, a balanced view of violent events needs to include information from the victim's perspective—which is generally not obtained in self-report studies.

Extremely serious violent events (for example, intentional stabbing or shooting, homicide, gang rape, aggravated assault during a robbery, injury requiring long-term hospitalization of a victim) were not reported by these respondents, despite questions and probes to elicit reports about such events. Although some subjects may have intentionally concealed such events or described serious violence as involving only minor harm, these youths reported a variety of crimes, some quite serious. Moreover, they were generally relaxed and comfortable with the interviewer by the time these questions were asked. The implication is that gratuitous violence or extremely serious violence was quite rare—even among highly delinquent youths recruited from the streets or group homes or interviewed in the local juvenile detention facility of the study community.

## Notes

1. Tables 6–1 and 6–2 distinguish between *experiences* with violence and *involvement* in violence. Experience with violence indicates knowledge of violent events due to one's own involvement or the involvement of a significant other (for example, family or friend as victim). Involvement indicates the subject was a party in the event.

2. When asked if they carried a weapon, those who did (or had done so in the past) explained that it was for self-defense. Perception of the need for self-defense is

usually associated with perception of violent contexts. For example, it is believed to be necessary either to avoid or to carry a weapon in certain neighborhoods. Similarly, weapons are carried by the youths when someone is "after" them or when they are carrying a lot of money or drugs. Even though these are not descriptions of actual incidents of violence, they suggest the youths' own theories about where violence is likely to occur.

# 7
# Delinquents' Perspectives on the Role of the Victim

*With Margret Ksander*

An important line of inquiry in research on juvenile delinquency addresses how youths themselves define the illegal activities in which they become involved. This chapter analyzes one aspect of that topic—the perceptions that underlie delinquents' selection of victims for their illegal behavior.

Sykes and Matza (1957) have delineated several "techniques of neutralization" invoked by delinquents; these take the "form of justifications for deviance that are seen as valid by the delinquent but not by the legal system or society at large." One of these techniques, "denial of the victim," holds that the crime "is not really an injury; rather, it is a form of rightful retaliation or punishment" of a victim who is perceived as a wrongdoer. The victim may be physically absent, unknown, or a vague abstraction (such as a public building). Similarly, "denial of injury" permits the delinquent to feel that "his behavior does not really cause great harm despite the fact that it runs contrary to the law." Property destruction is "having fun," creating "mischief," or doing "pranks"; autos are "borrowed"; fights are "private disputes" (Harlan and McDowell, 1980; Jensen and Rojek, 1980; Sykes and Matza, 1957). These two themes, denial of the victim and denial of injury, are apparent in the extracts from the interviews quoted herein. In addition, however, the extracts demonstrate how a positive intention to avoid harming individuals limits some youths' delinquent behavior. This, in turn, suggests the potential effectiveness of simple precautions against theft.

The data for this analysis come from interviews with 42 youths who reported involvement in criminal activities. Of the 42, 12 had been involved only in episodic, minor crimes, such as vandalism and shoplifting, and 30 had been involved in serious juvenile crime. Recall from chapter 2 the criteria for defining crimes as serious: (1) crimes that caused bodily harm to victims; (2) crimes of theft regardless of whether accompanied by property damage; (3) crimes involving property damage (including vandalism) or destruction alone; and (4) crimes involving systematic drug sales and otherwise minor offenses (such as petty theft or minor vandalism) that were reported as being common activities for a given youth.

Each respondent's interview transcript was read carefully, and every account of an actual crime, a planned crime, or an illegal event that the subject reported but was not involved in was noted. Answers to questions about hypothetical situations involving honesty or trust (or avoidance of crime) were also reviewed. As the following findings indicate, victims were not defined in the abstract, but in relation to different kinds of criminal events. Youths also shared some of their understandings about the role of the victim in a criminal event. Several themes emerged from the analysis of the transcripts: (1) the careless person is an appropriate victim of theft; (2) an individual who offends the juvenile or who victimizes others is also an appropriate victim; (3) family members, friends, and individuals who are "innocent" or who are particularly vulnerable are inappropriate victims; and (4) crimes are legitimated if there is no perceived individual victim.

## Careless Victims

The most common crime reported by sample members was property theft. A dominant theme in the reports of such thefts was the ease with which victims whom they defined as "careless" could be located. Not only is it easy to steal from the careless, whether they are individuals or business establishments, but their inefficiency in protecting their possessions makes them "responsible" in part for their own victimization. This view, that the careless victim has "asked for it," was articulated dramatically in a 16-year-old's report of the theft of his own bike stolen from the driveway of his home:

A: Well, I was out riding my bike and I heard the phone ring and I rode in, put my bike in the driveway, was talking to you, and when I hung back up I went outside and my bicycle was gone. And I admire that person whoever did that.
Q: Why?
A: They deserve the bike. They were, they had nerve, they were fast, for sure. I mean, it was broad daylight, it was like maybe six o'clock, not even, and it was, how long were we on the phone, you know, that takes . . . I admire them!
Q: So you're not concerned or upset about having lost the bike?
A: They deserve it, I think, and they deserve it more than I did.
Q: How much was the bike worth?
A: $180 that I paid for it with the money I earned myself.

This same youth, although he was involved in chronic drug use and sales, vandalism, car theft, and burglary, had never been apprehended. He elaborated on the theme of the careless victim in a discussion of business establishments that fail to apprehend shoplifters:

*Q:* Have you ever told somebody in authority that somebody else was stealing something?

*A:* No.

*Q:* Have you ever been in that kind of situation where you could have? I mean where you saw someone?

*A:* Yeah.

*Q:* How come you didn't tell?

*A:* Because if someone stole, and they allow people to steal from their store, and a store should either safeguard against people stealing or you know, if they can't catch them . . . like I felt about my bike. If they don't get caught, they deserve it. I don't really, I don't feel that way to the deepest of my heart, but, you know, that's a general rule. No sucker deserves to keep his money, you know.

Of the 42 youths in this subsample, 25 reported frequent incidents of taking cars either for joyriding or for extended use or sale. The ease with which they located vehicles vulnerable to theft because of the owner's carelessness dominates reports of such criminal activity.

A 17-year-old involved in, though not arrested for, repeated episodes of auto theft, theft from autos (including stealing a police revolver from a patrol car), and drug selling provided an account of a typical incident.

*A:* Um, this guy was up on Lowell Street, down toward Underwood more, and we were walkin' by, and he, uh, parked his car and left it runnin' and went in this house; we just jumped in that sucker, and we were gone.

*Q:* How long did you have it altogether, then?

*A:* Three days. We just, I would just park it, couple blocks away, and then go get it when it got dark out. And that was it.

A 13-year-old, who was in the group detained by the juvenile authorities when interviewed, talked about taking a car in similar fashion on a street in downtown Yule City:

*Q:* What happened with the car?

*A:* I don't know. I was walking down, I skipped school, I was walking down Eve Street and I saw a key . . . a car with the keys in it. I looked around, I jumped in it, I started driving away.

A 19-year-old who admitted drug selling, auto theft, and gambling described the theft of a moped from a careless owner. In his recollection of the event, the carelessness of the owner not only made him a likely victim but, in the subject's view, negated the criminality of the act altogether:

*Q:* How old were you?

*A:* I think I was 10. Stole it, and I didn't really steal it, it was at the store, and somebody must have planned on keeping it running, running right in and running right back out. I just jumped it and went off. Then I gave it to this older kid, and he took it from me. And I didn't never see it again.

Although the subjects depended on carelessness on the part of victims, they also conceived of victims as careless even when the victim may, in fact, have taken routine steps to prevent theft. This conception facilitates the neutralization of theft as "borrowing." Subjects' spoke of taking vehicles in such terms:

*Q:* What do you mean "we borrowed a car"?

*A:* Well, the keys were in it, underneath the car, you know, one of those hide-a-key things? They're great. A lot of people have those. And it was late, about one o'clock in the morning. We borrowed the car and I don't know what we did. We brought the car back about five o'clock in the morning.

*Q:* Put it back where you found it?

*A:* Yup, didn't damage it or anything. We might of even put a couple bucks worth of gas in, I'm not sure though.

In many interviews subjects also reported searching for careless victims. An 18-year-old respondent from the purposive sample, well known from field work for "rowdy" delinquency, described both searching and borrowing:

*Q:* Have you ever stolen anything like a car or motorcycle and stuff?

*A:* Uh-huh.

*Q:* When was that?

*A:* See, we didn't steal cars, we borrowed cars.

*Q:* Oh, okay.

*A:* We would . . . take the car, see we just looked for cars with keys in them, and we'd drive it around, let it run out of gas, and then bring it back to where we took it from.

*Q:* Uh-huh.

*A:* . . . leave the keys in, leave it. Exactly where it was that means, you know. . . .

Another 18-year-old in the purposive sample (involved in auto theft, burglarizing automobiles and houses, property destruction, and drug sales and distribution) described a search for a careless owner in the following account of stealing a van in order to burglarize a rival drug dealer:

*Q:* So tell me how you managed, how did you get the van and everything?

*A:* I stole that from the airport. In the airport they leave the keys underneath the floor mat.

*Q:* Well, the people out at the airport must have known the van was missing and come after you or something.

*A:* Nope, 'cause people go on weekend trips, you know, or, you know, sometimes they'll come back early and they take the car without anybody knowing.

*Q:* Oh, you mean it was just parked in the parking lot out there?

*A:* Yeah, I just hopped in.

*Q:* It was unlocked?

*A:* No. I busted the vent window. I busted that, reached in and unlocked the door, and that's how I lift up the floor mat and there was the key. Um, and all that.

Despite the owner's precaution of leaving the van locked and in a paid (presumably controlled) lot, the delinquent viewed the owner as having left himself vulnerable to victimization.

## Deserving Victims: What Goes Around, Comes Around

Whereas careless victims are typically viewed as having "asked for it," "deserving" victims are viewed as "having it coming." The delinquents used the adage, "What goes around, comes around." That is, those who injure others will eventually be injured themselves.

One 16-year-old boy who sold drugs explained, for example, how he refrained from becoming a deserving victim:

*Q:* You ever, um, been tempted to do that to somebody [cheat his customers on the quality or amount of drugs]?

*A:* Oh, many times, I could do it with speed in a second.

*Q:* Why don't you?

*A:* Because, what goes around comes around. And it . . . you know, they would definitely, you know, I sell them the speed, they don't speed, you know, they'd know something was up, they'd come back to me you know, so . . .

Schools and their personnel are common targets of vindictive vandalism for wrongs inflicted on delinquent youth (also see Gold, 1977; Harlan and McDowell, 1980; Toby, 1983a, 1983b). In a representative account from a 16-year-old boy who had been detained, breaking and entering and destruction of school property are revealed as retribution against the principal:

*A:* Okay, coming back from a party, and I'm going to, uh, on the way home, I dropped Ivy off and I was with Irwin. And we got out to take a short cut, we got to go across the field at Ashdale. So I, you know, he said, well man, want to break in? Yeah, let's do it!

Q: Well, how'd you get the idea, how did that come into your head?

A: Cause its principal, remember I told you about the principal?

The subject goes on to detail the vandalism and destruction perpetrated in the school, including the following symbolic victimization of the principal:

Q: . . . and the, uh, I found a set of handcuffs in his [the principal's] desk. We drew a picture of, um, Mr. Sutton with the, like the handcuffs hanging off the wall right by the thing. "It's going to be you when I get done with you," stuff, kinds of things.

This retribution was because the principal had earlier suspended the boys from school for behavior they defined as a minor infraction of the rules.

Another very clear theme in the interviews was the youths' sensitivity to being treated without respect by adults, especially those in authority. Retribution for such perceived insults was sometimes immediate and direct. For example, a 16-year-old detained youth involved in burglary and chronic shoplifting described a physical altercation with a teacher:

A: Yeah, and I hit the teacher, man, cause she be talkin' smart about that math, man, and if I can't get an answer from her, throw a pencil on the floor, ya know, she came over, ah, "The poor little baby," ya know, and I curse her out for callin' me a baby, and threaten her, man.

On the other hand, retribution may also involve considerable planning. An 18-year-old youth in the purposive sample, for example, described an elaborate burglary of a neighbor's home. In discussing the incident, he implied that the neighbor, a drug dealer, had been an appropriate victim because he failed to "respect" the youth's maturity and skill. The burglary had netted an expensive stereo and a large sum of money, but the primary goal was fifty pounds of marijuana, which provided the youth with a two-year supply for personal use and sales. The victim had refused to sell the youth marijuana and had treated him like "just another kid down the street."

Another type of "deserving" victim is a commercial establishment that "rips off" the delinquent, peers, or the general public. One youth who stole an expensive stereo noted that stealing from individuals was not a routine crime for him. He only did that when he got "rowdy" and had the support of others. He was, however, a skillful and persistent shoplifter and was unabashed about it:

*A:* I only do that when I get real rowdy. I don't like doing that, that's mean, you know, that to a person, I mean if you did it, to a store, it's all right if you do it to a store, I think, that's, at least I do. Store robs you anyways. So you can steal from them, who the hell cares. But if you take from a person, man, they, they got to work for their money. It's not right.

One youth had worked out a sophisticated scheme with his friends for going to the movies without paying:

*Q:* Have you done that since?
*A:* No, that was justifiable by the way.
*Q:* Why?
*A:* Well, I may be fifteen, but how come I can't get into an R-rated movie alone? But I have to pay adult prices, so I figured I pay one out of two movies I see is fair.
*Q:* You thought it was fair then?
*A:* I know it's fair.

The subjects' discussions of retributive crime suggest that these acts help restore injured self-esteem and respect among peers.

Still another category of "deserving" victim includes those who engage in some illegal activity themselves. This may involve other delinquent peers, such as those who shoplift or steal and those who prostitute or fence goods. Take, for example, the following account given by Kevin, a 20-year-old self-reported drug addict with a long history of delinquent involvement and detention. (Kevin's case study is included in chapter 9.) When asked about types of persons against whom he might use force in order to take money, he ruled out his mother, brothers, and fellow students, but reported that one category whom he and his associates routinely victimized were fellow delinquents:

*Q:* Tell me about that one.
*A:* We used to rob the robbers—other people that robbed—when they hit something, you know: "Hey, give me some money." They would give it to us, I can remember a couple of times we went out and checked his pockets.
*Q:* Did you do that by yourself or who did you usually do that with?
*A:* Ivan.
*Q:* How old were you then?
*A:* Fifteen.
*Q:* So that was the same period in here with stealing and robbing?
*A:* Yeah.
*Q:* Okay, you ever get caught?
*A:* Doing something like that!

*Q:* Yeah . . . you say you "robbed the robbers," you make it sound like there was this whole huge network of people who were robbing and stuff. Was that a pretty common type of thing among the people you hung with and stuff?

*A:* Hmm-mmm.

Persons involved in drug sales, either as dealers or as buyers, were particularly vulnerable to being victimized. Expectations of dealer/buyer victimization routinely characterized subjects' accounts of drug dealing. Often, knowledge of drug networks and supplies led to a fellow user–dealer being marked for victimization. A 16-year-old delinquent in the purposive sample, for example, described how he and three close friends acquired their "head stash" by cooperating in the theft of a large marijuana plant from the garden of a known dealer.

In our study, respondents who sold drugs were almost in a class by themselves as persons who "deserved" to be victimized—because they were expected to "rip off" the customer in some way. Dealers were well aware of their dual role of victimizer and potential victim (see also Goldstein, 1985; Johnson, Goldstein, et al., 1985; Johnson, Wish, et al., 1983) as the following account shows. A detained boy justified his practice of holding out "three or four joints" when selling marijuana to someone he did not know well. Friends to whom he sold would, he said, get him high as part of the transaction. Strangers to whom he sold might not acknowledge this convention, so he took care of himself. This practice, he argued, was expected.

*A:* . . . a person I don't know buys it from me, I don't know if he's gonna get me high, if he does, he does, if he doesn't, he doesn't. But if I always got four joints, I always know I'll get high after. You know, see you make a little profit out of it.

*Q:* What would you think if somebody did that to you?

*A:* It's always bein' done. I don't mind . . . But I always get mine. . . . I never buy from strangers anyways.

## Inappropriate Victims

The respondents were asked to discuss not only actual criminal behavior but also hypothetical situations. In these discussions, many explicitly rejected the possibility of assaulting or stealing from people they knew. They also expressed an unwillingness to harm "innocent" or helpless persons. The subjects reported several strategies for avoiding harm to other individuals. In the case of theft, they often selected victims they thought could bear the loss, avoided friends and relatives, and chose impersonal victims such as corporations.[1]

Among these seriously delinquent youths, very clear norms define empathy for and identification of one's family or friends of one's family as inappropriate victims. A 16-year-old girl commented about stealing:

> *A:* I mean from my mom's friends. I would never steal from them.
> *Q:* How come?
> *A:* I don't know. I just wouldn't. I have no respect for that.

An 18-year-old in the purposive sample emphasized both the self-protective and empathic content of this behavior:

> *A:* I don't steal from people that I know.
> *Q:* The burglaries and all, were you usually in some white neighborhoods, or black neighborhoods, or did it matter?
> *A:* Usually, white neighborhoods, upper class. But I, I wouldn't steal anything unless I knew it wouldn't hurt anyone.

It was important to a substantial number of these delinquent youths that no underserving person suffer. An 18-year-old member of the purposive sample explained his reasons for refraining from crime in some situations:

> *Q:* Could you tell me about times you could easily have taken things and gotten away without punishment, but did not do so?
> *A:* Well, I could take all kinds of stuff from the labs at school. And the only way of anybody knowing it is me.
> *Q:* Why don't you?
> *A:* It's mean. Someone else is going to suffer from it.

The subject goes on to explain the distinctions made in deciding whether or not a crime is "mean," decisions informed largely by norms regarding empathy:

> *Q:* I'm a little confused, then. How about when you took the, um, hub-caps? How come that wasn't mean?
> *A:* Cause the insurance will pay for that.
> *Q:* But is that mean to the insurance company?
> *A:* I don't give a shit about big insurance companies. It's multimillion dollars.

A 16-year-old boy was explicit about not wanting to hurt those who are innocent:

> *Q:* Okay, um, how about, ever throw stones or snowballs or rocks at windows of cars or buses?

*A:* Yeah, in the winter I always chuck' em at buses. Raptram buses; I don't do it to school buses or cars 'cause I might scare them and make them lose control. I always hit the bus from the rear.

*Q:* How come you do that?

*A:* 'Cause I just . . . I don't want to be responsible for anyone getting hurt if the bus driver swerves and runs into a tree or somethin'.

This theme of not being "mean," not "hurting" others, and protecting younger or helpless persons frequently includes specific references to empathy: "I wouldn't want anyone to do that to me," "I know how I'd feel." These youths may define breaking the law as only *formally* wrong if they have an acceptable motive. But they define violations of norms protecting certain classes of people from victimization as *morally* wrong.

When the crime involves personal contact, it is more difficult for youths to avoid not only injury but also an awareness of the victims' definition of the situation as unfair and frightening. No subject reported indifference to this problem; one solution was to select victims who were not "helpless."

A 17-year-old boy from the purposive sample who also had been involved in burglary talked about purse snatching with an accomplice. He specifically rejected helpless victims:

*A:* Would run by. One would knock the person down, one would grab the purse and take off. But, you know, that's a real nasty thing, now that I think about it, you know.

*Q:* Who, what kind of people would you do it to?

*A:* Um, ladies, you know, they're the only ones carrying their purses.

*Q:* Like old ladies, or . . .?

*A:* No, not . . . young, young ladies that would have a chance to fight back or would chase us or something.

This youth was asked if he had ever been given too much change by a cashier:

*Q:* What do you do?

*A:* I've—that's only happened to me once, and I had to bring it back, 'cause I felt guilty, stomach was churning, I was about to throw up. Because, um, there was this—I was at, going to the dentist and it was this blind lady, at one of those concession things. And, she gave me, one of those Susan B. Anthony dollars back instead, for a quarter. I said Otto man, shit, you know, Otto's always been with me when some of this shit's been going down and said, no, I got to take it back, took it back. And, um she told me to keep it anyway. She said keep it, keep it.

## Negation or Escalation of Harm to Victim

When, despite care in selecting victims, harm (from the victim's perspective) does occur, the victim's actions in the scene are seen as contributing to the nature of the victimization:

> *Q:* Did you ever hurt the people when you did it?
> *A:* Well, one lady, would not let go of the purse. Did not want to let go of the purse, and like, my brother like dragged her a few houses down and she, you know, it was on grass, though, you know. We, she was walking like, and we went by, knocked her over and dragged her onto the grass, you know; it didn't hurt her or nothing. . . . But, no, we never really hurt anybody.

If the woman had let go of "the purse" (notice it is depersonalized in the subject's account, not "her purse"), she would not have been dragged or physically harmed. In this and similar accounts, subjects expressed their perception that they did not "hurt" the victim(s) and that whatever harm occurred was the victim's own doing. The victim here was viewed as causing the incident to become atypical or problematic in the sense of converting a simple purse snatching into something not intended by the perpetrators.

In other instances, however, the victim's "overreaction," in the delinquents' terms, may lead to the youth's discontinuing their behavior. That is, interaction within the setting of the criminal event may make clear that, in fact, the target is an inappropriate victim and may lead the delinquents to cancel the criminal encounter rather than violate their own norms regarding victims. A clear and colorful example of such a foiled encounter is detailed in the following account wherein the subject was discussing the choice of victims for robbery. The account shows how an individual deemed appropriate by usual standards can come to be seen as inappropriate.

> *Q:* What kind of people would you usually do that to?
> *A:* Suckers.
> *Q:* How can you tell?
> *A:* You can, I can tell a sucker a mile away.
> *Q:* White, black, old, young?
> *A:* Any—there's always suckers; any race, any color, any age; there's always a sucker, "a sucker born every minute." . . . But, um, one guy, this was was pretty funny, it's not funny, but it is funny. Because we're sitting there, right? And we jumped him. He gave us this watch, his wedding ring, and his wallet, and he said, "Just don't beat me, man, come to my house, take my TV, my stereo, take my wife," you know? We were dying, we were laughing. The guy, we said, "Here, take your stuff, we don't want it."
> *Q:* How old was he?

*A:* He was, uh, about 35. Hispanic, guy, Andros Ramon or something like that.

*Q:* You knew him?

*A:* No. We just looked at his watch and go "Andros? What's an Andros," you know. I was getting pretty, I said, "Man," I said, "you want us to take your wife? Take your stuff back." We gave him all his stuff back.

Here, an apparently appropriate victim (a stranger, not too young, not too old, in possession of watch, rings, and so forth) was found by the subject and his companions to be, in fact, inappropriate because he behaved contrary to their expectations. As the subject and his friends viewed the interaction, the victim was never in danger of being beaten. The victim's humorous and inappropriate response in offering his wife and his general overcompliance conflicted so sharply with the youths' expectations about the event as to lead them to abandon the intended act.

A victim's refusal to behave positively, however, may lead to an escalation of the criminal event. A detailed subject reported on such an incident, the one that had resulted in his arrest:

*A:* I was going for his tape player man, it was all really nice shit. The dude wouldn't give it up, I told him to just give it up, man, and we could forget about it, you know. . . forget about it man, he just wanted to be. . . the dude wouldn't give it up, man. I was hitting him and he was still holdin' it there.

*Q:* You have to start over; we've got half the story here, from the beginning, who was with you, when did it happen, what time of day?

*A:* I was by myself. I went up there, ya know, I [got old friends] there; went to the house and jes kicked the door in, ya know; and I didn't figure nobody was there, it's a little small apartment; I went inside, [saw] a tape player, man, I started pullin' it, ya know, it was dark; and he'd pull it back again, ha, ha, ha; and I'd pull it, and pull it back again. . . . And all of a sudden, the lights came on, and [he] say, "No, you can't have my tape" and I say, "Don't mind jes givin' the tape" askin' we can forget about this, I mean, we ain't got to go through. . . I pull it, pull it back, man, and he wouldn't let go, man, and I was hittin' him, ha, ha, ha and um, damn! man, I got caught at it too, man. . . White guy damn! Dude wouldn't turn it loose, damn! I mean, that the least he could've did, man; turn it loose, man, at least could've listened to some music. They wouldn't turn it loose shit, man! And I got mad, I was kickin' him, man, hittin' him.

Within this encounter, the delinquent lost control of the situation. Lack of cooperation—in the form of physical resistance by the victim—led the youth to redefine the situation as calling for more serious harm to the victim than he had intended. Moreover, the subject saw himself as having been placed at greater risk in terms of the seriousness of the crime committed, the possibility of being physically harmed himself, and the possibility of being caught. In either type of event (escalation or negation), being an inappropriate victim amounts in practice to displaying behavior that does not comply with the delinquents' own expectations and that causes the delinquent thereby to lose control of the criminal event.

## Victimless Crime

Some of the criminal activity reported by the respondents did not involve a victim from their perspective. Rather, objects in their environment were used in ways they found appropriate. Many of these events involved financial loss or discomfort for others, but such losses were not part of the youths' definition of the situation. From their perspective, they found impersonal targets, not personal victims, for their activity—what Sykes and Matza (1957) call "denial of the victim."

A 17-year-old girl from the purposive sample, herself involved in routine shoplifting from stores and school, vandalism, and occasional theft from houses in which she babysat, characterized her own family's victimization by vandalism in just such terms:

> A: Yeah, and they wrote terrible rude and crude words on my house.
> Q: Same kids?
> A: Yep, as far as I know.
> Q: What did they write it with?
> A: Crayon. Says "come fuck" or something fuck.
> Q: When was that?
> A: I don't know, I just noticed that the other day because I was pulling

out of the driveway. I guess, um . . . and that little, our little garage thing on the side of our house, they kept going in there. Breaking stuff that was in there, playing around with it, and that's about it.

> Q: Why do you think your house has become a target?
> A: I don't know.
> N: No idea?
> A: Just it's available I guess, I don't know.

Of interest is the subject's matter-of-fact assessment that the victimization had no direct relationship to her or her family but, rather, was more or less incidental to the act of vandalism—any "available" garage would have been equally appropriate.

Objects incidental to settings similarly become targets of criminal or delinquent acts precisely because they are characterized as "nonvictims." In his description of deliberate property destruction, a 17-year-old male representative of the purposive sample was clear about recognizing when a circumstantial object is appropriate to delinquent activities:

A: Oh yeah, I've done that a couple of times, that was fun, though. But you know there's this—they were going to tear it down, you know, condemned to be torn down, I just—I had my pellet gun, I just put out a couple windows. But I'm not into damaging other people's things, you know . . . I'm on, I told you I'm on that "do unto others" kick!

In this incident, the subject already had his gun with him, so it was not a question of intentionally securing the gun in order to inflict the damage on the building. Rather his encounter with the target object was incidental and, because the building was "condemned to be torn down" (which, in fact, was not true) and not perceived as belonging to another person, circumstances—in the youth's view—provided the target of the delinquent activity. The important point is that in this and each of the other incidents reported in this subsection, the precise object targeted for criminal activity was, in and of itself, of little or no significance to the delinquent. The object's impersonal or public character constituted its appropriateness for the particular act. By such reasoning, subjects may clearly "deny the victim."

An additional theme that is evident in subjects' accounts about circumstantial targets is that the acts perpetrated served no purpose other than "fun" or expressivity. Consider the following account from a 16-year-old regarding an incident of arson that resulted in his expulsion from elementary school:

A: I set the bathroom . . . bathrooms—bathroom's at St. Mark's—on fire before. . . .
Q: Okay, what did you do?
A: Took a lighter to school and just wanted to play around with it, and I lit the paper towel roll on fire, the gas line, and the toilet paper, and the garbage can. And anything that would burn, I'd burn it. And then when I opened the door and all the smoke just poured out and I went down to the room, some kid asked to go to the bathroom and came back up and said, "Ah. . . ." The teacher said, "What's wrong?" He says "There's a fire in the bathroom."
Q: How did they catch you—how did they know it was you?
A: They found the lighter on me. I kept the lighter.
Q: What—did you do that on purpose? I mean did you want to set the bathroom on fire?
A: No, I just wanted to watch it burn!

This subject was subsequently suspended from junior high school for another incident involving playing with fire.

Note that shooting out the windows, as described in the earlier excerpt, was similarly characterized as "fun." Subjects routinely reported the "thrills" involved in being what they call "rowdy"—a residual category of behavior used by all types of subjects in referring to any boisterous, usually spontaneous behavior that might be conventional or unconventional, but was definitely not, from their perspective, "good."

## Summary and Conclusions

The respondents in this subsample of youths who engaged in illegal activities were in substantial agreement about their expectations regarding persons they victimized and how they expected victims to behave during a crime. In some respects, their expectations appear to represent an extension of generally held social norms. They expressed an empathy for family and friends that ordinarily protected them from being selected as victims. In addition, children, the elderly, and the handicapped were not perceived as appropriate victims. Even among "appropriate" victims, there was a clear rule against imposing gratuitous physical harm.

Delinquents defined strangers as being appropriate victims, especially if they were perceived to be "careless." Such persons were believed to participate in their own victimization. ("There's a sucker born every minute.") Victims were perceived to be careless if they did not protect their property or took only routine precautions (locking a car but leaving a key hidden somewhere in the car, or leaving valuable possessions in a coat pocket or a locked car). Persons who took effective precautions (leaving cars locked with no key available) were generally not victimized. Similarly, stores that used effective security measures and prosecuted shoplifters were not victimized by youths who routinely shoplifted (see chapter 5); they generally went elsewhere.

Also perceived as appropriate or "deserving" victims were persons considered to "have it coming" because they had injured or insulted the perpetrator in some important respect. The delinquents in Yule City mentioned a maxim, "What goes around, comes around," which emphasizes reciprocal expectations. The delinquent perceived that he was being victimized or insulted by someone and in turn retaliated against such "deserving" persons. Delinquents also frequently victimized and expect to be victimized by others who engaged in illegal activity. When they were the victims, they were likely to engage in retribution against the perceived offender. Moreover, they also expected retribution from others. Sometimes this expectation of retribution prevented them from victimizing others, but at other times they accepted the fact that they would be victimized in a similar fashion.

"What goes around, comes around" is especially important to delinquents who sell drugs; dealers seem to be particularly likely to cheat or otherwise victimize their customers or to have their customers perceive that they are doing so. Thus, drug dealers are likely to suffer retribution from customers who may steal or burglarize their supply of drugs, inflict personal injury, or steer potential customers to other dealers.

Most of the crimes committed by our respondents were generally designed to avoid personal interaction with the victims. When an offense did require personal interaction between the delinquent and the victim, the delinquent expected the person to be a "good" victim—that is, to allow the delinquent to control the situation, to turn over money and possessions, and to offer no physical resistance. When the victim did not abide by these expectations, the criminal event might escalate in terms of seriousness (a purse snatch might become a robbery) and the potential for physical injury (the victim might be assaulted).

The tone of these delinquents' discussions of their criminal activities and interactions with victims was neither hostile nor aggressive. Rather, it was one of controlled risk taking; generally accepted norms defined which classes of persons were "appropriate victims" and how all parties should behave during the criminal event. The delinquents recognized, however, that society might impose sanctions if they were apprehended, and it was ultimately in reference to societal norms that delinquents evaluated their responsibility for involvement in criminal events.

## Note

1. As we saw in earlier chapters, some youths reported stealing small amounts of money or items from their parents and/or neighbors. Even in these cases, however, they were clear about not stealing from persons they viewed as unable to afford such a loss.

# 8
# Case Studies of Youths at Risk in Early Adolescence

There is currently much emphasis in the social science and policy-related delinquency literature on locating populations at risk of initiation into delinquent activities. Various studies in the risk literature focus on either personality (Blos, 1967; Freud, 1958), peer group (Coleman, 1961; Friendenberg, 1963; Mead, 1970; Suchman, 1968), age cohort (Brunswick, 1979, 1985; Brunswick and Boyle, 1979; Brunswick, Merzel, and Messeri, 1985), or family (Britain, 1963; Brook, Lukoff, and Whiteman, 1978, 1980; Clausen, 1966; Larson, 1974) variables as related to initiation into deviant behavior. More recent investigations have examined drug use specifically and the interconnection of family, peer, and personality variables in determining such use (Brook, Lukoff, and Whiteman, 1977; Huba, Wingard, and Bentler, 1980; Jessor, Graves, Hanson, and Jessor, 1968, 1976; Jessor, Jessor, and Finney, 1973; Potvin and Lee, 1980). Perhaps the most conclusive of these studies are those by Kandel and her associates (Kandel, 1980; Kandel, Kessler, and Margulies, 1978; Kandel, Margulies, and Davies, 1978) and by Elliott and associates (Elliott and Huizinga, 1984).

In this chapter we present case studies (Mitchell, 1983) of two 13-year-old subjects involved in both delinquency and drug use. Specifically, we explore the factors that precede initiation into drug use and the way such drug use fits into other activities of the two youths. We look closely at the youths' worlds from their perspective, focusing on how they define themselves and their relationships with peers and parents and their current involvement and attitude toward future involvement with alcohol, marijuana, other drugs, and minor or serious delinquency.

## Background

Kandel and associates (Kandel, 1976a, 1976b; Kandel, Kessler, and Margulies, 1978; Kandel, Margulies, and Davis, 1978) found that both personal and interpersonal factors—personality, relationship with parents, and relationship with peers—are influential in initiation into drug use. They outline the nature of such factors and argue that "at least four distinct developmental stages in adolescent drug involvement can be identified: (1) beer or wine; (2) cigarettes and/or hard liquor; (3) marijuana; and (4) other illicit drugs" (Kandel, 1980:6). Among their findings on the relationships of drugs consumed, Kandel (1978: 34–35) reports the following:

> These longitudinal data indicate that many of the factors previously found to be associated with various types of drug behaviors at one point in time . . . in fact, precede the use of these drugs. There may be continuous processes whereby these interpersonal characteristics change further as a consequence of drug use. Jessor et al. (1973) have shown that involvement in delinquent activities which predicted the use of marijuana, progressed with continual use of the drug.

The five-year prospective longitudinal study by Elliott and associates arrived at similar conclusions and provided new insights about the patterning of delinquent behavior and drug use prior to and during the teenage years. Huizinga and Elliott (1981), for example, report that only a small proportion of youths (under 25 percent) initiate both delinquent behavior and drug use. Among those who initiate both, onset of minor delinquency and index delinquency generally occurs in the year prior to alcohol and/or marijuana initiation.

Elliott and Huizinga (1984; see also O'Malley, Bachman, and Johnston, 1977) report that patterns of initiation, frequency of involvement, and cessation of delinquency and drug use evolve in different ways during the adolescent years. They also show that age 13 is a critical year in early adolescence for a variety of delinquent behaviors. At age 13, they report, many youths initiate (and possibly continue until age 18) involvement in felony theft, felony assault, minor theft, marijuana use, alcohol use, and illicit drug use. Although a majority of youths are not involved by age 13, youths who do engage in index criminality by age 13 are quite precocious in comparison with other 13-year-olds, and their delinquencies are most apt to persist into adulthood. On the other hand, those engaging in vandalism, minor assault ("hitting others"), and minor thefts by age 13 are likely to desist from such behavior in the late teens. Thus, patterns of behavior and life-styles exhibited at age 13 may have important consequences for behavior in middle and late adolescence and as young adults.

Kandel and associates (also Hendin, Pollinger, and Ulman, 1982) suggest that social factors, mainly the growing importance of peers in early adolescence, are significantly associated with initiation into marijuana use. They suggest that youths at risk of *marijuana use* are those for whom not merely sociability but also peers and their activities are important predictors at this level. These youths exhibit: (1) acceptance of a cluster of beliefs and values that are favorable to marijuana use, (2) acceptance of beliefs that are in opposition to standards upheld by adults, (3) involvement in a peer environment in which marijuana is used, and (4) participation in minor forms of deviant behavior.

Psychological rather than social factors carry more weight, according to Kandel and associates, in characterizing adolescents at risk for *illicit drug use* (other than marijuana and alcohol) than for youths at risk for alcohol or marijuana use. Illicit drug users are those whose lives are characterized by: (1) poor relationships with parents, (2) exposure to parents and peers who use a variety of legal and illegal drugs, (3) psychological distress and depression, and (4) personal characteristics that are somewhat more deviant than those exhibited by novice marijuana users.

For the present analysis, two subjects were selected for case study. One (Norris) meets the criteria noted here for being at high risk of regular use of illicit drugs and serious delinquency; the other (Elizabeth) meets the criteria of being at high risk for marijuana use and nonserious delinquency. In terms of models of stages of drug use and delinquency, Norris is clearly farther along than is Elizabeth, and both are quite evidently at risk. These two subjects were selected from all subjects who met the criteria for being at risk not because they are particularly articulate or interesting—indeed, they are not—but because their biographies include features found regularly among comparable youths. Both appear to be typical youths. Both are white 13-year-olds being raised by their mothers after family breakup; thus differences in age, ethnicity, and family structure have been minimized. Their families and peers, however, differ in important respects, as will be discussed. Their perceptions of themselves and important others and their current delinquent and drug use behaviors permit an examination of the point in the life cycle at which initiation to alcohol, marijuana, and other illicit drugs becomes likely, as well as when serious delinquency may be initiated or continue.

## Case Study 1: Norris

Only 5 percent of all youths in the National Youth Survey reported committing a felony theft, but at age 13 Norris was arrested and sent to a detention facility for two counts of auto theft (he also reported committing other crimes, such as burglary). Norris is also among the 10 percent of 13-year-olds who use marijuana and the 2 percent who have used other illicit drugs (in Norris's case, pills and "mushrooms"). His reports of his delinquent behavior and drug use place him among the 3 percent of the nation's youth who are serious offenders and users of marijuana and alcohol (Elliott and Huizinga, 1984:37).

Norris had been involved in alcohol and cannabis drug use and in crimes such as burglary, major shoplifting, and car theft. He committed his first crime, stealing a bicycle, at age 8. At the time we interviewed him, Norris was living at a juvenile detention facility in Yule City, serving 12 to 18 months for an auto theft committed 6 months earlier. He was also awaiting sentence on a second set of charges: car theft, burglary, and the use of an unauthorized ID. Those charges stemmed from a second auto theft, a few days before the court date for the first.

Norris's parents divorced when he was 5 years old. For most of the time since the divorce, he has lived with his mother, her boyfriend of six years, and his two younger brothers. His mother was employed as a waitress. Her boyfriend, unemployed during the time he lived with them, had recently relocated for employment. Norris defined their economic class as "good"; when asked to put it in standard terms, he described it as "middle." (Using customary social-class scales, however, the family's income and occupational status would be classified as working class.) He depicted the neighborhood in which they lived as one in which a great deal of crime and drug/alcohol use occurred. He appeared to be ambivalent about his neighborhood and its effects on him:

*Q:* What do you like and dislike about living where you do?
*A:* I like, 'cause my parents are there. And they have friends. And, friends that get me into trouble.
*Q:* You like that?
*A:* Getting into trouble? No.
*Q:* Well, I'm confused; it sounded like you're lumping that together with what you like.
*A:* Oh. Yeah. No, I don't like kids that get me into trouble, no.
*Q:* Uh-huh. What do you dislike about living where you live?
*A:* Mostly the people around.
*Q:* How come?
*A:* I don't know, they're just different.
*Q:* Can you put your finger on what's different about them.
*A:* Yeah, they always want to get into trouble. Most of the kids.

Being troublesome and getting in trouble were major themes in Norris's description of himself and his life events. The two themes stand out in his reviews of his past, and they seemed to serve as organizing factors for how he perceived the present, himself, and his relationship with peers and parents.

Norris described growing up as "shaky," and his childhood, particularly the time in elementary school, as something he was pleased to "get out of." He took care of his brothers while his mother worked. At school he was "always getting in trouble." He failed seventh grade twice and attributed this failure to the fact that he "never went to school." He saw himself and his current behavior in the context of school as unchanged:

*Q:* What kind of trouble were you getting into in elementary school?
*A:* Talking back to teachers, pushing other kids.

*Q:* Do you think you've changed since then?
*A:* Not really.

Norris reported that in the detention center he was often sent to the office for making comments to teachers or for being late or skipping classes. His grades were just above the failing mark.

### Delinquency and Other Crimes

Delinquency and the rejection of authority appear to have been major aspects of Norris's relationship with his parents. His deviant behavior affected his relationship with his parents and vice versa. On the one hand, his parents imposed rules and punishments:

*Q:* Do your parents have rules for you, you know, kinds of do's and don't's?
*A:* Don't get in trouble. Do go to school. Do your chores. Don't do any drugs or alcohol.
*Q:* How do you know about these rules, I mean are they verbalized, or, you know, after the fact, or what?
*A:* Mostly after the fact.
*Q:* Do you think your parents are strict with you?
*A:* Yes.
*Q:* In what ways are they strict?
*A:* Can't do nothing. Get in trouble, get grounded for it, as long as they want you to be. Hitting you. That's about it.

On the other hand, the parents were not consistent in dealing with their son's deviant acts, either with each other (one parent would send him to live with the other as a punishment for his bad behavior and then take him back because his behavior deteriorated while with the other parent) or directly with Norris himself. For example:

*Q:* Do your parents know you get high?
*A:* Yeah.
*Q:* Do they care?
*A:* Yes.
*Q:* Do you ever get punished for getting high?
*A:* Yeah.
*Q:* Tell me about that, when did, how did they find out and . . . ?
*A:* My father's a lucky guesser, everytime. If I come in late, he'll say I'm high everytime I am. And he just smacks me around, and sends me to my room. My room.
*Q:* Why don't you just deny it?

*A:* I do deny it. But if I deny it, he smacks me.

*Q:* Can't you just play being, you know, real surprised, and saying, you know, what are you hitting me for, I'm not high?

*A:* Yeah.

*Q:* Doesn't work?

*A:* No. I, he must—one time he wanted to play a game with me, but if I lied he would hit me. All right, I wasn't high that time. And I go, he goes, are you high? "No," and he smacked me. I don't know. Just, he thought I was high and he smacked me around and sent me to my room.

Norris reports having run away from home four times. Each time, he said, he was responding to restrictions from his parents and to the easy opportunity to steal cars. His discussions illustrate how a chain of events can unfold, such that parents or another authority figure respond to a delinquent act and the perpetrator then responds to that response with more delinquency:

*A:* I was walking down, I skipped school, I was walking down, Eve Street, and I saw a key, a car with the keys in it. I looked around, I jumped in it, I started driving away . . . I ran away from home . . . When I got, stole the car . . .

*Q:* How come? What was going on at home that you wanted to run away from?

*A:* Everything was going on, I was being grounded all the time.

*Q:* Uh-huh. What would you have done if you didn't find the car?

*A:* Go home.

Later in the interview:

*A:* The Friday before Good Friday.

*Q:* Tell me about [it].

*A:* I don't know. Me and my friends were in school, we skipped school, and we ran away.

*Q:* Did that tie in at all to the car theft?

*A:* Yeah, we went back for the car. Spent a couple of nights in the car and then, we just, going down the road to get gas for the car and the cops picked us up.

*Q:* How come you decided to run away? What was going on that you decided to run away?

*A:* I don't know. I thought about it after I skipped school, that I would be dead when I got home.

*Q:* Would you have been?

*A:* Yeah.

*Q:* How come?

*A:* 'Cause my mother would have killed me . . .

*Q:* What was going on?

*A:* I don't know. We broke into a house, got a, get a bunch of beer and alcohol . . . and started drinking it . . .

*Q:* Let's start at the beginning.

*A:* At, Thursday, we were in, I don't know, I was in second period in gym. When my friends wanted to skip school. So I went with them. We ended up running away, to the car that I stole. And we just stayed in the car most of the day. Then we slept in the car; later on that night we broke into a house, got some beer and alcohol. Sat in the car and drank it. Fell asleep, woke up the next morning and got busted.

Norris said that television influenced him to engage in auto theft. "I'd see people stealing cars on TV. Seeing kids steal them, how easy to be able to drive. I wanted to try it." The media was one of three influences he cited throughout the interviews as consequential in his delinquency. The other two were his difficult relationship with his parents and pressures from his friends. In general, he seemed to believe that he lacked any internal controls; in answer to a series of questions aimed at identifying self-control, he consistently replied that "everything happens to me" and that he was not in control of his life.

## Relationship with Parents

Norris recalled the worst times of his life as his parents' divorce and their fighting about him. Family reunions and seeing his father were defined as the best times. These choices and Norris's telling of his story reveal a concern over his relationship with his parents. He described his relationship with his parents as "not good" and his mother's boyfriend as someone he "doesn't get along with." Closeness to his father, as opposed to his mother, was a product of having less interaction with him:

*Q:* Are you closer to one parent than the other?

*A:* Yes.

*Q:* Which parent?

*A:* Father.

*Q:* How come?

*A:* 'Cause I don't see him that much.

*Q:* How about your mom's boyfriend, how do you feel about him?

*A:* Not good. We never get along, can't do nothing wrong, he'll just get on you.

He reported that his parents had told him explicitly that they disliked him, and he indicated that he had been physically abused:

*Q:* Do you get hit or spanked, or what?

*A:* Hit. Punched.

*Q:* Have you ever gotten hurt, when you've gotten hit for punishment, or it's not that bad a hit?

*A:* Not by my father, my mother, but by my mother's boyfriend.

*Q:* What happened?

*A:* I don't know. He's like, he was using a ball, to throw me around.

*Q:* What had you done?

*A:* I don't know. I lied to him and started hitting him.

*Q:* And he just started hitting you? . . . what provoked you though, why, were you cursing at him, or saying things to him?

*A:* Because, he's always send me to my room, so I'll start cursing, then he started hitting me.

*Q:* Were you badly hurt, or you just felt like hurt?

*A:* It felt like hurt.

*Q:* You didn't have go to the hospital or anything?

*A:* No.

The household appeared to be characterized by disharmony. The parents often fought, and Norris was a frequent topic of dispute:

*Q:* How do your parents relate to each other?

*A:* What do you mean? How do they get along? Not that well . . .

*Q:* Do they fight when they're around each other, or what?

*A:* Yeah, sometimes.

*Q:* What do they usually fight about when they get together?

*A:* What do they usually fight about? About me. Most, um, my mother thinks it's my father's fault, 'cause I got in trouble, and my father thinks it's her fault. So I get in trouble.

*Q:* So they blame each other for your getting in trouble?

*A:* Yep.

*Q:* Whose fault do you think it is?

*A:* Mine.

*Q:* Do you tell them that?

*A:* No.

*Q:* How come?

*A:* I don't know.

*Q:* But you don't think it's either one of them?

*A:* Right. I always tell them it ain't, but . . .

*Q:* But you don't really believe that?

*A:* No.

*Q:* Who do you tell them is at fault?

*A:* I say, usually, it's because my mother and father are divorced. Something like that.

*Q:* But that's a crock?

*A:* Yeah.

*Q:* So you think if they weren't divorced you'd still be the way your are?

*A:* Yeah.

*Q:* What makes you think that?

*A:* I don't know, it's just—the neighborhood wouldn't change, the kids wouldn't change.

*Q:* What does that have to do with you?

*A:* 'Cause, I started, hey, I was good until like 10 years old, I didn't get in that much trouble. But then, when I hang around with the wrong kids.

*Q:* Uh-huh.

*A:* I was in all kinds of trouble.

*Q:* So why don't you hang around with the right kids?

*A:* 'Cause there's not that many right kids, that I know.

## Role of Peers

The foregoing excerpt suggests the special importance of peers to Norris's delinquency. Norris reported that all but two of his friends engaged in criminal activities. He had joined them for auto thefts, burglaries, and shoplifting. Sometimes he did so voluntarily, other times under pressure:

*Q:* How come you always go along with them?

*A:* I don't know. Do something.

*Q:* What happens if you don't? Did you ever say, I don't think I want to do that?

*A:* Yeah.

*Q:* What happens?

*A:* They [nag] me out and then I go and do it.

*Q:* How come you go and do it? Just because they nag you on?

*A:* 'Cause.

*Q:* How come you don't smoke then, when they nag you to smoke?

*A:* Cigarettes? I don't know. I tell them I don't want to, and they don't nag me about that.

*Q:* So you don't get nagged about that . . . but you do about doing crime?

*A:* Yeah.

*Q:* How come Annie didn't have to nag you to shoplift?

*A:* 'Cause I wanted to do it, too.

*Q:* So sometimes it's stuff that you want to do?

*A:* Yeah.

*Q:* What stuff do you usually do and what stuff do you have to be nagged to do?

*A:* I don't know. Sometimes break in the houses, I need to be nagged on it, but I don't want to.

*Q:* How come, how come you don't want to do that?

*A:* Well some houses I don't want to. Sometimes I don't feel like breaking into a house and getting into trouble.

*Q:* . . . Why do you commit crime?

*A:* For the money. And for the fun of it, sometimes.

*Q:* Uh-huh. Which is which, when do you, when do you do it for fun and when do you do it for money?

*A:* When I need money I do it for money. When I just, don't need, don't need any I just, do it for the fun of it, see if I can break in and not get caught. . . .

*Q:* Which do you do it more for, fun or money?

*A:* Money.

The influence of his friends becomes especially clear in regard to drug use. Norris reported that all but one of his friends used drugs. He was introduced to alcohol, however, within a family context, at a high school graduation party for a cousin. He first became intoxicated at another graduation party—for the sister of his girlfriend.

Norris said he drank and used drugs only when he was with friends, never alone. Asked why, he replied simply, "It's more fun." The motivation for such use was not always peer pressure, however:

*Q:* Do you think there are other reasons or other factors why people do drugs and alcohol and do crime than just 'cause it's cool or fun?

*A:* No. If they're mad or depressed.

*Q:* . . . So you think that people who are depressed do drugs, or alcohol?

*A:* Yeah.

*Q:* Who?

*A:* Me. And, Annie [his girlfriend].

*Q:* Uh-huh. You get high when you're depressed?

*A:* Yeah.

*Q:* Which, which happens more often, do you get high when you're depressed or mad, or because you, for the fun of it, or what?

*A:* Mostly 'cause I'm mad.

*Q:* What are you mad about?

*A:* Parents. At my parents, if something goes wrong in school.

Norris was introduced to marijuana by Ivan and Otto, two of the three other members of his major peer group. He was asked about that event.

*Q:* Marijuana. When was the first time you ever tried that?
*A:* Twelve years old. My birthday.
*Q:* Tell me about it.
*A:* I don't know, we camped out in the back of our yard, and two of my friends, Ivan and Otto, come over, and they had some pot, and we started smoking it.
*Q:* Who had the pot?
*A:* Ivan.
*Q:* Did he give it to you, or did you buy it, or what?
*A:* No, we just, sat there and smoked it.
*Q:* How much was that?
*A:* A nickel.
*Q:* So the three of you split a nickel [$5 bag of marijuana]?
*A:* Yeah.
*Q:* . . . How soon after that did you have it again?
*A:* How soon? The next day.

The final member of their friendship group, Carl, introduced him to prescription drugs:

*Q:* Has anyone ever offered you these drugs?
*A:* Not really. Except for a robin egg [a pill—unidentified].
*Q:* Uh-huh.
*A:* And I took that. But I didn't know if it was speed or not.
*Q:* When did you take that?
*A:* Six months ago.
*Q:* Tell me about it.
*A:* Um, I ran away from um, away from, um, home and went over to a friend's house. And we, he had beer, and we were just sitting there drinking it, and he brought it out and I took it.
*Q:* How many did you take?
*A:* One.

Norris reported that friends provided his main access to alcohol and marijuana, but family connections were also involved. He had been exposed to, invited to use, and supplied with drugs by persons who could be said to be peers, although they were somewhat more related to the family network.

*Q:* What about hash, when was the first time you ever smoked hash?
*A:* When my babysitter's friend came over with it.
*Q:* When was that?
*A:* It was like, a year ago.
*Q:* How soon after your first marijuana try?

*A:* How long after? Maybe a couple of days.

*Q:* How come you got high with them [babysitter and her boyfriend]?

*A:* 'Cause they asked me to.

*Q:* Do you get high with them often?

*A:* Yeah.

*Q:* They usually supply the stuff, or . . . ?

*A:* Yeah.

*Q:* Have you ever?

*A:* Supplied it for them? Yeah.

*Q:* Do any of your friends, um, use any of these drugs?

*A:* Yeah.

*Q:* Which, which friends use which drugs?

*A:* Um, Ellen, my babysitter, takes Black Beauties, and that, speed.

*Q:* Uh-huh. What about mushrooms, when did you first try mushrooms?

*A:* On my birthday.

*Q:* Which birthday?

*A:* When I turned 13.

*Q:* So this year?

*A:* Yep.

*Q:* Okay. Tell me about that. What happened?

*A:* I was sitting over my uncle's house one time and he asked me if I wanted to try some, so I tried it. . . .

*Q:* . . . How come you tried mushrooms?

*A:* Um, 'cause he didn't tell me what they were until after.

*Q:* What did you think they were?

*A:* I don't know. Food or something.

*Q:* Come on, what did you really think they were?

*A:* I knew they were drugs, but, at first I didn't know. So I tried it, I tried it, and after I had, and I asked him what it was, he said mushrooms. I tried to look it up, see what it was. Couldn't really figure it out.

## Plans for the Future

At the time of our interviews, Norris was not a serious user of prescription drugs, although according to findings from aggregate data, he was at serious risk of becoming so in the near future. From his own point of view, however, he was in complete control of his drug use. He used marijuana and alcohol because it made him "feel good"; he would take speed if offered to him at the detention facility because he "hadn't had drugs in a while"; and he wanted to try cocaine in the future, "just to see what happened." All other drugs, however, he said he would not use under any circumstances or any amount of coercion. He talked about an uncle who was killed trying to hop aboard a train while under the influence of drugs, and he expressed the fear that use of potent drugs would result in suicide or overdosing.

Q: How come you haven't tried any of these other drugs?
A: I'm afraid of them.
Q: What are you afraid of?
A: That I might just OD or something. Just, something might go wrong, I might commit suicide or something.
Q: . . . How about inhalants, like glue or locker room?
A: No.
Q: . . . What about if, um, a bunch of the guys got hold of some glue up here, and tried punking you out, you still wouldn't try it?
A: No.
Q: How would you handle that?
A: How would you handle that? I'd say no and I'd walk away.
Q: What happens if they start punking you out?
A: I don't care. You could die from that.
Q: If you would try cocaine, how come you wouldn't try acid then?
A: I don't know. I don't know.
Q: You sure you wouldn't? How about if Ivan and Otto came over and said, here's a couple hits of acid, you want to drop some acid?
A: No.
Q: Still wouldn't
A: No.

Norris had attempted to give up his crime and drug involvement by staying away from his heavily involved friends (Ivan, Otto, and Carl).

Q: So then you do avoid people that get in trouble a lot?
A: Yeah.
Q: How come? Tell me about it.
A: How come? 'Cause I don't want to get in trouble.
Q: Do you think just hanging out with that, those kids, gets you into trouble?
A: Yeah.
Q: How, how does that happen?
A: 'Cause every time I see them they always want to do something wrong.

Instead, he had chosen to spend time in another foursome, one in which he was the only male. Whether that group turned out to be less involved in drug use and crime is unknown, however. All three females had been engaged in minor delinquency, two drank alcohol and used marijuana, and one had used other drugs.) He said their major activities included "partying" and "getting into trouble."

> *Q:* What kinds of things do you do with your friends when you get together?
> *A:* I don't know, party. Get in trouble. Talk.
> *Q:* Are those the only activities you do with your friends?
> *A:* Yeah.
> *Q:* Do you ever do anything else like, picnic or go to the movies, or . . . ?
> *A:* Yeah, go to the movies or swimming or to the beach.
> *Q:* Uh-huh. Does that usually end up with the guys partying and getting into trouble, though?
> *A:* Yeah.
> *Q:* What kind of trouble do you get into with Annie and Arlene and Effie?
> *A:* I don't really get in any trouble with Annie, and, and, and Arlene and Effie. Annie, we always—got in trouble.
> *Q:* Just you and Annie?
> *A:* Yeah.
> *Q:* What kinds of trouble do you get into?
> *A:* Stealing from stores and that. Partying, in school.
> *Q:* When was the last time you stole from a store with Annie?
> *A:* Stole from a store with her? Um, two months ago.
> *Q:* Tell me about it, what store, what happened? Tell me the whole thing.
> *A:* Oh, we skipped school, and we were, walking around and, we stole, we went into every store at High Fashions [shopping mall] and we stole something from it.

As for the future, Norris saw himself as avoiding trouble. He viewed his future as a time when he would not have to steal for money, as well as a time when he would have responsibilities.

> *Q:* When you think of the future, say when you're, oh, I don't know, 23, what do you think you're going to be like?
> *A:* I hope I'm, I'm not getting into as much trouble as I am. Better person.
> *Q:* . . . Do you think things are going to be good then? When you're 23?
> *A:* Yeah, I hope so.
> *Q:* Think they'll be better than now?
> *A:* Yeah.
> *Q:* In what way, what's going to be better?
> *A:* I don't have to steal money, I'll be able to earn it?
> *Q:* Is that why you steal now, 'cause you can't earn it?
> *A:* Yeah.
> *Q:* Is that true?
> *A:* Yes.

*Q:* If someone was to offer you a job, would you take the job?

*A:* Yeah.

*Q:* Would that be what you'd rather do?

*A:* Yeah. Rather than steal. 'Cause everything I ever take I can get caught for.

*Q:* . . . What do you think your duties and responsibilities are, are going to be 10 years from now?

*A:* Have to earn my own job . . . stay out of trouble.

## Case Study 2: Elizabeth

Elizabeth is a 13-year-old female from the random sample who had tried alcohol and was involved in shoplifting. Based on the National Youth Survey (Elliott and Huizinga, 1984), Elizabeth has much company in her relatively minor delinquency and alcohol use. Forty percent of the respondents in that survey used alcohol, generally on an irregular basis, and 17 percent of the 13-year-olds reported minor thefts, such as shoplifting.

Elizabeth reported that she did not commit serious crimes like burglary, robbery, or grand larceny. Although slightly more deviant than the majority of 13-year-olds, who avoid delinquent behavior and alcohol or drug use, Elizabeth appears typical of 13-year-olds who have begun such activities.

Elizabeth described her childhood as one marked by frequent moves, leaving friends, and changing schools. She was happy to be settled now in Yule City. She lived with her mother and her younger sister in a neighborhood she described as friendly. It was underpopulated with youths her own age, however, and she was unhappy about that. She described her neighbors' socioeconomic status and that of her own family as middle class. Her mother was a graduate student at a local university and was employed part time as a research assistant. Her father died when she was 2 years old. Financially, she says, her family is "well off, not rich, but we're fine. It's not like we're suffering at all."

### Relationships with Family

Elizabeth described herself as unaffected by her father's death, but noted the consequences for her mother and the family:

*Q:* What would you say where the worst times that you can remember?

*A:* Seeing my mom upset. It hurts me more than anything. Because, um, there's no one around who she can talk to her own age. I mean it's just me and Inga [sister]; little kids, she really can't communicate with us, we're just younger and it's just, it's not easy for her. She has all these responsibilities and she has to do them all herself. I think it's really hard. They give some money from the government from my father and stuff. But still she has all of these responsibilities and all herself, and she, you know, so seeing her upset is the worst thing.

Q: Has there been a time when she's been real upset?

A: I can remember when my father died, seeing my mom cry. I saw her cry and I hated to see her like that.

One main consequence of her father's death, as Elizabeth saw it, was that her mother became "liberated" and, thus, so did she. She believed that had her father lived he would have kept her mother in the kitchen.

A: I wouldn't be the way I am if my father was alive. With my mom, she wouldn't be for women's lib or do protests or something because he wouldn't like it. Maybe he would, I mean he could change, too. But, uh, she was made to be in the kitchen.

Q: Really.

A: Yes.

Q: Is that how she describes it to you?

A: That's how I think it was. That's how I feel it was and I don't know. She just told me things. She didn't work but we were only two. My sister was only one year old, so, I don't know. Maybe she didn't get back to work yet. I don't think she worked though. I don't know, beats me. But cook his meals and give him this and give him that. My husband is going to cook meals, too.

Her mother's liberalism and political activism were evidently very important to Elizabeth, notably in terms of their implications for her relationship with her mother. On the one hand, they provided a link between Elizabeth and her mother; she attended functions with her mother and shared her mother's persuasions. On the other hand, her mother's activities placed her in a deviant or marginal position among her friends and her extended family. In the following lengthy passage from the interviews, Elizabeth explains:

A: She's just a great lady. Um, she's um, she is the type of lady, she is different from [her] family. So every time we [have] a family get-together they always have a discussion, and arguments. They would say she's very woman lib type and we have been in protests, like at the college stadium. And when Alexander Haig came we had a big protest. Me and my sister came. We always go on these protests . . . and my grandparents don't like that. And my grandfather and my mom always usually get in an argument and my mom wants U.S. out of El Salvador and all these different things. . . . A lot of kids in my school, they think I'm crazy or something. "Oh, there goes Elizabeth's mom again." . . . And they see the papers and I say, "Oh, I was there." And they say, "It figures." But that doesn't say that they don't like me. I mean they agree with me once I explain it to them, but see the point is, a lot of people don't know about all this stuff. And that's the problem. So I tell all of my friends, and the parents probably want to kill me or something. . . . We're much different than our cousins, and before I get married I want to live with someone, and I got a letter from my boyfriend at my aunt's house and I told her that and she almost had a fit. She started yelling at me. . . . So when I'm around my grandmother and aunt you have to really watch what you say. I don't like doing that but it's something you got to do unless you want to get tore down. . . . I know [my mother] brought me up good and I'm, nice family. But protests and stuff like that I think are important. My kids are going to be doing that too.

The "difference" between her family and others is played out in other areas of Elizabeth's relationship with her mother. For example, unlike her friends, she is not treated by her mother like a child:

*Q:* Does your mom have a lot of rules for you, do's and don't's?
*A:* Not really. She makes rules that are fair. She treats, like adults, like fair things instead of a parent . . . control over child. It's a friend to friend really. Or a person living with another person having responsibilities. . . . I've seen some of my friends' mothers and parents and I would hate to live with them. But that's partly because I've grown up with my mom, but, uh, they are so unfair. Parent-to-child things that I don't have at all.

## Role of Peers

Her mother's pursuit of education, and her life-style more generally, resulted in the family's changing residence several times. Elizabeth said this resulted in a childhood in which she "never really had a permanent friend." Elizabeth said she was "very shy, because I kept on having to lose my friends, and that made me more so." More recently she had lost some of her reserve, and she attributed that to having a close and steady group of friends. She repeated in her interview, "Friends mean a lot to me."

A tension appeared to be developing in the relationship among Elizabeth, her friends, and her mother. Although Elizabeth described her relationship with her mother as extremely close and positive, she now preferred to be with friends and, in fact, would disobey her mother in order to be with her friends.

*Q:* How would you describe your relationship with your mother?
*A:* Special, very special. Once in a while she will get on my nerves. Lately she's gotten a lot on my nerves but that's because she's so pressured and this is her last week [of school]. I'm so happy. . . .
*Q:* In what ways do you think your relationship is special?

*A:* 'Cause we just like each other and like being with each other. I don't as much anymore, than being with my friends, but she's just, I like doing things with her . . . last summer I got in so much trouble. I was grounded all summer long. I was grounded all the time.

*Q:* What did you do?

*A:* It all had to do with the two boys. Me and Henrietta and the two boys. Always we spent the whole summer together and we always got in trouble, always. I don't know. I was just grounded all summer long. What a boring summer that was. Actually the times that I had fun made up for the boring times.

Elizabeth enjoyed school, and her description of this part of her life reveals the emphasis she placed on being with her friends, many of whom were black:

*Q:* Do you enjoy going to school?

*A:* Yes. See a lot of my friends. I love that. 'Cause when sometimes you don't see half of the friends you like. It's hard to get together with them all. So, when you're in school I like it. I don't like going to do work. I just like going to see my friends.

*Q:* . . . What do you like the most about school?

*A:* Going to see my friends.

Indeed, for Elizabeth friends were a first priority. Friendship was more important than success in school.

*Q:* What kind of student would you describe yourself as?

*A:* I'm not dedicated to my work. I don't run my life around schoolwork. I do it around my friends and my responsibilities. I get my homework done and I, you know, I do stuff, but I'm not the best student.

This movement toward peers and their values was also related to how she distinguished herself from her sister. Elizabeth said her grades were not as good as her sister's; she got mostly 70s and 80s, her sister got 90s. She attributed this to differences in their personalities. She defined her own personality as "fun loving" and peer oriented in comparison with that of her sister. Elizabeth saw herself and her sister at opposite poles and talked about this with reference to peers:

*A:* We are totally different. We're very different. She's very quiet and smart and I'm very rowdy and like to have fun.

*Q:* What do you like to do with her?

*A:* Nothing. That sounds mean but I'd rather be with my friends than with her any day. . . .

*Q:* Well how about when you were younger, was it different then?

*A:* Yeah, when we were real young we always hung around each other. We always played together, we did everything together. As we were growing up we did everything together, too, but I've changed and she's always stayed the same 'cause we came to Yule City. She doesn't have all that many friends, either. She's a very shy person. You know I'm rowdy and strange and weird and like to have parties. She likes to do that stuff, too, but not anywhere near as much or anywheres quite as loud, and I don't know, different from me.

Elizabeth reported that her usual activities with friends consisted of "just hanging around with a box," listening to a portable stereo while walking in the neighborhood, at a park, or sitting in someone's home. She emphasized, however, that she also had responsibilities around the house and a part-time job delivering advertising circulars.

## Drug Use

Elizabeth described most of her close friends as relatively "straight" in terms of drinking and drug use; two of them smoked cigarettes, three had had beer, and some had tried marijuana. Although her first experience with both cigarette smoking and drinking was with friends—and she knew of parties at which drinking and marijuana smoking took place—she described only one instance of engaging in such activities with her peer group:

*Q:* Do you remember the first time you had any kind of liquor?
*A:* Not really, I remember the first time. I remember the only time that I did. It was last summer. The summer before . . . I just had a friend of mine, me and Henrietta, there was other people. And we had Eddie, this guy, get us some pink champale or something. Two bottles of it and then we just went and got drunk off of that.
*Q:* Well, what were you doing. Where were you and what was going on?
*A:* We were just fooling around up at Al's drug store and got ice cream. And he came up there and we asked him to get us some.
*Q:* Why did you ask him to do it, to get it for you? I mean why did the whole idea come up?
*A:* Because we thought we wanted to get drunk. Have some liquor, and we asked him to get us some.
*Q:* . . . Do you remember at all why that time you decided you wanted to get drunk and other times you haven't?
*A:* I was feeling rowdy and wanted to do something, so we went and got something . . . the kids that were with us, they had some of it. They didn't really drink it, they just had, everybody, you know, at least tried it.

Elizabeth did not have any specific reasons for not drinking more and envisioned herself as drinking more in the future—when her friends were "old enough to get it."

*Q:* Do you have some reasons for not wanting to drink a lot?

*A:* No, I just haven't. I just haven't gotten around to it or something. I haven't felt like it.

*Q:* Do you think in the future you'll probably drink more?

*A:* Oh, probably.

*Q:* Why do you say that?

*A:* Because, uh, the kids in my grade will be old enough to get it. So they'll have it, they'll have it, I mean my friends, too, so they'll have it around more, so I'll drink it more.

*Q:* So you don't have any serious reasons for not drinking other than you just haven't done it?

*A:* Right.

Later in the interview she expressed a belief in moderation and control of one's drinking and consequent actions and the idea that these come with age.

*Q:* Do you think it's really wrong? I mean obviously it is against the law, as you said, for kids your age. But other than that do you think it's bad and stuff to do?

*A:* I think if you know how to control, I mean if you don't drink all the time. If you know how to control yourself like, uh, I know some people who drink every week. You know, a lot of beer and stuff like that. I don't think it's good. Especially because we're under age.

*Q:* Why?

*A:* Because they don't have control of themselves to drink that much. You know that's how a lot of crime goes on. They don't know how to control themselves. They drink too much.

*Q:* Is it important to you to be in control of yourself?

*A:* Yes, very important to me. I don't want to be, and if I don't have control I don't know what I would do. So I have complete control over myself.

Similarly, Elizabeth gave no specific reasons for not trying marijuana and said she could see herself trying it sometime in the future. As with alcohol use, she saw herself using it—with friends and because they were doing it. She punctuated such statements, however, with comments about people who were involved in such use and how she really had "no desire to try it," further suggesting that she was in a transitional and ambivalent stage in her own usage.

*A:* I just have never tried it [marijuana] and I haven't been around my friends when they have. And I wouldn't like marijuana anyways because you have to smoke it. And I don't like smoking. And I have heard that it makes your mouth real dry and I don't know, I just have no desire to try it. I would never try it myself. Maybe around my friends I might try it sometime, but I would never try it myself.

*Q:* You would never try it alone.

*A:* No, or with some of my better friends. You know, if you have a gang, maybe a bunch of kids, maybe I would. I don't know. I don't know. I have no idea.

*Q:* Do you have some personal reasons for not wanting to try it?

*A:* Not, well, I don't know. I just haven't tried it, you know.

*Q:* Do any of your friends use drugs like marijuana?

*A:* A lot of my friends have tried it but not really use it.

*Q:* Do you think that you may use marijuana or any other drug in the future?

*A:* I don't know. I have no idea.

*Q:* Why or why not? I mean why wouldn't you?

*A:* Because my friends are doing it. I wouldn't want to because I don't think I would like it . . . I have no desire to try it.

*Q:* Why not?

*A:* 'Cause I just don't. I am fine and happy the way I am, I've got no problems. I don't want to take that stuff.

Elizabeth said that if she wanted to get some marijuana, she would ask her friends to get her some. She also talked about youths at school who were not her friends and who used marijuana (for example, "Nanci, her parents even do it, that's how she started out"). She said she didn't get along with drug-using groups and maintained social distance from them:

*Q:* You hang around with those guys at all?

*A:* No, no.

*Q:* You don't get along with them?

*A:* No, not at all.

*Q:* Why?

*A:* 'Cause they do, they're creeps. They drink all the time. They smoke all the time, they'll sit on the corner before and after school, stand there and smoke. I don't like them. They're no fun.

## Delinquency and Other Crime

Although Elizabeth and her friends were only lightly involved (if involved at all) in alcohol and drug use, they were more involved in minor criminal activity. Her female friends engaged in shoplifting and her male friends had stolen hubcaps and a bicycle. The bicycle was taken from an abandoned house that the boys broke into and vandalized. One of those involved was her boyfriend, Alfred, whom she described as "straighter" than she was in terms of alcohol and drug use. She explained his involvement as due to peer pressure: "Alfred was with his friends and his friends were doing it, so he did."

Elizabeth herself was quite involved in petty theft, particularly shoplifting. She stole for the first time when she was about 10 years old. She expressed amazement, in retrospect, at the execution of her clever plan for stealing some accessories for her doll from her neighbor:

A: I was a smart kid. I was, uh, I took a bunch of baby clothes and I kept on telling my mom that she [the neighbor] was giving them to me, and then one time the father, her husband, came home. I saw the keys, I don't know how I thought of this . . . not being around people who shoplifted or anything. So when I saw the keys on the TV I shoved them in my socks. And I said, "Oh, I think I hear my mom calling." So I got out and go down to the car and take the stroller out, right? It was a baby stroller. So I took it home.

Elizabeth continued to steal, now by shoplifting. She was once apprehended for shoplifting, which influenced her to stop for awhile. Later, however, she began again:

A: I didn't, after I stole those records I didn't do it for a long time. Then my friends started doing it so I started doing it. Only little things mostly . . . just like necklaces. Little things. . . .
Q: Do you think that's a pretty common thing?
A: To steal?
Q: Shoplifting?
A: Uh-huh. 'Cause it is. Everybody does it.

Elizabeth thought that being female insulated her from many criminal activities. The boys she knew who engaged in crime "only do it with a bunch of guys, they wouldn't take a couple of girls with them." When asked about more serious criminal activities, Elizabeth stated that she was not involved but cited the involvement of her male friends and acquaintances. Certain crimes, such as stealing from her mother, from which she was not so insulated by her sex, were acts she simply would not engage in, for moral reasons.

Q: Have you ever taken anything, well like your friends took hubcaps off the side of a car, mirrors, antennas, anything like that?
A: No, Eric stole a tape out of a car. Out of his friend's car.
Q: Were you with him?
A: No.
Q: Um, how about ever taking a car or motorcycle or truck or anything like that?

*A:* Andy, you know the boy that took me to dinner, he stole a car and was going past the border with it.

*Q:* Oh really?

*A:* Yeah.

*Q:* Were you with them then or . . . ?

*A:* No way.

*Q:* . . . but you've never done anything like that or been with Alfred or Eric or Eddie or anybody who would have taken a car? Just go for a ride or anything like that? No.

*A:* No.

*Q:* Um, you ever used checks illegally, like use your mother's checks or . . . ?

*A:* No. I would never steal from my mother.

*Q:* You never have?

*A:* I never would.

*Q:* Why wouldn't you? Why do you say that so strongly?

*A:* Cause she pays a lot of things for me. I would never steal from her.

*Q:* Um, you ever broken into a house or a store or a car or anything like that?

*A:* Nope.

Although she seemed to emphasize the role of peers in her own and others' involvement and desire to become involved in deviant activities, Elizabeth saw herself as in control of such involvement:

*A:* I'm in control of what happens basically, a lot of things that happen in my life. I'm in control of what I do and what I don't do. And like, if kids go around drinking and I don't want to, I have control of that. I won't, it's not like they're going to put it in my face, and I'm going to back out and do it if I really don't want to I won't. . . .

## Plans for the Future

Elizabeth seemed to "want to" engage in criminal activities, such as shoplifting, more than she desired to engage in drug use. She legitimized it in terms of "everybody does it" (at least in terms of shoplifting that seems to be an accurate statement). On the other hand, she and some of her friends had been exposed to alcohol and drugs, and some had had experiences with these, but no one was actively involved yet. Elizabeth did not rule out the possibility of becoming more involved in drug and alcohol use. At 13, however, she saw it as a bit dangerous and, therefore, she simply did not pursue it further:

*Q:* The shoplifting stuff, I mean, why do you get involved in that at all? That you are very serious about not taking drugs and drinking a lot and stuff?

*A:* I don't know . . . I just want something and so instead of paying for it, I don't want to, and also taking drugs it ruins you. And I don't like it so why should I do it?

Elizabeth's vision of her future was vague. She was not sure what she would be doing, except that "it will be a lot of fun," she will own a car, and she will be with friends.

## Discussion

Norris is among the 2 percent most delinquent and heaviest drug-using segment of American youth. He was enmeshed in a circle of delinquent friends, he lacked straight friends, his family situation was unstable, and his school performance was poor. The prognosis for Norris at his interview was toward persistence of serious delinquency and escalation of drug use. It must be noted, however, that predictions of individual outcomes as serious adult offenders are frequently wrong (Robins and Wish, 1977; Shannon, 1982; Smith et al., 1980). Many youths with histories as disturbed as Norris's manage to straighten out in early adulthood. He, in fact, saw himself as avoiding trouble and taking more responsibility for his activities in the future.

Elizabeth is typical of a larger group of 13-year-olds who engage in minor delinquency and have begun alcohol use, but who are unlikely to become serious delinquents or routine users of illicit drugs. Her circle of friends (who were very important to her) were beginning to experiment with marijuana (and other substances). But her strong ties to her mother and a strong sense of self-control appear to be associated with her denial at interview of interest in marijuana. Perhaps subtle pressure from friends in later adolescence may lead to marijuana initiation. Escalation to serious delinquency, however, appears unlikely, although minor offending may continue.

The value of case studies is twofold. First, they put some "meat" on the findings of survey studies by illustrating how key variables become manifest and influential in the lives of actual individuals. Second, they permit the development of additional hypotheses about the questions at issue. With those two goals in mind—rather than for actual purposes of generalization, which would be impossible with two cases—we compare Norris and Elizabeth.

A striking similarity between the two youths concerns the point at which they became vulnerable to initiation into patterns of delinquency. In both cases, such initiation took place at a time when peer relations played a significant role within the family context. In Norris's case this was especially apparent: he evidently engaged in crimes and truancy as part of a pattern that involved his divorced parents (as well as his mother's boyfriend) doing battle over rearing him. From a very early age, his acts were part of a cycle of attack and response by the members of this family system. He maintained friendships with youths who engaged in delinquent activities, but, depending on his family situation, he moved in and out of active participation with these peers. He was unable to find nondelinquent peers ("There are not that many right kids that I know").

In Elizabeth's case, there was an obvious bond between her and her mother, which involved mutual respect and a shared ideology. As a result of her mother's frequent relocations, however, Elizabeth developed an intense desire to have friends and to be closely tied to those friends. Part of that tie entailed involvement in their delinquent activities.

Reflective of their general life circumstances was the youths' ability to control their activities. Norris was in a no-win situation at home and in terms of his school performance, he had no guiding belief system or direction, and he described an external locus of control. He reported a need for drug use and delinquent activities. Elizabeth, on the other hand, had resources at home, adequate school performance, and a strong sense of self. She reported an internal locus of control and the ability to choose (within a range) her involvement in delinquent activities.

Both Norris and Elizabeth were marginal persons in Yule City, and that contributed notably to their risk of involvement in drug use and crime. Norris lived in an unstable family and neighborhood environment; Elizabeth lived with a mother who engaged in activities that were considered extremist both by her extended family and by Elizabeth's school peers. Both ended up with other marginal youths as peers: Norris with those who "always get in trouble," Elizabeth with black youths (in a mostly segregated peer culture). Elizabeth was less often invited into criminal events than was Norris, however, in part because such activities are the province of boys rather than girls.

# 9
# Case Studies of Seriously Involved Youths

*With Margret Ksander and Mary F. Stuck*

T his chapter presents extensive case histories of two youths on the threshold of adulthood who are (or were) prototypical polycriminal substance abusers. The two youths, Kevin and Gallo, were selected from among 41 subjects who were seriously involved in crime and heavy drug use (as defined in chapter 2). For a number of important analytic reasons, they were selected to represent two extremes of adjustment to extensive drug use.

On many important dimensions, the two youths are very similar. Both were daily substance users and frequent drug sellers. Both reported committing several serious crimes, such as burglary, robbery, major thefts, and assaults. Both were from broken families and had poor relations with one or both parents. Both reported that contacts with police and contacts with the criminal justice system affected their criminal behavior.

But Kevin and Gallo were also very different. Kevin describes himself as having lost control of his drug use. He was arrested, punished, and "forced" into treatment. Gallo, on the other hand, always managed to keep his intensive drug use under control and to conceal his serious criminality from the law—although he did have brushes with the police.

Kevin appears similar to many youths (see Elliott and Huizinga, 1984; see also chapter 8) who begin minor delinquency in late elementary school and initiate marijuana and other drug use in their early teens. As drug use increases, the severity of their crimes and the frequency of commission also increase. Kevin was known and officially labeled as a delinquent and drug user. Cycles of arrest, criminal justice punishment, and drug treatment extended through his teenage years and into adulthood. Finally, under criminal justice pressure and with the support of a girlfriend and family, he entered a drug program. At the time of his interview, he appeared to be rehabilitated from drug abuse and crime.

Given the nature of the purposive sample drawn for this study (see chapter 2), not many, if any, of the subjects would fall into a category of individuals who once were seriously involved in drug–criminal activities but were no longer. In point of fact, Kevin was the only such subject in the sample. More common in our data are youths who become routinely involved in delinquency and drug use and who, over time, exhibit a pattern of continued involvement in certain forms of delinquency but a lessening involvement or desistance of involvement in other forms. Gallo exhibited this type of pattern.

Gallo appears to represent youths who are seriously delinquent but are rarely seen by the criminal justice system (Dunford and Elliott, 1982; Dunford, Elliott, and Huizinga, 1983a, 1983b; Huizinga and Dunford, 1985). Yet he was extreme on most dimensions of deviant behavior: early onset, planning, seriousness, frequency, criminal and drug-using peers, and so on.

Despite his delinquent tendencies and extraordinary drug use, Gallo completed high school and had clear objectives—to enter the military and have his own auto shop when he returned to civilian life. Above all else, however, Gallo said he was "in control" of everything in his life. If he planned a crime, he decided whether to do it "stoned" or "straight." If he sold drugs, he was sure to protect himself from ripoffs. If the sales didn't pay, he stopped. If he liked a drug (other than marijuana or alcohol) that was habit forming, he limited his consumption. He reported that he had a violent temper and that although he had fought numerous times with his siblings, he had managed not to lose his temper in most situations.

In presenting these case studies, we have organized the material around a theme that is frequently overlooked in research, that of the *processes* by which youths make changes in their life-styles, particularly those involving substance use and criminality.

The literature is replete with theoretical explanations (for example, Cloward and Ohlin, 1960; Cohen, 1955; Sutherland, 1947; Sykes and Matza, 1957; Yablonsky, 1959); information and aggregate data about adolescents and their criminal and drug involvement (for example, Gold and Reimer, 1975; Huizinga, 1982, 1986; Jensen, Erickson, and Gibbs, 1978; Richards, Burke, and Forster, 1979; Weis and Sederstrom, 1981); and factors related to adolescent and criminal activity (for example, Brown, 1982; Lyerly and Skipper, 1981; Weis and Sederstrom, 1981). There is, however, little if any information (see Kandel and Yamaguchi, 1984) in the literature that describes the processes by which an adolescent makes the change from a life-style of involvement in crime and drug activities to a life-style of noninvolvement or reduced involvement in such activities. In addition, little is known about the differences between youths who remain committed to involvement and those who have changed from commitment to noninvolvement. It is toward these gaps in knowledge that this analysis is directed.

## Kevin

Kevin was a 20-year-old, Catholic male who had been expelled from high school for truancy. He reported that he had used all drugs except heroin and cocaine, had dealt drugs, and had committed a number of index offenses, principally burglaries (for which he was arrested). Kevin himself, however, made the point that he did not commit "violent crimes" (although he did commit robbery).

Kevin became involved in criminal mischief— "getting in trouble"—around the age of 10 or 11. He saw this as a result of "hanging out" with his cousin:

A: I was hanging out with my cousin Allen. . . . He sort of influenced me to things that, like, I didn't think were wrong. I had a wild imagination. We used to build fires and see who could build the biggest fire. . . .

During his early adolescent years, Kevin's behavior was influenced by different schools and different peer groups. On transferring to a middle school where he was tested as brighter than previous tests had shown and was moved ahead a grade, Kevin found himself "hanging out with a bunch of jocks":

A: Everyone was into doing their homework first thing and then going and doing their sports. I had really good grades. I was like fourth on the high honor roll in seventh grade.

But when he was switched to another class and got to know yet another group of peers, Kevin, now 13, became further involved in proscribed activities, this time the use of drugs. He attributed his involvement to his peers:

A: And then eighth grade I got switched to another class that was a smart class but like a lot of people in the class they were getting high and everything. I think the reason that I got high was that, I was, I don't know, I think it was mostly peer pressure, 'cause like I was a little scared the first time I got high . . . I didn't want everybody to say, "Ah, he's a punk." I've got to do this so people don't look down on me, so I don't feel funny.

As Kevin's use of drugs went from smoking marijuana to the use of psychedelic drugs, he started skipping school, his grades dropped, and he became seriously involved in criminal activities (specifically burglaries of houses), for which he was arrested "seven or eight times within a month." In speaking of this period of his life, Kevin stated:

A: I put my mother through a lot, and I was putting myself through a lot at the time, but I was so screwed up I really didn't care. I was, like, pointing the finger at everybody else because things were going wrong in my life. But when you point the finger at somebody, three fingers point back at you, you know.

Kevin's home life was a prominent factor in his involvement in drugs and other criminal activities. His mother had remarried when he was in the seventh grade, and he did not get along with his stepfather, who "used to be an alcoholic":

> *A:* I use to, like, hate going home, I really did, because of my father mostly, because he'd be drunk all of the time . . . every day. He'd bum me out a lot because I could tell I was running in competition with my mother with him. He'd be pissed off about something, and he'd start yelling at me . . . he'd drag me into their argument, bringing up something that I did, and I just got jerked around all the time, and it wasn't a very good environment for me to be in. I didn't like to go home, and there wasn't anything else happening on the streets except get in trouble, or get high. And that's what I did.

This last explanation for his involvement in both crime and drugs is supported by studies that have found that drug users, though not necessarily alienated from parents, are less apt to report positive relationships (Adler and Lotecka, 1973; Hirschi, 1969; Tudor, Peterson, and Elifson, 1980).

Kevin's delinquent, criminal, and drug activities brought him into fairly routine contact with the criminal and juvenile justice systems. At age 14 (eighth grade) he was sent to a youth camp for seven or eight months. Kevin described the program as "strict in a way . . . a pretty well structured program," but also as a "big front." During this time, he reported, he cut down his drug use but did not stop getting high. A short time later, he spent a few months in a detention home, whose setup he described as "stupid" and which he likened to a prison. Although he still did not cease his involvement in drugs and criminal activities as a result of that time in the detention home, his comments about being sent away provide a glimpse of components of the process of change from involvement to noninvolvement:

> *A:* My view is that you can send somebody away but the only way they're going to change is not 'cause you're telling them to change, it's 'cause they want to change. It's got to come from in here, your heart. . . . When you're in prison, doesn't do anybody any good, only if they want it to do any good . . . when I got sent away, I came out and I hated the world . . . I didn't learn my lesson, didn't suffer enough.

On release from the detention home, Kevin returned to using drugs and committing robbery. His drug use at the time (age 16) was quite heavy. He was drinking and using marijuana daily, taking prescription drugs (barbiturates and Valium®) regularly, and using and dealing cocaine. He also lied to his probation officer and to an attorney who represented him on earlier charges.

As a result of violation of probation at age 17, Kevin once again had direct contact with the courts. This time, the court-appointed attorney had him placed in Drug Freedom, a drug-free residential program, where he spent about eight months. Kevin went through the program faster than most, indicating that during the first four months he was "really serious . . . really upfront." During the fifth month, however, he started getting high. He alleged that "the guy that ran the operation was like real crooked . . . and backed me every time anything went wrong." According to Kevin, he was "phased out" of Drug Freedom because the staff suspected him of having sex with a girl in the program.

Kevin's response to the program, to the alleged "corruption," and to his being phased out early reveals an awareness, which he was not yet able to articulate clearly, that he was in need of and probably benefiting from the program. This foreshadows later explanations of his process of change to noninvolvement:

*A:* They phased me out because they thought me and this girl were having sex, so they, like, let me go, and I knew I wasn't ready to leave but I hated it there, and I went back home, and things didn't work out well at home. I was home; I OD'd . . . I woke up in a hospital. And that didn't even teach me a lesson . . . the situation at home wasn't any better. My father was still drinking a lot, you know, I felt really bad 'cause I knew I hurt my mother, and I felt that I didn't want to live anymore, I just didn't want to see anybody, all I wanted to do was get high. I didn't want to kill myself either, 'cause I didn't have the guts.

Kevin's family life, specifically his stepfather's drinking, which he had indicated was important initially in his getting into trouble and using drugs, once again became a major factor in his life—this time in his overdosing after being phased out of Drug Freedom. The overdose and resultant hospitalization, in a sense, might be seen as signaling a major turning point for Kevin.[1] He seemed to have hit bottom with the overdose and suicidal feelings; the only way to go, then, was up.

Seven months after leaving Drug Freedom, Kevin—still involved with drugs and crime—violated probation again and was once more brought before the court, which, according to Kevin, "this time around didn't want to hear shit." This time, as he described it, "I copped out as a drug addict," explaining to the lawyer that "I have a drug problem."

*A:* Because . . . this is what my intentions were at the time: being in a jail, okay, I'll go to Rehab House, and I'll bluff my way through the program and then get out. It was an easy way out instead of being in jail. Because I didn't want to deal with jail.

Kevin (still 17) was, in fact, sent to Rehab House, another residential drug treatment program. Although his initial motivation was to avoid jail and to bluff his way through treatment, he actually worked with and through the program: "I got something out of it." He stayed approximately eight months, after which he emerged rehabilitated.

The specific elements of this process seem to be in large measure subjective, internal decisions and value changes, although a significant other (a girlfriend) and heavy legal pressure were also a part of the process. (The elements of this process were, of course, dynamic and interactive and are being separated here only for analytic purposes.)

A major motivational factor in Kevin's desire to change was his fiancée (whom he had met about 17 months before entering Rehab House):

A: Debbie, my fiancée, has had a lot to do with me wanting to change because I really love her, and I hurt her a lot, I know I did . . . but she stuck with me through the whole deal; she was behind me all the way, and she supported me a lot. She was part of my motivation or inspiration or whatever you want to call it.

Regarding Rehab House itself:

A: Rehab House is a real good program, it really is, I couldn't say anything bad about it . . . [the] Rehab House program was more structured than [Drug Freedom]; it was just really good. I don't know if I can—I can't really tell you what goes on there because that would be a breach of confidentiality.

Though choosing not to talk in detail about the Rehab House program, Kevin did speak at length about the changes he had gone through and, in the discussion, alluded to procedures of the Rehab House drug treatment program. His comments reveal Kevin's perceptions of the effects of his family structure. As a result of this family structure, he indicated, while he was actively involved in drugs and crime, all he cared about was money and not people:

A: I was brought up spoiled and, like when I started getting into drugs, my mother used to give me money all the time and my grandparents, and I'd always have a lot of bucks, you know. Then I started getting into drugs and they stopped giving me money and everything. And I'd just steal and stuff. And the only thing I valued, like I didn't care about other people, all I cared about was money. Material things.

I used to just value money, material things, I didn't even care about myself . . . it was just like the payoff I cared about. It was never like, look what you're doing to your body, and your mind, and what you're doing to the people that love you. I was really being selfish in a negative way. I really sucked. I was, I don't know, a delinquent . . . all I wanted to was rob something so I could get some drugs . . . like I wasn't in control then 'cause drugs had taken me over and my values were all money and drugs, money and drugs, and I was just obsessed with that and it was like, I don't care about anything else, I wasn't doing anything productive.

During and as a result of the drug treatment program, however, Kevin reported:

*A:* My values changed a lot . . . like values changed. It's just like what I said before, you have to go through, I think it's true for anybody, you have to experience a lot of pain before you change, if you're only into negative shit like that [not caring about people, only money]. I'll tell you, this is true, had a lot of fun, I really did. I had a lot of fun, but it's not worth it in the long run, it isn't. You're just screwing yourself over, you go nowhere fast. Usually, you think you're going somewhere, but you don't know where, and you don't care. Like now, money's something but it isn't everything 'cause, like before, now say I'm broke, I won't go out and rob something. I'd rather be broke and be on the right side than be on the wrong.

Whatever the particular, specific mechanism(s), the *process* Kevin needed to undergo to change from involvement to noninvolvement was a personal, subjective change in values, apparently facilitated by the structure of the drug treatment program: "I like myself and feel really good. I got something out of it [Rehab House]". When asked what caused these changes in values specifically, Kevin answered:

*A:* Well, uh, I just got sick of it, you know, I just really looked at the situation. Other people helped me look at it too. You know, people, like before I'd say, ahh, what the fuck do you know, thinking I knew everything, you know. But I don't and [I'm] never going to amount to anything. Well, what do you want to do, do you want to spend the rest of your life in jail, have other people control your life? This is your life, you know. And that, before, I hurt people . . . never listened. I've started listening.

Similarly, Kevin explained his choice not to use drugs as related to a change in his feelings and a desire not have "old feelings" return:

*A:* I didn't want any drugs in me, I really don't. If I started . . . I'd kick off these old feelings around here, it'll be some more of this, and some more of that. That's why I don't do drugs anymore . . . I just think it's stupid to put all the things in your body. I don't want to take the chance of setting myself up again. I let my life go down the tubes a couple of times from doing drugs. I'm not going to let it happen again. The only way to do that is to prevent myself from doing any drugs. So I won't do them. I get pissed off if people keep, like, c'mon man, 'cause I don't play that shit no more . . . letting other people do my thinking for me. I used to be a follower for a long time. I don't follow anybody now.

For Kevin, then, change in his values about money and people seemed to be related to (and possibly produced by) changes in his attitude toward himself and his desire not to spend the rest of his life in jail, not to have other people control his life.

The process of change for Kevin was also related to a change in his group affiliations. Kevin indicated that since "graduating" from Rehab House (approximately a year before this interview) he never saw his old friends (with whom he used to do drugs and burglaries). The reason was:

*A:* Because they don't care about themselves, how can you care about them. If they don't care about themselves, they don't care about anyone else either. So they can't do anything for me . . . after I sat back and looked, just looked back on things differently . . . I thought they were my friends. They really weren't. They weren't doing anything for me . . . I got my life and I know that they're probably still in the same sort of things [drugs, burglary] so I don't have time for them.

Well, when I went to Rehab House, stopped seeing them altogether. No I figured, that's another thing, that's another thing that I know that they're not my friends. They don't even see what I'm up to or anything like that.

Another type of change that occurred after Rehab House was that Kevin's family relations, specifically the relationship with his stepfather, improved:

*A:* Well, me and my father, like we used to never shit with words . . . it was like, "Hi, good-by, kiss my ass," nothing, you know. We talk. I don't know, I just sat down with him one time, not too long ago, I think it was on Father's Day. I got him a card, and it didn't say anything in it, and I wrote a couple of pages, like, we know each other . . . we were close at one time, but we were very far, and I wish things would change. My mother told me when he read the card he started crying. Things have changed a whole lot in my life. I'm happy. When I got out of Rehab House, all my relatives and everything noticed the change in me. Like I could be open and talk about things I did before. Like I couldn't do that [before], and like, look people in the eye and talk.

The change in friendship structures and the improvement in relations within the family structure were both part of the process of Kevin's change from a life-style of involvement with drugs and criminal activities to one of noninvolvement. A most interesting question, and one that perhaps cannot be answered, is whether the changes in the friendship and family structures were both product and producer of Kevin's changes in values and life-style.

## Gallo

Gallo (nicknamed by friends after the wine of the same name), a 17-year-old male, was selected for the case study because of his active drug use and involvement in dealing. In addition, he was a primary source of information on such activities for one field-worker. This field-worker spent an extensive amount of time with Gallo and came to know him and his everyday activities quite well. The rich field data on Gallo supplement the interview data in this account.

Gallo was the third youngest of his mother's 13 children, the first of three children born of the marriage between his mother, a self-employed babysitter, and his father, a security guard. The marriage between his mother and father, who had been separated for three years at the time of our interviews, was the second for both of them. Gallo was living with his mother and three siblings in a neighborhood that he described as "down in the ghetto,"[2] a "rowdy" place where many people are "getting stoned, breaking windows, and slicing tires." His parents' economic class, according to Gallo, was "average." (Standard social science criteria would place them in the low economic class.) He saw his father as someone who could "handle" his money, whereas his mother foolishly spent whatever money she had. Thus, his father was "pretty well off," but his mother was "not a lot." At the time of the interview, Gallo was about to graduate from an alternative vocational high school program within the Yule City public school system. He had had various jobs (some funded by the government) throughout his adolescence.

*Self-Perceptions*

Throughout the data on Gallo, his perceptions of himself emerge in three separate but interrelated themes: (1) Gallo as "cool," (2) Gallo as "expert," and (3) Gallo as family man. The themes are particularly meaningful in terms of Gallo's delinquent activity. Common within and among these themes are patterns we refer to as *presentation of self* and *mentorship*.

**Gallo as "Cool."** The essence of Gallo that emerged from our data is aptly captured in the following comments included in field notes describing an interaction with him:

> One gets the impression, from watching this kid, that he feels very sure of himself. There is nothing tentative or affected about his gestures, demeanor, clothing, etc. However, one gets the impression that he is carefully trying to project an image that is clearly in his mind—a very "cool" image at that. . . .

According to the data, Gallo was quite interested in making a particular impression on others. He presented himself as cool, and, as observed in field and interview settings, worked very hard to be all that the cool image (in his eyes) entailed—including not having to work at being cool. This presentation of self, studied and orchestrated for effect, is part of everything about Gallo, from his nickname, to his physical appearance, to his talk. This is quite apparent in both sets of data—in the physical descriptions of Gallo recorded by the field-worker; in the way he relishes the descriptive details of his various drug, crime, and family escapades in the interview; and in the bravado he engages in with his friends in their observed and reported interactions. Consider the following excerpts from field notes which first describe Gallo and his interactions with other youths:

> About halfway down the block, we meet another boy [Gallo] similarly dressed, but dark hair; he is walking a Doberman puppy. The boys are clearly buddies and greet each other by name. . . . We stop and the boys take out cigarettes and light them up. They talk about the dog, its owner claiming he's "ferocious" and will attack on command. . . . There is much talk about drugs—about not having any pot.
>
> . . . [Gallo] is wearing his usual outfit consisting of faded jeans, buckled with a marijuana leaf–shaped buckle, a rock group logo t-shirt underneath a green army fatigue jacket, heavy work boots, a leather visor imprinted with "Gallo." Gallo is very thin and seems kind of hunched into the jacket, but his gait is loose, almost ambling and casual; as he walks he is smoking a cigarette, which for the most part he lets hang from the corner of his mouth.

In the following account, Gallo and his friend had arrived at a party "evidently drunk/high enough not to be able to function as he normally does." He attempted to roll a joint and was unable to do so. The field notes continue:

> (As I've noted earlier, Gallo tends to pride himself on his ability to roll paper joints, which as I've seen, turn out very thin and neat.)
>
> As Gallo turns this task over to Ben, there emerges quite a bit of teasing banter about the fact that Gallo messed up. . . . This teasing took the form of Ben belittling Gallo's ability, and somehow insinuating that he (Ben) was more experienced and older, and "of course" would be able to roll the joints. Gallo responded by saying such things as "fuck man, I was rolling joints when I was 5 years old!" Ben scoffed, challenging him with "5 years, huh? Sure, when you were 5 years old, I'd been smoking dope for 5 years."

Part and parcel of creating and sustaining this image for Gallo was the resource he had in an appreciative audience. He found an eager audience in a group of friends who were, for the most part, younger than he; one was his brother and the others were rather young, typically immature, and somewhat disaffected boys from a group home in his neighborhood. An additional audience was provided by the researcher, who was eager (in the sense of being "disinterestedly interested") to appreciate without challenge Gallo's presentation of himself and his world.

For Gallo, an audience was a resource that could be tapped for practicing and performing and, thus, for nurturing and perfecting his presentation. Both product and producer of this performance was Gallo as "expert."

**Gallo as "Expert."** Part of being a cool and experienced "stoned little hippie," as Gallo called himself, was to present a knowledgeable self in terms of everything he did. As one might anticipate from the preceding self-reference, this included to a large extent drug use, dealing, and other delinquent behavior. Gallo assumed the role of expert quite easily and, we might add, not only for the audience provided by the researcher–interviewer. As seen in the previous example, in his observed daily interactions as well as within the interview, Gallo readily presented himself as an expert. He legitimized his expert status by citing his experience or the experience provided for him by significant others—his mentors— in matters of delinquency and everyday life. His mentors for the most part were family members. In turn, and as an expert, he took pride in mentoring others:

*A:* Like, uh, Sunday. We went out, well, we were, were getting pretty well blitzed and everything, but a friend of mine was starting his bike and he had a fucking flat. He had slipped underneath the bus on Clover and East Street. The bus driver got out and started bitching and shit, saying uh, "I hope you learned your lesson" and shit, and it wasn't his fault. It was an accident. And this dude is coming out there and getting all mouthy and shit, we were gonna beat the hell outa his ass.

*Q:* But you didn't . . . how come?

*A:* 'Cause I told everybody, come on, let's go. And then, you know usually everybody listen to me. 'Cause you know. I know more about law than they do. 'Cause my brothers and shit. And uh, they will listen to me 'cause I got good advice most of the time. When I tell them to do something, you know, they usually will keep cool about it. Like if, we do something rowdy, I'll tell them what not to do and what to do. They can take my advice or they can leave it. Usually they'll take it. You know, 'cause I don't really give a fuck if they don't take my advice. Just someone's grave and coffin, not me. That's the way I feel about it, and I tell them that. Tell them right to and you do what you want to do. But I'll tell you now. I'll tell them what I got to say. If they listen, if they don't, they don't.

As is evident here, the role of his family is very important, particularly in the sense that it provides another resource for the construction of the "Gallo" image.

**Gallo as a Family Man.** References to his family as a unit as well as to individual family members are pervasive in Gallo's remarks. He painted a bittersweet picture of his family life. His parents had been separated since he was 14, only one of the "innumerable" times they had split up. His father was an alcoholic who, according to Gallo, had stopped drinking, except on those occasions when he was with Gallo's uncle. His mother was what Gallo described as (among other things) "messed up." When his parents were together, their relationship was filled with conflict over how to raise and discipline the children.

Gallo saw his father in a much more positive light than he did his mother. In fact, he often framed his discussion of either parent in terms of a dichotomy he drew between them. He expressed disrespect for his mother, describing her at different points in the interview as "foolish," an "idiot," a "bitch." He said that he doesn't "get along with" his mother, "never has" and believed that she hated him. She didn't like "anything about me" and nagged him constantly. According to Gallo, the feeling was mutual; he said that he didn't love his mother.

In contrast, his father was typically described as a strong character. He managed money well, could control his drinking when he chose to do so, knew how to discipline children properly, didn't strike women, taught Gallo things, didn't nag him about his drug use, and would (if he could) let Gallo live with him. Their relationship was rooted in mutual respect. It was more like "brother to brother than father and son." He knew his father loved him, and he loved his father.

The rest of the family also sided with one parent or the other. Indeed, "taking sides" was at the same time a result and a reinforcement of the split between the parents:

*A:* He [his father] lives by himself. He wouldn't like nobody else living with him. He only liked me, my brother Artie, and my brother Iven. And, uh, two of my sisters, that's it. You know, he like, um, my little brother Webster, he used to call him a cockroach and shit, get up on the table and pound on his feet and call him a cockroach and shit. And he couldn't stop him, 'cause my mother couldn't allow him to. See, the ones he corrected, he got to correct. It was me, my brother, my older brother, and sisters. He got to correct us. Because, you know, my mother thought we could take it. But the ones she babied were hers. And the ones that was his was his. He could correct them any way he wanted to. And she didn't say nothing. But her babies, he couldn't correct them. And that's the way it was, and then they broke up, my mother's marriage broke up 'cause my little brother Webster kept on doing this shit, and my brother got corrected by my dad, and my mother didn't like it. So my dad told her plain and simple, hey, he's my damn kid too, he's got my blood in him, you know, if I can't correct him, fuck it, I'm leaving. My mother said good then, fucking leave. Plain and simple.

*Social Darwinism — class causes of crime*

'Cause most of them, most of them around the neighborhood, most of the families are together, but my family are apart. It's like black sheep, and then there's white sheep. And then there's idiots and then there's brilliances. You know. Like that in my family there are different categories, like this one, Victor, Artie, Eros, Webster, and my mother are idiots. All right. And, uh, my brother Iven, my brother Ray, my sister and my sister Holly . . . and Dwayne.

Gallo spoke of his older brothers—that is, those on "his side" of the family split—in much the same way that he did his father. He saw their actions as legitimate, even in family fights in which he was the victim.[3]

*A:* Uh, I always got into fights with my bigger brothers always. No matter what, you get into a fight with them, but if somebody messes with you outside the family, then they would, they get on your side, you know, they can, they were the only ones that could beat you up. That's the way it goes. . . .

The theme of mentorship emerged in Gallo's descriptions of his brothers. His older brothers were mentors *and* peers in many activities that had come to be important to Gallo and his presentation of self.

*A:* I learn from their screw-ups, I learn. Not to screw up like that, 'cause that's what we talk about. Most of my brothers, if they tell me, they'll say don't do that. And after they tell me I won't do it. I won't get into a screw-up mess like that. 'Cause I'll know how to keep myself out of there. . . .

The most pervasive of these activities (in terms of his brothers' mentorship and his involvement) is drug use. In fact, Gallo seemed to be cognizant to some degree of carrying on a tradition. He took seriously his role as a "model" for his younger brothers. The fact that one of his younger brothers was quite babyish, coddled by his mother, and—in Gallo's estimation— "uncool" disgusted Gallo. In contrast, he delighted in another younger brother, Dwayne, who models his behavior and appearance on Gallo's, "hangs out" with him, and in general, emulates him. Dwayne was 12 at the time and, according to field notes, was a pint-sized Gallo. Gallo showed obvious concern for this brother—a concern that is clearly geared toward initiating him into the "cool life." Gallo described these relationships:

*Q:* How about Dwayne?
*A:* Yeah, he's my buddy. He's my chum. See now he's my buddy. I'm his older brother so, you know. That's the same, Roger's my older brother, you know. That type of way that he hangs around with, that's it. And Webster, he's an idiot.
*Q:* How come?

Cohen
develop
mental
subculture
1) common problem
2) communic on basis of p
3) interact around the problem
4) Develop Solution to the problem

4) Maintain + confd
Cloward & Ohlin
Criminal Gangs
Retreatist Gangs
Conflict Gangs

1) Attachment
2) Commitment
3) Involvement
4) Belief

Cohen
Status frustration
Durkheim
'social integration'
Crespo — fail = delinque
O'brieck

*A:* 'Cause he is. He's just plainly idiot, you know. Just because he's momma's suck a tit, that what we call him, momma's little suck a tit. He hides behind mommy and all this other shit. He don't know how to fight yet. He won't fight with black dudes in the neighborhood. And they can pick on him all they want, you know. That type of situation, that's an idiot.

*Q:* . . . Did you turn Dwayne on?

*A:* Yup.

*Q:* When?

*A:* When he was, uh, turned 8.

*Q:* And he never smoked at all before then?

*A:* Nope, never smoked in his life.

*Q:* And now he does?

*A:* He does. He's a heavy partier now.

In this way, family is very important for Gallo. It provides a world in which activities, as well as their "cool" status, can be learned and viewed as legitimate. Thus, through his family, Gallo continues to have resources for his cool and expert statuses.

*A:* Nope. No adult. 'Cause ain't nobody going to be like me. You know I got my own way of living.

*Q:* Where do you think you got that way of living?

*A:* From my brother. Like, I'm combined from my brother Iven. I'm combined from my brother Roger. I'm combined from my brother Victor, I mean my brother Ichebod. . . .

Family is also important in that Gallo views himself as the man of the family, taking responsibility for persons in the family (again, expertise emerges as a pattern). Despite his conflict with, and disrespect for, his mother and certain of his brothers and sisters, Gallo was protective of his family as a whole. He indicated an understanding of his mother, best exemplified by his talk of her "moving to the other side."

*A:* . . . Like my mother had this dream that her first husband and my Aunt Bert came back in her dream and told her that they wanted Nancy [one of the children]. You know, and the next day she [Nancy] was dead. Really flipped her out. And, you know, that's mainly why mother is like she is now, 'cause her first husband, he said he was gonna die, and that would, you know, kind of move you somewhere else. You know, and then that dream. That dream would move you somewhere else, too. You know, that wouldn't keep you in reality. That would push you back. And that's what it did, you know, it made her kind of messed up a little bit. 'Cause she was a nice lady before, because you know, my aunts and uncles we talk a lot. And they tell me things like that. She was a very, you know, highly sophisticated lady. You know, she was a nurse and shit like that. And then it just moved her. You know, it put her out.

*Q:* So you think she kinda, maybe like a nervous breakdown or something like that, a mental . . .

*A:* Yeah, something. Mental, messed up . . . see my dad tried to straighten it out, but he couldn't. So it wasn't any fun.

Although Gallo complained about his mother, one gets the sense that this was to some extent part of his image; inasmuch as she wasn't "sophisticated," she didn't quite fit this image, yet he still showed an understanding of her as well as a sense of responsibility toward her. In addition, he defended her, as he did his entire family, to any outsiders. As he said about his brothers, "we can do anything to each other but nobody else better mess with any one of us." It seems that his identity as a "man" and as one who is responsible binds him to a loyal and protective attitude toward his family. This is played out in his interactions with other youths, as observed in the field as well as in his remarks in the interview.

### Development of Delinquent Career

The formal patterns of presentation of self and mentoring that underlie the aforementioned substantive themes play a significant role in every aspect of Gallo's life. In this section we focus specifically on the history of his involvement in delinquency and on other life events surrounding that involvement. We then turn to a discussion of Gallo's movement from or commitment to various delinquent activities and the role that one form of deviance (drug/alcohol use) played in another form (crime). Gallo's descriptions of his delinquent career and his attitudes toward involvement illuminate the themes introduced earlier.

**Delinquency Begins at Home.** Gallo reported that his delinquent career began at the age of 4, when he was introduced to marijuana and began to use it regularly. He described his older brothers as both peers and mentors in his initiation and subsequent early use. They provided the marijuana, invited him to share it, and assured him that it was not harmful.

*A:* I was in Appleville. I was 4 years old. My brother came home late one night and he was stoned. He came to us, so me and my brother. . . .

*Q:* That's the way, he just came in and said . . . ?

*A:* Yeah, "You guys want to try something?" And then we said, "Yeah." And he goes, "What?" My brother Roger took the first toke and I took the second. I told my brother Roger, "You try it first." And my brother Roger tried it. And then, ever since then we were getting high every day. . . . Yeah, I was scared. I was scared. That's why I said to my brother Roger, "You take the first toke." I'm not dumb. If it don't hurt him, it shouldn't hurt me . . . we took two or three hits. And then, after that, we started taking two or three hits every day and then gradually went on. . . . I got high [the first time], I got a little bit too buzzed and I went to sleep and I passed out. My brother carried me to bed that night. . . . I thought it was pretty cool. Plus, uh, when I went out with my brother's friends the next day and, uh, his, my brother's friend turned me on. You know, everyone was doing it around me so why shouldn't I?

*A:* When I was 6 I started smoking a lot. That was just with my brothers. I never smoked with none of my friends until I was 11 . . . because none of my friends, you know, they were all, you know, like I had friends of Reynold's, my older brother's friends, you know, and my other brother's friends but they were older people. But my age group didn't get high. When I was getting high, they didn't get high. A couple of my friends just got turned on [a few] years ago. You know, being that old.

In addition to continuing to smoke marijuana, at age 6 Gallo was introduced to cigarettes by a brother who smoked.

*A:* I asked him for it. I said, what do they taste like, and he said, here taste it . . . I didn't really like it . . . I didn't know how to inhale.

At 7, he was introduced to sex:

*A:* . . . I had sex when I was 7.
*Q:* Really?
*A:* Yeah.
*Q:* How did that happen?
*A:* My brother Iven. . . . he told me how to do it and I went in the other room and did it with my girlfriend. So, you know, I found out how to do it. . . .

When he was 8 he learned how to inhale cigarettes properly, again, within a smoking activity with his brothers. He subsequently got "hooked," thought it was "cool," and thus began to smoke daily cigarettes that his brothers purchased for him. His brothers were also influential in teaching him other things at this age that were to become very important to Gallo.

*A:* . . . He told me, he taught us a lot. I mean he did. He taught [me] how to fix automobiles, mechanics. When I was 8 years old I started working on cars. . . .

Gallo also had his first drink at age 8, for his sister's graduation: "We had to have a little celebration. So we were getting ripped." Gallo drank wine on this occasion and continued to drink it at family functions on special occasions. During this time he continued to use marijuana with his brothers.

At age 9, Gallo was introduced to hashish. The situation was similar to the marijuana smoking with his brothers, except that this time hashish was mixed with the marijuana. At 10 he was introduced to hard liquor (in the form of Black Velvet and ginger ale) at a New Year's Eve party hosted by his brother. He said that he didn't really like it because his brother was "pushing it on him" and that he continued to drink hard liquor only on special occasions. He did, however, begin to drink beer on the weekends (this in addition to smoking marijuana) with his brothers, who always bought the beer and shared it with him. Also, he said, this was the time when he began smoking marijuana by himself and buying it for himself, albeit still from his brothers. Much like his initiation to marijuana, alcohol, and cigarettes, his use of other drugs took place under his brothers' supervision:

*A:* [They'd buy me] . . . a pack of cigarettes a week. That's what I always smoked, three or four. You know, they didn't let me get too heavily into it until I got to be a teenager.
*Q:* So they did kind of watch out for you.
*A:* Yeah, they watched out, but they never really said anything. They never let me get into pills or anything until I was 14, 13, 15, never, it was always hashish, beer, reefer, and cigarettes.

**Expanding Delinquent Horizons.** Entering middle school seemed to be a turning point for Gallo in terms of both increased delinquency and delinquent acts with peers outside the family. He described this early activity with his school peers as the "best times" he can remember and cited entering school as a benchmark for an increase in drinking alcohol. About the same time that he entered Every Middle School, he began to drink wine during the week and on weekends.

*A:* When I started going to Every School I started drinking Gallo and, uh, what was it midnight train express, or some shit like that. Just cheap wine you know. Taste like grape soda and shit.
*Q:* . . . when you got to Every School you started drinking it [wine] more just out by yourself or with your friends?
*A:* Yeah, with my friends and we get together and we get a couple of quarts and we'd get a couple of nickels [of marijuana] and we'd get high. Get a cheap high you know.
*Q:* Then about how often would you drink wine then?
*A:* About, oh, everytime we got money.
*Q:* About how often was that?
*A:* About every other day.
*Q:* So even during this time, when you were 11, 12, and you'd have beer sometimes on the weekend, during the week you'd be drinking wine?
*A:* Yeah, yeah, if I wasn't drinking beer I was drinking wine.

This increase was marked by his friends christening him Gallo, a name that he continued to wear both literally and figuratively with pride.

*A:* . . . Oh yeah, most of them [his friends] almost every one of these guys drink Gallo. They're all lovers of me. What can I say.

*Q:* How did you get that name anyway? When did it start?

*A:* Uh, a friend of mine named Clarence, he used to drink Gallo and I used to call him the Gallo King. So he didn't know my real name and I didn't know his real name so he called me the Gallo Kid. And then I finally knew his real name and started calling him Clarence. But then, he kept calling me Gallo. So then everybody got the name 'cause, like he used to call me down the street and shit, hey Gallo, and all my friends used to be with me. Oh your name's Gallo, uh. You know.

*Q:* That's not a bad name.

*A:* I know it's not. Everybody thinks it's a pretty cool name. They wonder how I got it, and I have to tell them that big long story.

The partying image suggested by his new nickname was one that Gallo sought to live up to during this time.

*Q:* So ever since you were at Every School you drank wine pretty much all the time on weekends, during the week?

*A:* Yeah, me and my buddy [J.D.] used to get into that all the time boy. We used to get stoned, blitzed. Take a quart of wine and shoot up at our girl-friend's. That's when I used to have girlfriends, you know, go over to their house every day and bullshit like that. Then we used to go over there and get drunk, get stoned, fuck with their mom. Squeal away and get stoned. And even when I didn't drink that much. You know, even though it was wine.

*A:* . . . How often did I drink? Well for a week we drank it everyday me and my friend J.D. For a whole straight week you know, and then we started doing it every other day for a couple of months, then we stopped.

*Q:* How come you were drinking so much then?

*A:* 'Cause we were getting into partying really heavily and really wanted to get drunk bad, so there was liquor or nothing. Plus his mother had a whole cabinet full, of liquor . . . like we went straight through a week on full, every-day drinking hard liquor and then we started drinking every other day for about two months and then we stopped . . . because we did, burned ourself to the ground. And plus we were running around without our T-shirts and you know liquor is warm for you and we just got toasted. We used to get totaled all the time. Our girlfriends used to yell at us because we were too drunk.

Gallo reported beginning to smoke, on average, a half-ounce of marijuana a day during this time. But when his girlfriend at the time bet him that he couldn't stop smoking for two weeks, he won the bet and was awarded an ounce of marijuana, all of which he smoked in one day. It was also during this time at Every School that he began to buy marijuana from persons outside of his family.

He was still, however, mentored by his brothers in the ways of drug use. When he was 12 his brother introduced him to amphetamines:

*A:* . . . My brother gave it to me, and I was tired that day and I wanted to go to school and pass out there in school. Here, do a couple of these. I said all right, sounds cool.

*Q:* Did you know what they were? Did you want to try them?

*A:* Yeah, I knew what they were. Yeah, I knew what they were. Just that, you know, never really wanted to get into them.

*Q:* Were you scared and all about what would happen?

*A:* No.

Gallo continued amphetamine use "once in a while" on days that he didn't feel good because "it brings you up. It makes you zoom around and not go to sleep."

Gallo's time at Every School was also marked by trouble. He stated that he "got kicked out" of school "practically every day" because the principal at Every didn't like him as a consequence of the disdain he held for Gallo's older brothers, who had preceded him there. Consequently, according to Gallo, he failed seventh grade. During his remaining two years at Every (ages 13–14) his parents separated. He continued to get in trouble at school and was eventually suspended after striking the principal, who accused him of possession of drugs and attempted to search him. (Gallo recounted this incident with pride as the same type of situation that both of his older brothers had been through at Every—both also struck a school authority.) Gallo ended up spending most of his weekday afternoons at a vocational center, where he began to study auto mechanics, something he regarded as an important aspect of his life:

*Q:* Oh, so when did you do that, when you were going to Every School?

*A:* Yeah, when I was going to Every School. Like when Parker [principal] didn't want me for a full day he sent me down to PAT and that's what I was doing everyday, I was down at PAT, and that's a vocational center down here. I was going down there every day after school, but it was for my benefit, but he didn't know it and he didn't like me at all. But it was still my benefit because I learned a lot. Got to know a lot of people.

It was also during these years (ages 13–14) that Gallo first purchased hashish and experimented with noncannabis drugs other than amphetamines. The first of these experiments, with LSD, took place at a rock concert. His description of the event was matter-of-fact, restricted to how he got the LSD and what he did with it. He was given ten hits; he sold eight and took two.

> Q: Did you buy it on purpose, or . . . ?
> A: No. I got it gave to me. 'Cause he happened to have, uh, a bunch of it. And he wanted to get rid of some. And he gave me some to get rid of to sell. And some to do up myself.

The second experiment occurred when someone brought marijuana treated with PCP (Phenocyclidine, or "angel dust") to school. Gallo said he wanted to "check it out."

> Q: Did you know it was angel dust?
> A: Uh-huh.
> Q: Did you want to do it, did you want to try it?
> A: I wanted to try it to see what it was like, 'cause everybody said, you know, it gets you more stoned then regular reefer. I said oh yeah. Let me check it out. So a friend of mine, he and us, we checked it.

One of the other youths who tried it "started freaking out in class" and ended up in the hospital. Another youth who was involved reported the one who had provided the marijuana to the authorities. The drug seller, a friend of Gallo, was put in jail. Gallo was very angry with the person who "squealed" and, in fact, took revenge by "beating his ass." As for the youth who was hospitalized:

> A: . . . nothing happened. He just went on a bad trip that's all . . . he was one of them, young, still, you know, smokin' a joint, half a joint, and getting fucked up. He was that sort of person, you know, and he tried to keep up with us and he just couldn't take it. So he winded up fuckin. . . .

**Criminal Activities Other than Drugs.** Gallo reported involvement in delinquent activities with friends—shoplifting and stealing from houses—in addition to his drug use during his last two years at Every School. He described how he and his friends used to steal lumber for the father of one of the boys:

> A: Rip off houses and shit like that. Just go out and steal like for Vann, his daddy owns a lot of houses and we used to go out and steal 2 by 4s and all this other shit like that, and sell them to him, you know. He'd say go get me how many 2 by 4s he wanted, and he'd tell us how much he'd give us. And pay for gas to get out there. He gave us a truck to use.

He also described a specific house theft that he engaged in when he was 14. He and his friends had spent the night in a suburb of Yule:

*A:* And I went to [suburban town] and we robbed this lady 'cause, like, we were hungry and shit. Me and a couple of friends. This door was unlocked so we walked in there and helped ourselves to the food. Walked in there, opened up the refrigerator. Oh yeah, check this out. Started munching down, cooked couple of things and walked out. We cooked, uh, what was it, steak or something. Went into the backyard and ate it.

He and his friends also took cars from parking ramps and went on joyrides.

*A:* We used to go up there and steal Trans Ams, Camaros, Firebirds.
*Q:* Who?
*A:* Me, P.T., and a couple of other people.
*Q:* And what would you do with it then?
*A:* Just cruise around the city. I drove one up Edwards Falls one time. Drove it off.
*Q:* With you in it?
*A:* No.
*Q:* And you never got caught at all?
*A:* Nope, I just let the sucker go into neutral. I threw a brick at the gas pedal and shut the door.
*Q:* Must have been pretty weird.
*A:* A friend of mine had, uh, a Firebird, and I just ran up the hill got into the Firebird and hauled ass.
*Q:* Don't you ever worry about getting caught?
*A:* No, if you think about it you'll get caught. If you look like you're nervous, you're going to get caught.

They did get caught that year stealing lights from road barricades. The police officer who caught them was quite angry because the absence of the warning lights they had taken had caused him to drive into a ditch. This situation culminated in one of Gallo's literal "brushes with the law."

*A:* . . . And, uh, he was, uh, driving up the street, you know, and he had us in the car and shit . . . and, uh, so he was all pissed off because he fucked up the underneath of his car and, you know, he would have had to pay for it or somebody would have to pay for it. And he was thinking that he had to pay for it. And he was all pissed off, so he goes, "I ought to beat your ass you little fucker." And I said, "You'll regret it" and that's all. And he goes, "Oh, yeah," stops the car in a hurry, opened up his door and opened my door. The minute he opened my door, I smacked his ass with my belt and I said now get back in there and sit down.

At that moment Gallo's brother-in-law, who was a sheriff, arrived on the scene and the fight ended abruptly.

The year he was 15 Gallo stole a radio and some money from an acquaintance. The youth had left the radio at Gallo's house. Gallo's brother wanted it, so Gallo kept it and sold it to his brother; he told the friend that the radio had disappeared from his house. The same youth had given Gallo some money to purchase some marijuana for him, but Gallo kept the money and gave him no marijuana in return. The impetus for these thefts was that, according to Gallo, this acquaintance was "a fucking idiot."

As alluded to in the foregoing scenario, Gallo began to sell drugs at Every School, at first only occasionally and then by the joint. He became more involved in dealing (which he distinguished from "selling") after his one and only "big" theft activity—the burglary of a house in his neighborhood owned by a known dealer who would not sell to young people, not even to Gallo. This fact, along with "getting reefer," were what he cited as reasons. Gallo committed this theft alone after planning it carefully. The plan began with the theft of a van from the airport.

A: I wanted a van because I knew I was going to take his stereo and I knew I was going to take a lot of shit. I wanted something I could, you know, wouldn't be in the back seat.

He took fifty pounds of marijuana (which was stored in trash barrels), a stereo, and some money; he loaded it all into the van and "drove down the block a little ways. Pulled up in my mother's yard because she didn't have the fence at the time. Just pulled up into the back yard and stashed everything down in the cellar way and hauled ass with the van." He took the van to a nearby parking lot, "locked it, sliced the tires, busted the head lights, busted the windshield," and left it there. Gallo felt that he really "overdid it" with this theft and said he would never do anything like that again.

His bountiful acquisition turned into profit. That was when Gallo began to "deal."

A: How did I get into drugs? Selling? . . . Uh, by the dealer down the street, ripping him off.

Q: You never did it before then?

A: No, never dealed really. I maybe sold two or three joints out of a bag I bought, but I didn't deal, deal, deal. But when I got down to fifty pounds I had to do something.

That was the start, but dealing became more of a business for Gallo when he became employed, because with an income he could build up a drug stock, as well as have income to fall back on if he got "ripped off." He mainly dealt in marijuana; he sold amphetamines for a while but stopped when he found that they turned too little profit.

After leaving Every, Gallo entered Oxford High School and was subsequently advised to enter the vocational-technical program of the Yule City Public Schools.

*Q:* So how did you get into that?

*A:* 'Cause my brother Roger was in it and he was an A student. So Miss Laymen goes, "You must be one too." You know, old me?

*Q:* Did you want to do it?

*A:* Yeah, I wanted to. You know, I wanted to go in there because like, I'm an auto mechanic and I already had two years in auto mechanics and I wanted some more training, which I'm going in the military for training too. And I wanted to go in there and get more training and that's what I did. I went in there.

He continued his already heavy use of marijuana, increased his use of cigarettes to a pack a day, and purchased beer from a store for the first time, although he was underage. He explained:

*A:* I couldn't find nobody to buy it for me so I finally said fuck it. I'll go in and see if I can buy it myself.

After finding that he could successfully purchase beer, he started buying for friends, which, he says, contributed to his increase in drinking. At this time he also tried cocaine and Quaaludes for the first time:

*A:* Well, it was just everybody was sitting around and nobody had no reefer or anything. Some dude had some coke . . . a friend said, "here's some coke, do you want to snort it?" I said, "Yeah."[4]

Gallo described the first time he used Quaaludes as a product of "just wanting to try it."

*Q:* What was it like?

*A:* It was a downer. It brought you to the ground.

*Q:* Did you like it?

*A:* Not really.

*Q:* How come you did it? I mean did you want to try it?

*A:* Yeah, I wanted to try it. I always like experimenting.

He was, however, cautious about his experimentation:

*A:* I got it and did it at home. 'Cause, you know, if it made me pass out or anything, I was going to be home. No way was I going, you know, to be out in the streets or anything.

Finding his experiment with Quaaludes to be enjoyable, he was not reluctant to use them again four months later.

*A:* . . . 'Cause I thought the first time was pretty excellent.

*Q:* Well, what was it like? Was it like getting high?

*A:* No, it was like getting high but you were brought down to the ground, you know, you were down, you know, you didn't feel like doing anything. Just, oh, and got you into it.

This was also the year that Gallo came to the attention of the criminal justice system. He became a "person in need of supervision" (PINS) after running away from home and staying with his girlfriend and her parents for six months. His girlfriend's parents were "cool," got stoned, gave him drugs, and didn't mind his staying there. Despite this change, Gallo's life went on as usual. He continued to go to school, which he viewed as too important to miss, and would go to his mother's house when he knew she wasn't there to pick up clothes and eat. Eventually he got caught.

*Q:* Why did you go back home?

*A:* 'Cause my mother put [PINS] and all this other bullshit out at me. I had the cops looking for me and shit. They finally caught me. And I went home and my mother said, "Wow, all I want you to do is stay here," and all this other bullshit. I said all right. And after that, that's when I got in trouble.

Gallo's criminal activities continued (in addition to his dealing) with two violent incidents (which he considered legitimate), for one of which he was convicted. The first incident, the firebombing of a house, was, to Gallo, an act of deserved revenge in the name of his brother. He described the situation and what led up to it:

*Q:* He stabbed my brother. I burnt down his house, and I told him he better have good fire insurance . . . well, I don't know if it burned down the whole house but . . . I don't know, if it hurt, it might have hurt some people though. I don't know . . . yeah, he had a family, I guess, I don't really know who he was really . . . I know where he lived, and I know that.

Prior to the firebombing Gallo got "stoned," but he was not explicit about the substance.

*A:* Got stoned on purpose. So I'd bring my courage up. 'Cause when you're stoned, you're right. It just so happened I was stoned and had a cocktail.

The second incident, assault of a policeman, Gallo viewed as an act of protection of personal property. In this case, as in the previous incident, his temper (which he described as difficult to control) was provoked to the point of violence. He described the situation as one in which he was as "straight" as if he had just "gotten out of the shower," when:

*A:* Okay, well, somebody called the cops about my dog. And they came to look at my dog, and they said it was anemic pink eye. The puppies were pink eye, not the dog, but the puppies. And so, my mother had to sign papers for them to take the dogs, so she did. And, uh, they had left with my dog, you know, and bit him and shit. They had to put a muzzle on her.

*Q:* So cops came? Were, like cops from the Humane?

*A:* No, cops came, and cops came and called the Humane Society. And it bit him, and so he put a muzzle on him. And I called up the veterinarian when they were outside talking and, uh, he said there was no such thing as pink eye. I went out there and asked the lady when I was going to get my dog back. She said never. And I saw the dude kicking my dog. So I say, "Hey, stop that." And he wouldn't stop it, so I went over to him and that lady goes, "You stay right there." And I smacked her and beat, beat that cop up. And then another one came and I beat his ass with the other dude's club and another came and I hit his ass with the other club. That's all that happened. Then my brother came around the corner.[5]

Gallo's brother took him down to the courthouse, where he was charged and detained for three days at his brother's request "to cool his attitude down" and to show him that "it [jail] ain't no fun." Gallo, however, thought it was funny and said that he "laughed right through" his jail experience.

As a consequence of this charge and his mother's requests, the court was ready to order that he be "sent away," but his older sister would not allow it and agreed to take custody and have him live with her. Gallo lived with his sister for several months but, as Gallo puts it, "after a while, you can't, you begin not to be able to live with your sister, 'cause you know your sister has been living with you all your life and you just can't get along sometimes." Eventually, Gallo recalled, after an argument with his sister he said, "Fuck it, I'll move." He moved to his father's apartment.

Gallo celebrated turning 16 with the help of his brothers, who "partied" with him and provided him with "magic mushrooms" and a Quaalude as birthday gifts. This was the first and only time he used mushrooms, which he didn't like because they "smelled and tasted bad." It was his third use of Quaaludes but decidedly the last. He explained:

*A:* . . . that time was when I passed out because I was drinking and shit. And the next day I got up and I wasn't feeling good. So I didn't want to mess with them [Quaaludes] anymore.

Later that year he experimented with opium provided by a friend of his brother. He used it for three days in succession (he stayed overnight at the friend's house) and had not used it since. We see that his brothers' direct and indirect mentoring continued to influence Gallo's drug use:

*A:* . . . he just got a new shipment in. And he knew it was good stuff. And it was stuff he would keep for his head [stash]. You knew it wasn't hard, hard, hard, it wasn't bootleg or anything it [that] was gonna fuck you up, that's why, you know, he said, "Here you go." He's my brother's best friend. And he knows a litttle bit better than to fuck around with [my] brother. So I did it three days in a row.

New Year's Eve of that year brought (as usual) a big party. Gallo described "partying" so heavily that night that he became quite sick—in his words, "too fucked up." As a result, he decreased his drinking considerably for six weeks after the new year began. He described this decrease as "not hard to do" because he doesn't "like the taste of beer anyways . . . just like to get drunk."

At 16, Gallo's criminal activities continued. He sold the turntable he had stolen in the house burglary referred to earlier, continued dealing, and was involved in a shooting incident related to his dealing activity. Gallo and his friend Vann were in the park selling marijuana. Because Vann had the "reefer" in his pants, Gallo carried Vann's gun in his. (Gallo was very matter-of-fact in telling this story; he acted as if carrying a gun in this situation was "no big deal," although he didn't always carry a gun when dealing.) According to Gallo, the situation called for violence in the interest of protecting valuable property:

*A:* . . . And this dude came over and he wanted four pounds . . . we didn't know he was coming, somebody told him where we were. And the dude came up and asked us for four pounds [$1,200 worth]. And, uh, he checked it out and everything and he liked it. And then he went to haul ass . . . and Vann said shoot his ass. Bang.

*Q:* You shot him?

*A:* Yup, dropped down on the ground. Shot him in his left leg. We picked up the reefer and hauled ass.

*Q:* . . . Why didn't you just leave and not give him the dope? Why did you shoot him.

*A:* Because he had the dope in his hand and started running.

At another point in the interview he made reference to this incident in terms of necessary violence for protecting property:

*Q:* Well, I don't doubt that, it's just that it seems like pretty heavy stuff, you know, all these guys running around shooting?

*A:* Well, they don't shoot them unless they have to. Like, you ain't going to let somebody walk, run away with $1,200. No way, you ain't going to let him run away with it. You going to get him and you might as well get him right there while he got it still on him, 'cause if you get him the next day he might not have it, and you're just out. You're just going to kick his ass whoopie shit.

Gallo never again heard of, nor was he questioned about, the man he shot that day.

*"Settling Down"*

At the time of the interview, Gallo had just turned 17 and was finishing his final year at the vocational high school. He was happy to be at the school and believed that if he was not there he would still be "getting into trouble, guaranteed." It seemed this was so because at the vocational school he didn't get in trouble for the same things that would get him in trouble at "regular school," like taking cigarette breaks and being "independent." In addition, he was going to graduate:

> A: When I got in ninth grade, from there I just went up taking my aptitude tests and things like that, and I did well. So I [started] liking school a lot more. Because, you know, I get my thing done, I do what I do, you know. I'm graduating at the age of 17 years old, which is good. A lot of my friends don't even have their diploma and they're 18, you know. I'm getting mine at 17, which is good.

The only criminal activity in which he had been involved in the recent past was minor vandalism (breaking a light in a parking lot) while "partying" and playing frisbee with his friends.

> Q: So did you do it on purpose?
> A: Yeah. We did it on purpose because we were fucking out. We got drunk, then, you know . . . like, you know, we just were fooling around yesterday and got rowdy so we busted it right.

Four months prior to the interview, Gallo had moved back into his mother's house. Although his father "liked having him there" with him, he couldn't stay because the neighbors complained about his loud music and parties, and the landlord said he had to move.

For the first three months after he moved back to his mother's, Gallo began to use amphetamines more frequently—daily, in fact—rather than occasionally. He explained that this increased use was a product of the more active life-style that accompanies the business of selling drugs.

> A: 'Cause, uh, I was doing a lot more activity. You know, getting into a lot more things. Going around and selling dope and shit. Running around to the west side and the east side, and all that bullshit. Also while I was riding my bike I was doing speed.

During this time, Gallo reported taking an amphetamine five times a day for three months. One month prior to the interview, he decided to control the frequency and amount of his amphetamine use. This decision was based on advice from his brother:

*Q:* . . . and you really made a serious decision that you thought you were doing too much or what?
*A:* Yeah, because my skin was starting to turn yellow and, you know, my brother was always warning me about that, your skin is starting to turn yellow. You're doing too much . . . I don't use it that much now. I quit using it, 'cause after a while, if you use it too much, your skin will start turning yellow and shit and you can die.

Dealing, for Gallo, had been reduced to selling, mostly to friends. In the days prior to the interview he sold drugs five times, all to friends. Other than this type of selling, his activity had taken the form of acting as a go-between—finding buyers for or providers of drugs. He was often paid for this service in drugs, but sometimes in cash. He no longer dealt in the same way he had before because he saw it as too risky:

*Q:* Why did you stop?
*A:* I was dealing. Like black people in the neighborhood. I didn't want them guys to know so I stopped and then I cut off and on so they wouldn't really know. They didn't know what time I was dealing or anything, so they couldn't rip me off. 'Cause, you know, when around my fucking neighborhood they rob your fucking house. They find out you got reefer.

His selling was also limited to certain people and certain drugs. (One gets the sense that this is why he called it *selling* rather than *dealing*.) These limitations were also due to perceived risks:

*Q:* Uh, do you sell to younger kids?
*A:* My little brother.
*Q:* Dwayne? Is he the youngest?
*A:* Yup, he's about the youngest, I, nope he's not the youngest in my family, but he's the youngest one I sold it to. [Dwayne was 12.]
*Q:* Would you sell to someone younger if they came around?
*A:* No.
*Q:* Really?
*A:* No, because I don't want their momma coming back and, you know, yelling at me. I bought it from so and so. Yeah.

He would not sell and never dealt PCP or Quaaludes, and he now avoided selling amphetamines:

*Q:* Did you ever buy it for other people, deal?

*A:* No, I never got into angel dust except for that one time . . . not that many people getting into it 'cause if you get busted with angel dust you'd be in trouble. It's just like cocaine or heroin.

*Q:* Worse than reefer?

*A:* Yeah, you'd be up shit creek without a paddle.

*Q:* . . . Quaaludes?

*A:* No, no never got into dealing with them 'cause they're, I tell you, you'll go to jail easily.

*Q:* . . . speed?

*A:* . . . you can go up for seven years. . . .

As noted earlier, after a period of regular and frequent use of amphetamines, Gallo had decided to cut down. In the thirty days prior to the interview he had had three "hits" of amphetamines, all of which were taken on a single occasion at a brother's house.

Gallo now bought beer, wine, and cannabis for himself and had these for other youths. He typically consumed alcohol, mostly beer and wine, over the weekend, starting with Friday night. He reported being high on alcohol for at least fourteen or fifteen days of the thirty days preceding his interview. Although he said he wasn't "into" drinking, parties were occasions for increased and indiscriminate alcohol use.

*A:* . . . I don't really like drinking that much even though I'm 17 now. You know, I just drink maybe three or four beers on the weekend. Sometimes I'll drink a lot when we have parties you know. I paid money for the beer, you know, I'm going to drink my share, you know . . . but I don't drink that much. If it was up to me to buy it all the time I wouldn't buy it. I'd buy maybe a six pack a week . . . 'cause whatever I drank, but I drink a lot because when I got to parties and things I just drink . . . forget it. I get drunk, fall down and go boom. All kinds of little things. We get alcohol.

He was trying to decrease his cigarette smoking because he wanted to join the military and "you need good lungs for that." That sort of concern does not deter him, however, from smoking marijuana.

*Q:* . . . Don't you think reefer does the same things to your lungs?

*A:* Not really. People have lung cancer and shit, they prescribe reefer for them.

Gallo had great faith in marijuana. In fact, according to Gallo, cannabis played an important and ritualized role in his everyday life. This is evidenced in his description of his typical day:

*A:* . . . An average day? . . . Get up early in the morning and go to school. Start smoking on the way to school. We get up early in the morning me and Barry and smoke a joint . . . and then bring three joints to school. Smoke them and then come home and get a couple joints to smoke them. Then we hang around all day long and just get reefer and beer and shit. Go out and play, and whatever, after we get stoned. You know, just like that.

When asked to go through his day hour by hour, his day was recorded as follows:

| | |
|---|---|
| 6:00– 7:00 | gets up—1 joint preshower |
| | 1 joint postshower |
| 7:30– 7:45 | before leaving house—1 joint |
| 7:55– 8:30 | meets Barry—2 joints on way to school with Barry |
| 8:30– 9:10 | first period |
| 9:10– 9.20 | break—1 joint with Barry |
| 9:20–10:00 | second period |
| 10:00–10:10 | break—1 joint with Barry |
| 10:10–10:30 | third period |
| 10:30–10:45 | break—1 joint with Barry |
| 10:45–11:45 | lunch—3 or 4 joints with Barry |
| 11:45–12:12 | fourth period |
| 12:15–12:30 | 2 joints on way home with Barry (Barry to work) |
| 1:00 | home—usually alone in room—2 or 3 joints |
| 2:30 | T.J. comes over—2 or 3 joints |
| 3:30 | Woody comes over (T.J. leaves)—2 or 3 joints with Woody |
| 5:00 | J.J. comes over—6 or 7 joints with Woody and J.J. |
| 5:30– 6:00 | dinner—usually at brother Mike's—2 or 3 joints with hash with brother |
| 6:30 | Barry comes home from work—5 or 6 joints each |
| 8:00– 9:00 | Woody/other friends come over—reefer and beer depending on money |
| 10/11/12:00 | mother kicks friends out, "passes out in bed" |

Although much of Gallo's marijuana smoking was with friends, he did not wait for his friends in order to engage in the ritual.

*Q:* You don't like to smoke by yourself?
*A:* No, not really but, you know, if I want to get high, shit I'm going to get high, fuck that.

Drugs and drug use were an important part of his identity—that of a "drug-using hippie." He prided himself on knowing much about the pharmacological aspects of various drugs and often cited his many years of experience with drug use. He also took pride in the fact that he had tried just about every drug, except for heroin, and stated that he "always likes experimenting." Gallo did not see himself as an "addict," however. He separated himself from that category of people who get "hooked" or lose control when they use drugs.

Although his drug use was engaged in for its effects, it did not affect his day-to-day responsibilities and obligations, such as school, work, and management of his money.

> *A:* . . . . when there was work to be done, we would do it, you know, even though we were stoned we did our work and we did it right. . . .
> *Q:* Well, how are you responsible for your money?
> *A:* 'Cause I know how to spend it and things like that. You know, if I have to pay a bill or something, I won't go out and spend that money on drugs. I'll pay my bill with that money. I'll put it away. That's responsible. . . .

He said, in relation to a friend who owed him money, that using drugs should not make one shirk one's responsibilities: "I don't consider going out and getting stoned more important."

In the context of talking about using cocaine:

> *Q:* Would you do it again?
> *A:* No.
> *Q:* How come?
> *A:* I only try. I always do at least once, twice, three times. And then I don't really get into it after that. Marijuana is my favorite, then hash. The rest of it, you know, I'll do once in a while. Like speed, you know, I used to do that regularly. It gets to you after a while. If you did all this stuff, you know, you'd realize. I don't want to be a burnout, you know, before my time. 'Cause after you do cocaine and that shit, that burns out some of your brain cells. If you do too much of it, you will just be zap. A fried one. I have friends who have fried their brain. And all they do is, duhh! Get out of here you fucking burnout. It's just what they are is fucking burnouts.
> *Q:* What are they doing there?
> *A:* Nothing. Sitting at home, sitting on their ass, looking at a wall . . . most of them live with their parents. Bunch of burnouts. There's a couple of them that are in group homes. It's 'cause of that, they got theirselves too fried. They got into it too much. That's why I take it easy. Maybe, maybe three or four years from now I'll get back into it, you know, doing once or twice again, but I won't do it, you know, after, after, acid again, things like that.

He referred to himself as an "experimenter," and a knowledgeable one at that. This knowledge was, for the most part, a product of his brothers' mentorship and his own experience. "I've been a long-haired hippie and getting stoned since I was four years old."

> *Q:* You never, it sounds like you've never been scared to try any new drug.
> *A:* No, 'cause my brothers always warn me how much to take and not, you know, things like that. You know I was never dumb about doing things. I was always warned and I always took that warning. I never, you know, said, "Oh fuck

them, they don't know what they're talking about." I always, you know, went through their standards 'cause, you know, they all tried them theirselves, too, you know. They know what they are. They know what they do and shit like that. And I just took their advice. . . . I know, you know, I see a few people with the shit. I don't know them, but I see them. And I don't want to know them.

Q: Why do you feel that way?
A: 'Cause that's just going too far. That's going too far. I could see, you know, if you could do it without getting hooked on it. But I don't want to get hooked on it. When they get hooked on it they start shaking and shit, if they ain't got it. Go out and rip off their own mother and shit. To get money to buy it. I don't even know them. I don't want them coming over to my house ripping me off. . . .
Q: How come [you didn't do it again]?
A: 'Cause, I mean, that fries too much. Acid's one of the deadliest things there is. See I know just when to do it, and when not to do it. My brother is the same way. He won't do acid three times in one year. Even though, you know, that, it fries. Fries you a lot.

Although he was an experimenter, Gallo's *regular use* was limited to particular drugs. In the context of a discussion of amphetamines and Quaaludes:

A: . . . I don't get into drugs.
Q: Never? You've never done them?
A: Yeah, I've done them. I've tried them. I don't get into it though. I get into reefer and beer. Most of the time I don't drink beer. I drink Gallo.

He expressed a commitment to marijuana and alcohol that was not matched in terms of other forms of delinquency:

Q: When you're on probation aren't you supposed to quit [using drugs]?
A: Yeah, I'm supposed to. Yeah, but what I'm supposed to do and what I do is two different things.
Q: You're just, is that partly why you're careful about getting caught? Getting involved in harder drugs and stuff?
A: That's partly why I don't do that much shit crime now. That's why you don't hear nothing over 16.

Q: What kind of person are you?
A: Just an average person. You know. I don't like doing things that's against the law; partying you know that's against the law, but I do it anyway. But I don't, you know, don't get into too much trouble. I didn't get caught . . . a lot or get too rowdy. I only got caught two times by the law, well three times. Once for sleeping in the backseat of a car, once for stealing barricades, and

once for that fight. And that was it. That's all I've been in trouble with the law, but that sleeping in the car and the barricade didn't even go on my record . . . that was the only big hassle, getting in the fight with the cops. After that, like I did used to rob houses. I got three or four when I was younger. Never got caught. After that I said, you know, I didn't say, "Oh I'll never get caught." . . . And that's the way it was, you know. Did it two or three times if I didn't get caught I would quit doing it. Like, I robbed the dude down the street two times. I just quit, you know, plain and simple stop. Said, "Forget it, there's no sense in getting arrested over it." Like a friend of mine, he robbed about twenty-six houses and got busted . . . he got busted. I got three houses and I don't do no more.

## Crime and Drug Relationships

The sequence of Gallo's initiation into and use of cigarettes, alcohol, and drugs was unusual. Cigarettes and alcohol, respectively, typically precede use of cannabis and noncannabis drugs (also respectively), but Gallo began with marijuana and later included cigarettes, alcohol, and other drug use. He was not introduced to cigarettes and alcohol by peers but, rather, by older brothers who became his "peers" in drug use until his friendship groups were initiated (as he puts it, "caught up with him") into alcohol and drug use.

Unlike most youths (Elliott and Huizinga, 1984; Huizinga, 1986), Gallo began using alcohol and drugs before his initiation into criminal acivities (at age 14). Moreover, he ceased criminal activity, with the exception of drug selling and minor property damage, when he turned 16. Also, unlike his drug use, his criminal activity was not directly mentored by his brothers, although he engaged in some criminal activities for his brothers or in their name. He did, however, cite his brothers as mentors in the ways of the law.

Gallo's criminal involvement was serious, not so much in terms of frequency as in terms of the *types* of crimes he reported. Violent crimes, such as assault (twice, with one conviction), arson, and assault with a weapon, were among the most serious Gallo reported. In addition, he reported two breaking-and-entering incidents (one of which included theft of a vehicle and resale of stolen goods), two petty thefts, one minor property damage, some vague references to shoplifting and joyriding incidents, and extensive involvement in drug dealing.

Similar to his patterns of drug use (commitment to marijuana and experimentation with other drugs) was his extensive involvement in one type of crime (drug selling) and his dabbling in other types of offenses. As with drugs, Gallo committed certain crimes once or twice but indicated that he would never do them again. Also, similar to his talk of drug use is the role he assumed in terms of crime—again, he was the expert. Indicative of this is the pattern of "knowing of" an instance of every crime he was questioned about in the interview, although he himself had never been involved in most of those crimes. This is also indicative of his efforts to create and sustain his "cool" image.

In Gallo's case, the role of drugs and alcohol in his criminal activity varied from no role, to one involving possession or acquisition, to a significant role as disinhibitor. Drugs, however, were typically not the overriding or single factor in Gallo's criminal activities. In two burglary events, direct acquisition of marijuana was the goal; in petty thefts and resale of stolen goods, money was sought; in another breaking-and-entering incident he took food. Thus, theft as consumption is apparent in Gallo's case, and drugs are one of the many consumer goods he values and seeks out. Drugs also played a role in violent acts, because they were highly valued goods requiring swift and serious protection.

In terms of drugs playing a role as disinhibitors, Gallo stated that his recent vandalism was a form of alcohol-induced rowdiness. A planned arson for revenge was made "easier" by taking a drug for its disinhibiting effects.

Gallo also admitted that drugs could disinhibit him by feeding the fire of an already hot temper—yet his temper alone accounted for all the violent acts (except the arson) that he reported. In fact, he reported a belief in disinhibition for himself and others. Because he knew he could be disinhibited, he purposely avoided using drugs in certain situations or avoided certain situations when he was under the influence of drugs. He believed in such effects, then, and that drugs could play a definite role in crime because of those effects, but he argued (and gave support for) the fact that this was not the case for him.

Why? Because he was "cool," and not only do cool people not have to try to be cool, they are also in control of their drug use, their drug use is not in control of them. This was Gallo's main philosophy of drug use (and life, for that matter) and the reason he used or didn't use various drugs. According to Gallo, "different people do drugs for different reasons." Many people do drugs to be "cool," to be part of the crowd, because others do it, or because someone who is "cool" (like Gallo) does it. Others do drugs for the effects that they induce.

Part of knowing what you are doing in terms of drug use is not to allow drugs to affect you in "negative" ways. That is, to know enough *not* to use those drugs that disinhibit you at the *wrong* time—essentially, to be in control, to handle it, to use drugs and alcohol at the "right" time—to party, be rowdy, socialize.

Because of Gallo's interest in control, which was necessary to maintaining his image, drugs were given a role in events or situations when that role was an effectual one. Like everything else he did, he used drugs for effect, but the "effect" was on two levels. On one level, drug use had to do with the effect he sought to create, that was his image; on the other level, he used drugs for the effect they had on him. For example, he said he uses drugs in order to "do" and "get into" things. Drugs may be consumed to induce rowdiness for a concert, courage for an act, or productivity in school. Drugs also helped him shut out things and calm his emotions. Above all, he took drugs because it was part of having a good time with friends.

Q: . . . Why do you take drugs?
A: Well, I live with my momma. And, you know, that's based on, you know, my mother. She bitches a lot and shit. And I don't want to hear it. So I'll just go

down on my bed and just crank up the tunes and ignore her. Want to get away from her. But, you know, I do all kinds of different stuff for different reasons. Like when I go to concerts and shit, I'll get stoned at a concert, 'cause, you know, it gets you in a rowdy mood, you know. I get up there and jump around and shit. . . .

My temper. That's one thing I cannot control. Like, uh, my mother got me pissed that one time when my dog got taken away and I find out she's the one that called the ASPCA, and shit, and made up that bullshit about pink eye, and uh, I just went off the wall and shot her stereo out the window. Shot her couch out the window because, you know, I asked her, said do you love this stereo? And then she said, yeah, yeah, and I said I love my dog, too, and how about this. I threw it out the windows. You know I just went totally berserk. Instead of throwing everything, boy, I just didn't care if it was mine or hers or what. And then I went out in the back, to the shed, we got back there, and I started kicking the walls down. And then a couple of my buddies said all right, all right, calm down, let's go smoke a couple bowls. You know, got me stoned.

*Q:* But usually when you want to smoke reefer and get high and stuff, you just want to get together with friends and . . . ?

*A:* Yeah, we just have a good time. That's what a good time is. What is life. That's the way we feel about it. What is life. You ought to in life have a good time, 'cause you can die tomorrow. And if you didn't have a good time, today you know, it wouldn't be good. But if you had a good time today and died tomorrow, wheee!

According to Gallo, drugs do have an effect on people. That, in fact, was why he used drugs. The effects, however, vary in terms of individual physical and psychological reactions to each drug. Different effects are sought for different situations. Thus, knowing what drug to use (and how to use it) to create the best or avoid the worst personal effect for a particular situation is of utmost importance and is how one maintains control.

*Q:* When you do speed could you keep doing [what] you were supposed to do? In school and everything?

*A:* Yeah. Yeah, no, not really. 'Cause when you sit down in school and you don't feel like sitting down, you feel like getting up and doing this and that and the other thing. So you really can't get into schoolwork. . . .

*A:* . . . No, each time I did it was only about, well, that was one time I did it. That was the most I did it. But the other times I only did two lines [of cocaine] you know. I wanted to get off, but not, you know, flying and skying and shit . . . acting like a birdy.

Another way of maintaining control is to avoid universal, rather than situational, effects such as "burning out" or becoming "addicted." For Gallo, then, drugs could safely continue to be a part of life and thus of his image. Crime, however, was not profitable enough. Therefore, he purposely avoided circumstances in which drugs could play a role in criminal involvement or, if he was involved, increase the risk of getting caught, unless he desired that sort of effect. He cited actual circumstances and theory.

*Q:* How about this time, when you broke into that guy's house [were you high or drunk]?

*A:* No. . . . No. I wanted to have a clear head.

*Q:* And when you took the van?

*A:* Yeah, I wanted to have a clear head. 'Cause that way you don't get really caught. If you're stoned and shit, you might get, get really paranoid.

*Q:* And what would happen?

*A:* You might get caught. If you get paranoid and nervous and shit. You start talking slower, stuttering and shit, people understand, you know, "Oh, I see, he's a suspicious character." And you always gotta have a clear head when you plan something like that. You gotta have a clear head. You do. 'Cause you gotta know what you're doing. If you've stolen shit, sometimes you don't know what the hell you're doing and you get in trouble. . . .

*Q:* Do you think they're [drugs and crime] related? If you weren't into drugs and stuff, you might not have done that?

*A:* No, most of my fight, most of my fights was never dealing with drugs. It was always when somebody messed with me and I had a bad temper, that's all it is. I got a very bad temper. And, uh, that's most of my fights. If I'm stoned, it's even worse, you know, that type of thing, but . . . my temper gets faster, you know, it's faster. 'Cause you fuck with me when I'm stoned, and I'm liable to kill you or something. You know I'm a little bit crazier when I don't have a clear head, you know. I'll just beat the shit out of you if I ain't got a clear head. If I'm stoned, I'll shoot you in a minute. You know, that' why I usually try not to carry my gun when I'm stoned. But if you fuck with me when I'm stoned, I'll shoot you.

Gallo's awareness of what situations were to be avoided and what was at stake was, again, rooted in knowledge that he attributed to a mentoring relationship with his brothers.

*A:* Yeah, I try to be careful as much as I can. 'Cause, you know, I know that I can go to jail, and I know this and that and the other thing. 'Cause, hey, they changed the law. You go to jail at 16, but you can go to jail at 14, too. You know, that type of thing. And I know all that. And I know about the law. 'Cause, you know, 'cause my brother's one. You know, he teaches me a lot. My brothers teach me a lot about what to do and what not to do. And when to have a clear head and when not to have a clear head. And that type of situation. . . . Like that fire, I wanted to do it, Just, I didn't want to do it with a clear head. I wanted to do it stoned . . . I wanted to be stoned when I did it.

Gallo viewed his drug use as legitimate. It helped him to be productive, could act as a stimulant to violence that he deemed necessary, or in other situations could soothe his temper. His knowledge of which drugs had which effect on him under various circumstances enabled him to be in control and was what made his drug use legitimate. Nevertheless, he could see the negative effects of drugs on others:

*A:* And that's the way it is around my neighborhood. They want to be one of the crowd. Like all the black dudes. They don't go home and party reefer by theirselves. They go out with friends and shit and party and get drunk and rowdy. And get in trouble. You know, all my friends, us, once in a while we'll get rowdy. But we don't get rowdy all the time, like black dudes do and shit. Like that light bulb, that fire and shit. You know, that's once in a while, that's once in a great while.

For Gallo, then, drugs contributed to his cool image but did not "make" his image, as they did for the youths who did drugs "just to be cool," nor were drugs allowed to get in the way of his image.

*A:* We used to hang out with a bunch of Puerto Ricans too, on the west side. And they used to get in all kinds of trouble. I used to just walk away. Say, hey dudes . . . they'd look for trouble. 'Cause they were stoned and shit. They didn't care. You know, they would just go out. Hey man, wanna fight? Cut you ass all up. And I'd just say, hey, you know, that's uncool. Later. And that's the way it was with me. If it was uncool I didn't like. . . .

For Gallo, crime had too much potential for tarnishing his image. One would be stupid to violate the law (in such a way that one could get caught) after the age of 16. It simply wasn't worth it. Foolish drug use could lead to involvement in criminal acts with negative consequences. Gallo controlled (that is, limited the frequency of simple use) his use of those drugs that he believed played a role in criminal involvement.

*A:* 'Cause when you're a teenager you're rowdy. Nowadays you aren't rowdy. You know you just want to settle down because you can go to jail now. Your boy can put you into a detention home or bullshit. But you can go to jail now. Jail ain't no place to go.
*Q:* So you think you're more likely to get caught now?
*A:* Yeah, yeah, maybe, you never know when you're going to get caught. Wondering why I did it then, you know, I thought about it. Getting caught. But

I didn't really give a fuck. Now, you know, I think about it and I do give a fuck. I don't do it. That's called craziness.

*Q:* . . . And we're interested in how kids who avoid crime do that. . . .

*A:* Think about jail.

Knowledge of criminal activities and of the law (and the ability to act as expert) was more a part of the Gallo image than actual *participation* in crime. Similarly, the commitment to being "a stoned little hippie" ("partying" talk, experimentation, using drugs for the "right" reasons, being knowledgeable about drugs from experience, and so on) seemed to be more the story of Gallo than his commitment to drug use in and of itself.

*The Future*

Gallo's level of involvement in drug use and criminal activity at the time of his interview carried through to his vision of his future. He included drug use as a continued part of his everyday life. Crime, however, was not included.

As with everything else, Gallo was sure of his future. He planned to enlist in the military, where he would continue vocational training in automobile mechanics. After he served his time in the military, he hoped to own his own automobile repair business. This appealed to him because he could be his own boss and give rather than take orders, "cause I don't like people telling me what to do." Such a business would be fruitful and would enable him to own his own house and car, to meet his responsibilities with no trouble, and to maintain a "partying" life-style.

*Q:* What will your responsibilities be years from now?

*A:* Pay my bills and pay my reefer bills, you know. Drug bills, beer, you gotta pay that. But, you know, if I buy my own home I, you know, I'll have to pay taxes and things like that. And I'll just be the same way I would be in the military. I'll save my money for my taxes and my winter bills and I'll have to pay my light bill and my gas bill every week, you know. I mean every month. And that's about it. And maybe all the other money I'll just spend on dope and shit. I'll have a lot of parties and food. You gotta have food. It's necessary. But I don't think I'll get married until I'm at least 35.

Gallo projected ten years into the future and described what he believed would be a typical day in his life. The description was strikingly similar to his description of his typical school day, with school (thought to be too important to "skip") replaced by work—again, too important to avoid. Also parallel was the emphasis he placed on drug use as an important feature of his future typical day:

*Q:* Describe what a good day would be like ten years from now?

*A:* Skipping work and staying home and getting stoned out of my mind. You know, something like that would be a fantasy but, like, I don't like skipping work, you know, because it all depends, you know. To me it's easy. To other people who don't know what it is it's hard. To me I like it. I love it, you know, and I like building and having fun and have race cars and things like that. And that's what will be my average day you know. Going out and riding in my car and banging it up a little bit and coming home and fixing it and doing, you know, and getting stoned while I'm doing it. Just, I'm an average person. I like doing what I do. Getting stoned and working on cars. That's my life.

## Discussion

The case study of Kevin, a 20-year-old male, focused principally on his reason for changing from a life-style of involvement in drugs and criminal activities to a life-style of noninvolvement. The case study of Gallo, a 17-year-old male, focused on his initiation and continued involvement in drug use and his explanations for his current noninvolvement in criminal activities.

Kevin and Gallo are similar in the sense that they both have quite set and patterned images and presentations of themselves. They have their stories "down." Gallo's story is of a "cool," "drug-using hippie" who is completely in control of his life and his activities. Kevin's is a story of the old Kevin—in his own words, "a delinquent . . . I wasn't in control . . . 'cause drugs had taken me over and my values were all money and drugs, and I was just obsessed with that . . . I let other people do my thinking for me" —and the new Kevin, who was in control of his life and was no longer a follower. Kevin spent most of his interview comparing those two selves, using a vocabulary that had been provided to him by Rehab House.

For both youths, the resources for creating/constructing and sustaining their images were available. Gallo's resources were his brothers and the younger youths he mentored. For Kevin, the drug rehabilitation program provided him with the resources for abandoning his old image and constructing a new one— that of a reformed, responsible, *ex*–drug user, *ex*-criminal.

In Kevin's accounts of how he became involved with drugs and criminal activities, he placed the responsibility for the initiation of those activities *outside* himself. When discussing things he now viewed as negative, he blamed others: his cousins influenced him in his first criminal activity, fire-setting; his classmates ("peer pressure") influenced him to get high; his stepfather caused him to dislike going home, the alternative being to "get in trouble or get high." Similarly, the reasons for his not remaining in the first drug treatment program (Drug Freedom) seemed to him to be external: *they* phased him out when "[he] knew [he] wasn't ready to leave." His accounts of the causes of his drug/ crime activity are consistent with much of the literature, which presents and documents the position that external factors (groups, structures) are primarily responsible for the initiation and sustaining of drug use and delinquent activities (for example, Brown, 1982; Hirschi, 1969; Levine and Kozak, 1979; Weis and Sederstrom, 1981).

In contrast, although Kevin mentioned a confluence of factors—especially legal pressure, detention, and treatment exposures—his change to a life of noninvolvement, a good and positive occurrence, was an event for which he claimed most of the responsibility for himself (although he did grant that his fiancée was his "motivation" or "inspiration" and that "other people helped me look at it"): "I used to just value money, material things, I didn't even care about myself"; "I just got sick of it [his situation] . . . I've started listening . . . I don't follow anybody now. . . ."

For Gallo, on the other hand, his initiation into delinquent activities, his continued use of drugs, and his change from involvement to noninvolvement in criminal activities are all attributed to an inner locus of control. His brothers showed him how and invited him to partake in cigarettes, alcohol, and drugs, but it was he who made the choice to be initiated.

At those times when he felt things were "forced" on him, Gallo described the situation as unpleasant and stated that he didn't continue the activity for that reason (for example, his initiation to hard liquor). When he described his criminal activities (with the exception of those occasions when he was disinhibited by drugs/alcohol), he saw them as situations in which he was in control and chose to do things, although he now viewed such things as "not smart" to do and suggested that he and his friends were "rowdy" and "foolish" not to view such activities as joyriding and theft as risky.

Gallo continued to be involved in heavy use of cannabis drugs and alcohol, experimentation with other drugs, and drug selling. Unlike Kevin, he did not give accounts of any problems associated with those activities. For example, Gallo continued to do his schoolwork and did well in school even though (in his opinion, *because*) he used marijuana daily and was typically "high" during school hours. Kevin, however, cited drugs as detrimental to his schoolwork and as responsible for his poor performance and subsequent dropping out.

Gallo controlled his drug use so as not to let it affect his actions unless he wanted it to do so. Kevin, by contrast, saw others as responsible for his drug use and then saw drugs as responsible for his other negative and delinquent activities.

Kevin's case history includes many features well known in the drug and alcohol rehabilitation field. Bringing about a change from very heavy drug use and delinquency to one of noninvolvement is neither simple nor easily achieved. Such changes are complex and involve many factors that interact synergistically.

Many of the factors in Kevin's life—poor relationship with father; influence of drug-using, delinquent friends; poor school performance—persisted through his teenage years and contributed to relapses. His continued affection for his mother and a new relationship with a girlfriend, however, provided connections to the conventional world and reasons for his positive changes. Nevertheless, external pressures through his contacts with the criminal justice system repeatedly placed him in programs designed to control his criminality and prevented him from being at liberty. He also "bottomed out" and was hospitalized after overdosing on alcohol and pills. Both Drug Freeedom and Rehab House, as residential programs, almost certainly had treatment practices (Kevin did not describe them) by which to confront drug abusers like Kevin about their denials and rationalizations. Both almost certainly provided a set of explanations for Kevin's "negative" behavior as well as positive and alternative values, which Kevin learned, apparently internalized, and now articulated clearly. Although Kevin did not "succeed" in each treatment effort, he did absorb something from each contact.

Kevin made a clear choice to change his life. This choice involved changing his values, his reference groups, and the nature of his family interaction. He now emphasized subjective, internalized decisions and controls designed to avoid "old feelings" and to support new feelings, new relationships with others, and more conventional behaviors.

Gallo's decisions to continue his drug use and discontinue his criminal activities were largely subjective as well (there were some structural features or components, such as his brothers' mentoring and his audience). Thus, we might conclude that for these two youths, the *processes* of moving away from versus staying involved in delinquent activities are essentially the same. For both, the processes involved legitimizing one's activities and delegitimizing opposing ones. For both, they also involved having a ready vocabulary and audience for doing so.

These case studies can also be interpreted in terms of adolescent developmental processes. The literature in this area suggests that the processes Kevin and Gallo described (particularly in terms of drug use) involved needs that are part and parcel of the adolescent stage of development. Brunswick (1980:450) cites adolescent needs for "growth in competency and responsibility" as well as the need for autonomy and control (Brunswick, 1985; Brunswick and Merzel, 1986). Adolescent behavior such as drug use can then be interpreted as the "acquisition of a behavior to meet these expanding needs" (Brunswick, 1980:450).

In addition, these case studies show that the complexities of family structure, parental relationships, peer interactions and changes, legal structure, and deterrence considerations, among others, have important and continuing impacts on the lives of specific individuals. Even the most seriously involved youths make both gradual and rapid changes, sometimes planned and sometimes not, in the types and frequency of crimes committed or drugs used. No single factor appears critical or dominant in bringing about such changes in drug use and delinquency (see Jessor and Jessor, 1977; Kandel, 1978).

## Notes

1. After ingesting a mixture of "yellow jackets," a quart of Southern Comfort, and other alcohol, Kevin found himself in the hospital. He referred to this experience as "overdosing." Kevin had never used heroin or methadone, drugs typically connected with overdosing. He used and dealt cocaine from age 15 to the time he entered Rehab House.

2. Talking about the "ghetto" is significant for Gallo, who was explicitly prejudiced against blacks. His somewhat negative description of his neighborhood had a lot to do with the fact that his house was located near a low-income housing project, where many Yule City blacks lived. Gallo saw blacks as inferior and spoke about them as a group in terms of all activities and in the same patronizing way he spoke about individuals he believed were inferior to him in various aspects and situations of life.

3. Physical fighting with and among family members was common in Gallo's descriptions of his familial context. Violence was also a typical way in which Gallo's family dealt with conflict both within and outside the family.

4. Gallo reported having snorted cocaine six times since then: three times at parties and three times with friends (for one of whom he got the cocaine). He did not clearly state *when* those events took place.

5. Recall the excerpt from the field notes at the beginning of this chapter. Gallo was described in the context of walking his "mean," "ferocious" dog, which "attacks on command." As we have suggested, everything Gallo did was studied and played for effect. This included his dog. He didn't just have a dog—he had a "Dobie" (Doberman), prized for being ferocious and mean. Yet Gallo was probably as vulnerable about his dog as he was about anything on which we have data. This vulnerability was quite apparent in his description of this episode and is therefore important to note.

# 10
# Experimentation versus Commitment

*With Margret Ksander and Bruce Berg*

One common assumption that provides a rationale for delinquency intervention policies is that youths who are involved in habitual (routine or addictive) drug use are thereby forced into a life of chronic crime. This assumption not only ties routine drug use to criminal activity but, further, relies on indicators of such drug involvement as predictors of criminal activity. Empirical grounds for this assumption include statistical associations like those of Elliott and Huizinga (1984), which demonstrate that youths responsible for the bulk of serious crime are characterized by high levels of involvement in alcohol and drug use. Theoretically, in forming this assumption, there is a suggestion of a sequential model of alcohol and drug involvement (see Adler and Kandel, 1981; Kandel, 1976a, 1976b; Robins and Wish, 1977) that progresses toward use of "dangerous" and/or illegal substances.

Of particular relevance to the question of a drug–crime link are findings (Goode, 1972; Johnson, 1973, 1980) that suggest that the value of the sequential model of substance use lies less in its ability to predict actual drug use than in its indication of involvement in various subcultures and, perhaps, a parallel recreational delinquent life-style (see also Buffalo and Rogers, 1971; Haskell and Yablonsky, 1974; Short and Strodtbeck, 1965). The success of this sequential model, as Becker's (1963) work suggests, lies in its recognition that patterns of behavior develop in orderly social sequence wherein selective recruitment, interaction, and socialization at each stage (not naturally existing or pharmacologically produced predispositions) draw some individuals further along in the sequence or precipitate alternative activities (such as cessation or regression) for others.

Becker (1963), in his classic study of movement into deviant life-styles, argues that behavior that can be called "committed" occurs at a point in the sequence when, because of past actions or institutional routines, an individual finds that he or she must adhere to certain lines of behavior or risk jeopardizing other valued activities. Intermediate processes involved in the sequential progress toward such commitment, Becker suggests, include "entangling alliances," "special circumstances," a "taste for something known and experienced" (motive), and—significantly—being caught and labeled. If, as has been suggested both statistically and theoretically, a relationship exists between involvement in habitual or routine drug/alcohol use and chronic criminal activity, then we "must deal with a sequence of steps, of changes in the individual's behavior and perspectives, in order to understand the phenomenon" (Becker, 1963:23). That is, we need to investigate whether, when, and how the sequential process of becoming "committed" to alcohol and drug use and, relatedly, to a subcultural life-style "comes to" involve concomitantly delinquent and/or criminal activity (Empey, 1978; Empey and Lubeck, 1968; Jensen and Rojek, 1980).

In this chapter we examine the experiences of adolescents selected from our sample for their variable involvement in the sequential process of substance use: those who may be considered "committed" and those who progressed no further than an initial, experimental involvement. We examine their accounts of involvement in these behaviors, focusing on the natural history of their substance use and their involvement in delinquent and criminal acts. Of particular interest are (1) how the drug use experiences of subjects characterize their different stages of substance involvement and (2) how crime is or is not related to those experiences.

To identify youths at varying stages of involvement with alcohol, drugs, and related criminal or delinquent behavior, we categorized the total population of subjects, described in chapter 2, within a hierarchical typology based on their reports of the extent and frequency of their participation in each of the focal behaviors. For each focal behavior we identified three stages of involvement: (1) *initiation–experimental*—occurred only once or twice (ever); (2) *casual*—occurred monthly or less frequently; and (3) *routine* ("committed")— occurred weekly, several times per week, or daily. These definitions, though based on subjects' reports, must be understood as analytic rather than subjective categorizations.[1]

Initially, we categorized each subject separately for each of the three focal behaviors based on the highest level of involvement reported in his or her interview.[2] As suggested earlier, each general behavior category contains a wide range of types of specific substances or activities, not all of which are necessarily characteristic or even typical of each subject. When a subject reported involvement in the behavior only occasionally—at what were defined as "special occasions" (such as family celebrations, parties with friends, or dates)—those instances were categorized separately.

Beyond this initial categorization, we identified those subjects who displayed patterns of initiation–experimentation or committed involvement across focal behaviors. That is, we isolated those subjects whose involvement in drug use and in crime had not progressed beyond an initial, experimental stage and those whose involvement in both drug use and crime displayed a committed (routine or habitual) involvement. After identifying these subjects, we identifed other combinations of involvement, such as patterns of initiation–experimentation and/or commitment in: (1) alcohol and drug use but *not* crime, (2) patterns of drug use and crime but *not* alcohol, and (3) patterns of alcohol use and crime but *not* drug use.

In this chapter, we focus on two categories of subjects generated by the analytic procedures just specified, namely those displaying patterns of initiation–experimentation with drug use and those displaying commitment across all of the focal behaviors. These subjects facilitate an investigation of the two research issues posed earlier by providing contrasting sets of experiences with the focal behaviors. Such subjects may be considered to be characteristically representative of each of the stages of involvement in the constellation of behaviors of interest.[3]

Six subjects fit the analytic definition of "initiation–experimentation," and 15 met the "committed" criteria.[4] Of the 6 initiators–experimenters, 3 were from the random sample, 2 from the purposive sample, and one from the detained sample. Of the 15 committed subjects, only one was found in the random sample, 13 in the purposive sample, and one in the detained sample.

## Overview

Our analysis of the substance use experiences of both "initial" and "committed" subjects suggests findings similar in some ways to those of Kandel (1976a) and Adler and Kandel (1981), proponents of the progressive sequential model. Notably, we found that entry drugs are routinely licit ones (for example, cigarettes, wine, and beer) and that use of marijuana usually precedes (in temporal sequence) the use of other illicit drugs. Among the committed youths, use of marijuana usually also precedes the misuse of some licit drugs (tranquillizers, barbiturates, and some inhalants).

Alcohol was the initial drug used. Among the initiators–experimenters, marijuana was the drug of entry for only one subject, and among the committed subjects, it was the entry drug for three. For only one subject, one of the committed group, was a drug other than alcohol or marijuana, namely Valium®, the drug of entry.

Among our committed drug users, then, we did not find clearly distinct stages (Kandel, 1976a) that lead from licit (and/or "soft") drugs progressively to illicit (and/or "harder") ones. The typical temporal sequencing of drug involvement for committed subjects was not a simple continuum from less to more "serious" drugs, characterized by less to more frequent usage thereof. Our findings suggest a more complex structuring of substance involvement through which some youths come to be involved with certain licit drugs (particularly pills and inhalants) subsequent to or simultaneously with their involvement with illicit ones (for example, acid, cocaine, opium). Moreover, as will be seen, the use of what Adler and Kandel (1981) refer to as "other illicit drugs" is—as a routine, habitual involvement—*not* characteristic of our subjects.

Our investigation suggests that the following patterns characterize committed subjects:

1. Typically, committed youths are involved with one "primary drug of commitment" (a single drug that is habitually used and with which the subject identifies him- or herself, despite his experimentation or short-term involvement with other substances). Some youths indicate a "secondary drug of commitment" (a second drug that is regularly used, though less frequently than the primary drug). The "primary drug of commitment" is, besides being routinely available and/or accessible to the subject, defined as nondangerous.

2. Also typically, committed youths are involved in a pattern of *continuous experimentation*—short-term (though often repeated) use of assorted drugs other than the primary (and/or secondary) drug of commitment. Important in their patterns of experimentation is their differentiation between "safe" and "unsafe" drugs, as suggested earlier—a perception with little relation to a substance's legality or pharmacological properties.

3. Temporal sequencing of particular kinds of drug use appears from the data to be governed by both the *accessibility* of certain drugs (that is, which drugs can be purchased easily at any given point in time) and the *availability* of certain drugs (that is, which drugs become available to the youth at no financial or personal expense).

For virtually all of our committed subjects, the primary drug of commitment was marijuana. For those who indicated a secondary drug of commitment, it was usually a licit drug, such as alcohol (most frequently beer) or cigarettes. For only two subjects did the use of an illicit drug, namely LSD, appear to occur with sufficient long-term regularity to displace either alcohol or cigarettes as the secondary drug.

Our analysis suggests, then, that among the core of committed substance users there is a continuous orientation to experiment with drug substances generally, underscored by the routine use of a single substance (typically marijuana) that is either easily purchased at any given point in time or available without much expense of money or energy. Hence, youths' "committed" involvement in the use of any particular substance appears to be governed by environmental factors, whereas their commitment to substance use, itself, involves their orientation (characterized by certain limits) to experiment with many substances. These findings suggest that the category in question is perhaps most aptly characterized as *committed–experimenters* (committed to one or two substances and willing to experiment with other drugs).

By definition, the substance use of our group of initiators–experimenters progressed no further than one or a very few experiences and, as reported earlier, their initial usage appears consistent with that suggested by the progressive sequential model (see Adler and Kandel, 1981). Subjects' initial participation in substance use was often attributed to environmental factors, such as availability and accessibility. The experience, however, was generally one to which they attached no personal identification (that is, drug use may or may not be pleasant, dangerous, and so on, but whatever it is, it is *not* what "I" do). Although they may have referred to negative sanctions and so forth, most characteristic of their accounts was the perception that drug use was "not worth" their involvement because it either had no effect or was dangerous (and potentially addicting). Typically, these initiators–experimenters made little differentiation between "safe" and "unsafe" drugs; rather, they viewed substance use rather conventionally and generically as something dangerous that they (as an individual) "do not do." Drug use might not be viewed negatively in all cases, but a "habit" or "addiction" clearly was.

Although the substance use experiences of these two categories of subjects are marked by clearly different characteristics, their patterns and accounts of criminal activities are less distinct. That is, the types of crimes and degrees of involvement in criminal or delinquent behaviors (with the exception of drug selling) were fairly randomly distributed among all the subjects examined in both categories. In fact, the subject involved in the most serious offense (armed robbery) was an initiator–experimenter. One fairly clear distinction—somewhat parallel to their distinction regarding substance use—exists between the two groups' perceptions of what constitutes "really serious" crime as opposed to activity for which one can be held seriously accountable. Neither group referred to themselves as thieves, burglars, robbers, or criminals. Next we discuss some of the details of the substance use and criminal experiences of these two categories of subjects as they are revealed within their accounts.

## Committed–Experimenters

Our routinely drug-involved subjects reported frequent and repeated short-term use (experimentation) with an assortment of drugs, as opposed to any long-term commitment to illicit drugs (with the exclusion of marijuana). Often the use of a given drug amounted to having tried that drug once. Consider the remarks of a 16-year-old male from the purposive sample. In addition to daily use of marijuana and routine (weekly) use of alcohol (chiefly beer), he also reported having used hashish, speed, cocaine, and acid. In discussing his involvement with speed and cocaine, he indicated that he had used speed heavily for a period (several weeks) and had tried cocaine only once. When asked by the interviewer whether he would try cocaine again, he responded:

*A:* No, once is enough. The only thing I do is party now [referring to marijuana smoking]. I took my fair share of speed in my time, much too much speed. So I just don't want to do it any more. *I just want to say I did it, you know?* Even though coke is expensive, it's probably the better kind of drug to do. I think it is, maybe it isn't I don't know.[a]

(Our fieldwork indicates that *speed* usually refers to caffeine pills that are sold with labels suggesting amphetamine or barbiturates.)

Or consider the remarks of an 18-year-old male from the purposive sample who also indicated multiple uses of marijuana daily; routine use of alcohol (chiefly beer and distilled alcohol); and some use of tranquillizers, barbiturates, inhalants, hashish, hallucinogens, codeine, opium, and cocaine. In the course of describing his first experience with speed, this subject illustrates a generally representative attitude toward drugs among these regular drug-using adolescents, namely a willingness to try almost any drugs:

*A:* I was at a party on Unis street, me and a friend of mine [from the house next door]. And, ah, he hands 'em to me, and I just popped 'em in my mouth. [I asked] "What was that?" He said, "Speed." I took them out of my mouth and looked at 'em and put 'em back in—figured I'd try 'em. I've tried everything else [so] why not?

Although these youths indicate a willingness—almost an eagerness—to "try anything once," they are fearful of a few drugs. All indicated a fear and avoidance of heroin. With a single exception, they also indicated a fear of PCP (angel dust). This included those who had smoked marijuana that they later learned had been laced with PCP. An example may illustrate more clearly this aversion to certain drugs. When the subject just quoted was asked why he had never tried heroin, he replied:

*A:* Heroin's too addictive. I'm sure other things are too, maybe, but from what I hear of heroin, on the news or [from] people on the street, it's extremely addictive. And, I won't get into sticking myself with a needle, personally.
*Q:* How about angel dust, how come you've never tried that?
*A:* Never had a chance, I don't think I'd do it anyway.
*Q:* How come?
*A:* I don't like the idea of smokin' it. PCP is, from what I hear, dangerous, and I don't get into dangerous shit.

Similar remarks were made by a 15-year-old female from the purposive sample whose drug involvement included regular use of marijuana (at least three times a week) and use of alcohol, hash, tranquillizers, and pseudoamphetamines (caffeine pills produced to resemble actual amphetamines). When asked if she had ever had an opportunity to try PCP or heroin, she replied:

---

[a]Note: Here and elsewhere in this chapter, emphasis has been added by the authors.

*A:* Uu-huh. I had a chance to try PCP, um, I had a chance to do coke, I had a chance to do heroin.

When the interviewer asked why she had not tried these drugs, she replied:

*A:* Oh, that stuff will kill you. . . . I don't like that other stuff. Those are hard drugs. Those compared to marijuana, marijuana is mild.
*Q:* What's the difference between hard and mild?
*A:* Well marijuana, you can't freak out on. You can't see a lady sunbathin' in the rain, or something, you know? There's no way, and with that other stuff you usually, you see lots of things that aren't there.

Despite the suggestion that these habitually involved youths experiment with an assortment of drugs, the particular substance tried on a given occasion is often determined by chance, not choice. Stated more directly, when we investigated whether initial use of a drug was intentional or spontaneous (that is, the result of situational circumstances), we found a like number of youths usually fell into each category for every drug type. When differences did appear, they were usually in the direction of a new substance being offered by friends or drug-using associates. For example, consider the remarks of an 18-year-old male from the purposive sample whose involvement with drugs included multiple uses of marijuana daily, regular weekly use of alcohol, and repeated use of LSD (and other hallucinogens), hashish, barbiturates, tranquillizers, opium, and cocaine. When asked to describe his first experience with cocaine, he replied:

*A:* I've never bought coke at all, I've just, you know, done it up. [I've gotten it] from other people.
*Q:* When was the first time you tried coke?
*A:* Uh, '76, '75 around there. . . . Uh, I think there was a couple of spoons.
*Q:* Someone had shared that with you?
*A:* Yeah. . . . I think it was someone I met at a party or something like that. He goes, "Hey, you want to check this out?" and I go "Sure," you know, "I'll check it out."

Consider also the remarks of a female, aged 13, from the purposive sample. In addition to her regular use of pot on weekends, she explained she would "get high" at least once during the week and, if it was available, would smoke more often (particularly with her friends before going to school). She also indicated that she routinely drank (mostly beer and distilled spirits) every weekend and stressed that she would usually drink until she was "drunk." She had used speed, rush (a type of inhalant often sold in drug paraphernalia stores), and PCP (unwittingly). When she was asked by the interviewer to talk about her first experience with rush, she said:

*A:* It was last month, in the wintertime, after Christmas, I think.

*Q:* How come you started using that?

*A:* Just wanted to try it. I like to try things.

*Q:* Who were you with?

*A:* Um, I don't remember— I think Susie, Debby, and Nelly. And some guys, I don't remember who. We were in Highbridge Shopping Center and they bought some from the Old World Paraphernalia. And, so they asked me if I wanted to try it. And, then I said, "Well, what does it feel like?" And they said, "Just like sniffing rubber cement." So I said, "All right." So I tried it.

*Q:* Have you used it since then?

*A:* Yeah, a couple of times in school. Nelly had a bottle, and she brought it to school.

*Q:* Was it real soon after the first time?

*A:* A couple of weeks later.

*Q:* Did you just keep right on using it all through the rest of the school year?

*A:* No. Just for those few days she brought it and then when it was all gone we didn't use it any more. . . . Yeah, that was the last time we used it.

In these two extracts, both of the youths were willing to try new drugs for two reasons—because they were interested in trying a new substance, and because it was made available to them without cost or effort. Neither, however, indicated that he or she became sufficiently committed to the drug to begin spending his or her own money to purchase it. Another interesting point, and one characteristic of these habitually involved youths, is the lack of concern with personal safety when experimenting with drugs. For instance, when the 18-year-old male quoted earlier was asked by the interviewer if he was afraid that what was being offered at that party might not be real cocaine, he replied:

*A:* It was a college fraternity party, they wouldn't do it, you know. People, you know, younger people will bullshit you a lot. But older people won't really bullshit you a lot. Especially if you're kid, you know. 'Cause, they know if they give me something and I freak out, they're going to prison, you know. It's as simple as that.

The experimental orientation of these subjects seemed to involve a degree of tolerance and even faith vis-à-vis not only the properties of the various substances, but also the drug-using environments in which they came to involve themselves. Thus, a kind of neutralization emerges that allows these habitually involved youths to try various drugs as they become available to them, a technique that reassures them that the circumstances are safe for experimentation.

## Initiators–Experimenters

Like the committed–experimenters, the group of initiators–experimenters came to drug use along routes suggested by the sequential model. These subjects, however, "progress" no further than an initial experience. Significant among the themes characterizing the drug use experiences of these subjects is a rather clear perception that, whether any actual substance use event was experienced as pleasant or unpleasant, "scary," or even inevitable, substance use in itself was not worth the risk of involvement. The "worth" of involvement is generally assessed in terms of actual psychophysiological effects and/or social consequences. Closely associated with this assessment of worth is the subjects' ultimate identification with substance use. Not only do the initiators–experimenters associate little effect and/or value with substance use, they ultimately view such activity (whether "effective" or "consequential") as something that they, individually, do not "do." These themes are closely associated within each subject's account.

Take, for example, the following statements by a 17-year-old female from our random sample as she described her early experience with marijuana. The first experience described—the first of only three experiences with this or any other drug—occurred when she was 16 years old. This followed her absolute initial substance experience, which was with wine and beer, by only a matter of months. This subject perceived some involvement with drugs as inevitable and not particularly untoward, and associated pleasant ("relaxed") feelings with their use. Ultimately, however, she assigned virtually no effect or value to drug use in itself:

Q: Did it [marijuana] have any effect on you?
A: No, because I didn't do that much.
Q: How come?
A: I didn't want to. I didn't like the smell.
Q: Why did you try it?
A: I don't know. I guess I had to try it some day, so I just tried it.
Q: You didn't think much of it, sounds like?
A: No.
Q: When was the next time you ever tried it?
A: Um, I was 17.
Q: So there was not use of it at all for a year? . . . Did it have an effect that [the next] time?
A: Yeah.
Q: Tell me about it, what was that experience?
A: I felt light-headed. I don't know . . . I felt relaxed I guess.
Q: Was it better than the first time?
A: Yeah.
Q: Did it make you feel differently about it?
A: No.
Q: So, you didn't like it anymore?
A: No, I don't like it.
Q: How soon after that second time did you try it again?
A: Um, months later, about 5 months later, I guess.

*Q:* How come you didn't use any in the 5 months?
*A:* I don't know. I don't know. I really don't like it. I mean it's all right. . . .

The following accounts regarding first cigarette and alcohol use were given by a 15-year-old female from our sample of detained subjects. They are indicative of the substance use that is characteristic of initiators–experimenters:

*Q:* What did do it [made her quit smoking marijuana]?
*A:* *I made up my mind to do it myself*, my mind did it, me myself.
*Q:* How come though, that's what I'm interested in.
*A:* 'Cause I just got tired of it. And the aftereffects scared me, and effects . . . that . . . what it does scared me.
*Q:* Uh-huh.
*A:* So I started like just turning against it. . . .
*Q:* Do you have some reason for not drinking wine or beer or liquor?
*A:* I hate it. *It's not me.*
*Q:* What's that mean, "It's not me"? Tell me about that.
*A:* It's not ladylike and it makes you do horrible things and forces you to do a lot of stuff . . . you regret in the long run.
*Q:* What makes you say that?
*A:* 'Cause people, who get drunk, the majority of them, they go do something that they don't want to do, but that alcohol it influence them to do. And then they feel sorry for it later and by then it be too late to feel sorry. [Emphasis added here and throughout.]

Each of the subjects within our category of initiators–experimenters affirmed their lack of identification with substance use. With regard to cigarette use, an 18-year-old male from the purposive sample explained:

*Q:* Do you think you might ever smoke cigarettes?
*A:* Naw, I don't think so.
*Q:* How come?
*A:* 'Cause that's what *I plan to do: not smoke* cigarettes.
*Q:* What is it about cigarettes that you particularly don't like? What are you afraid would happen?
*A:* Well, I'm not, you know, afraid, it's just that, *that's not what I wanna do*, so, you know, I'm not anticipating it.

A 17-year-old female subject from the random sample described her initiation into alcohol use in the following account:

*Q:* Do you have some reason for not drinking beer?
*A:* No, I just don't like it.

*Q:* How about if someone just offered you one, would you take it?

*A:* No.

*Q:* How come? Why wouldn't you?

*A: Because I don't. It's just the way I see it.*

*Q:* You wouldn't even drink it if it was free?

*A:* Even if it was free.

A 16-year-old male from the random sample strongly expressed this personal perception vis-à-vis drug use generally:

*Q:* You, um, you ever use any other kinds of drugs?

*A:* No.

*Q:* Ever had a chance to?

*A:* No, I don't want to.

*Q:* But, even if you said no, has anyone ever asked you?

*A:* No, Black Beauties [speed] I've been asked to sell, pills, but not. . . .

*Q:* OK, um, do you think you might ever try it in the future, like when you move away from home, or. . . .

*A:* No. I can sit here and tell you a thousand times . . . you know, but I just can't see myself lowering, ya know, get lowered down to that standpoint using drugs, you know?

*Q:* Why do you think it's "lowering"?

*A:* Why? Just somethin' proven to me. I don't want to die. It doesn't do anything to me but worry me, you know?

*Q:* Well, how does it ruin you? I mean I know kids. . . .

*A:* Well various people, like you see her on TV, she talked about how drugs messed up her career, for example. *I'm just not interested . . . so why should I get into something I'm not in?*

The final, vehemently stated expression of these subjects' lack of identification with various substance use was given by the 15-year-old detained female in response to how she handled situations in which marijuana (and/or other substances) were made available to her:

*A:* I just tell them I don't smoke.

*Q:* And that's enough?

*A:* I say, "I'm straight!" Sometimes I say "I'm straight, I'm straight, I'm straight!"

Another important theme distinguishing these subjects from those progressing to committed involvement is their tendency to make fewer distinctions between degrees of danger associated with drug use. Like the committed users, these subjects tend to distinguish between "soft" and "hard" (dangerous) drugs, but they assign more drugs to the dangerous category. Unlike more committed subjects, who in some cases actually view some substances as benign, the initiators–experimenters tend to assign some measure of risk to all substances.

The following account, given by an 18-year-old female subject from the purposive sample, exemplifies the degree to which these subjects generalize the dangers of substance use. This subject referred to alcohol, marijuana, and cocaine generically in her response regarding the dangers of drugs. In fact, her generalizations are based solely on her experience with marijuana.

*Q:* If someone offered you marijuana or some other drug next week, do you think you'd use it?
*A:* No.
*Q:* How come?
*A:* Because I don't get high.
*Q:* But even if it was free and available?
*A:* No.
*Q:* How about if it was cocaine?
*A:* No. They'd have to . . . I mean they'd have . . . I'm scared of it. It's, it's just the unknown. I don't know what it's like. I know that I don't like marijuana which is an . . . I mean not that alcohol is not a drug. I just . . . I put them separate though. Um, it's just the fact that it is a drug and that it . . . I don't know what my reaction will be to it. I don't have a good reaction with marijuana, so drugs scare me.

When a distinction between more and less dangerous drugs is made, it is almost unanimously drawn between alcohol, marijuana, and all "other" drugs, as suggested in the following account given by an 18-year-old male from the purposive sample. To the extent that a more "dangerous" drug is used, it tends to be restricted to "speed."

*Q:* Do you have some reasons for not using drugs?
*A:* Yeah, you know, 'cause I don't, you know, really—really, you know, need that kind of high where, you know, gonna make you, like, see things or, you know, act strangely. I don't need that kind of high because, give me a joint and I'll be satisfied with that, I don't need no hard drugs.
*Q:* Do any of your friends use drugs like, ah, marijuana or do other drugs that we've been talking about?
*A:* Yeah, you know . . . yeah, you know most of these . . . most of these . . . all my friend use marijuana, you know, but none of my friends use like, you know, like that, um, heroin and all that. None of my friends do that.
*Q:* Do they use speed though, cocaine, anything like that?

*A:* Sometimes they'll, you know, like they do speed sometimes, you know, but other than that they don't have much use for that.

A final, and perhaps most characteristic, feature of these subjects' substance-use experiences involves their general and clearly expressed perception that, despite what may be said for or against substance use in itself, becoming "addicted" or habitually involved is not only to be avoided, but is a very real danger within drug use encounters—a feature of drug use that in and of itself is fearsome to these subjects.

The following extended quotation from the 17-year-old female from the random sample expresses the perceptions among initiators–experimenters of the danger of addiction and its role in their avoidance of regular drug use:

*Q:* Now you mentioned that you've never tried any of these other drugs on the list. Do you have any reason why you haven't at least tried them?

*A:* Um, I just couldn't.

*Q:* Why not though, that's what I'm interested in, why couldn't you?

*A:* Well, because, well the things that go through your arm, I mean they be needed them, you know . . . and I don't really get into that. Well, some of those things I don't even know what they are. I really never seen them out in the street, you know, I don't even know where to get them. So I couldn't try any of them. . . .

*Q:* What's your worst fear? What's the thing you feel most that would happen if you tried one of these drugs like cocaine, or LSD, or one of these pills?

*A:* Getting addicted to it.

*Q:* So what? What would happen if you got addicted to it?

*A:* Then I would have to have it an' then if I had it I'd probably . . . I don't know, you see so many things on TV. Here I go again. When they can't get it right, this boy had a fork trying to get his arm open and I just couldn't see myself doing it.

*Q:* How about if you knew the drug wasn't addictive? Someone you had faith in told you that, well, you can use cocaine because you won't get addicted?

*A:* No, I still couldn't use it.

*Q:* How come?

*A:* I don't know I just couldn't use those things. I couldn't see myself with those things.

*Q:* So you don't think that if you used it once it would be okay, just to see what it's like?

*A:* No, I wouldn't try it.

*Q:* How many times do you think you'd have to use, like heroin, before you get addicted?

*A:* I don't know . . . about five times. I don't know.
*Q:* So you really couldn't get it from once then, probably?
*A:* I don't know. I'm not going to try it.

A 16-year-old, randomly selected male subject, when discussing his beer consumption, expressed his sentiments regarding "committed" use in the following way:

*Q:* Um, you usually drink beer when you go to the party, if they have it, don't you?
*A:* Yeah.
*Q:* About how much do you usually drink when you do?
*A:* One can.
*Q:* Really? You, you don't really like to drink that much or . . . .?
*A:* There's nothing wrong with it but, I don't make it a habit, you know.
*Q:* Why, do you think, do you think, it could get to be a habit?
*A:* No. Just that I, ha, ha, really to be honest with you I don't know. No, it's just that you know, I, I, if I go to a party, and have one just like everybody else, so you know.

An 18-year-old female from the purposive sample echoed these perceptions in declaring that, although she does smoke cigarettes on occasion, a "good day's without smoking." Later in the interview, when asked if she *might* use marijuana and/or other drugs in the future, she responded:

*A:* I think I'll never use marijuana. But I could see myself trying things, but nothing I would not want to get into the habit of, you know . . . I do drink, I would never want hey, "I'm going out to do drugs," you know. I'm sure if my interests . . . if there's an interest there I will do it, but I'm . . . I also get really scared, too. . . .

The 15-year-old incarcerated female best expressed the feeling by suggesting that to use a drug (in this case, cigarettes) is not necessarily negative, but to use them to such an extent that one has to resort to borrowing or become desperate enough to "feign" (cheat, steal, or "weasel" them from others) for them is definitely perceived to be so:

*Q:* When, if ever, did you start smoking regular?
*A:* I don't smoke regularly. I, I smoke, I smoke when I get a cigarette, but I don't buy them and I don't feign for them. I just smoke them when . . . most of the time I smoke them when I'm nervous.
*Q:* How come?
*A:* 'Cause I just feel like I want a cigarette.

## Criminal Orientations

Our analysis did not indicate unique patterns of criminal behavior for each of these two types of subjects, but we did find one striking distinction between the two groups in what they defined as "serious" criminal or delinquent behavior. The perception of "seriousness" involved not only types of crime in themselves (effect), but also the potential risk associated with involvement therein (consequence).

In a way not unrelated to their broader definition of "safe" drugs, the group of committed–experimenter subjects appeared to hold a more restricted view of what is "serious" and therefore to be avoided. Stated differently, the delinquent or criminal experiences of committed subjects, like their substance use experiences, tend to be characterized by less caution or, conversely, by a higher risk orientation. They appeared less concerned about actual or potential practical consequences, thus, in a sense, "freeing" themselves for greater involvement. The initiator–experimenters, on the other hand, appeared quite sensitive to even such informal and intrapersonal consequences as "embarrassment"; these sentiments were virtually absent in the accounts of the committed–experimenters.

Typical of the less-than-cautious orientation that is characteristic of committed subjects is that of a 16-year-old male from the detained sample. In the following excerpt, he describes the negligible concern he felt on discovering the presence of the homeowners in a house that he and his friends had broken into for the purpose of burglarizing, until one of his companions bungled their attempt:

*Q:* Is this the first time you were with him, first time you did it?

*A:* Yeah, well, what . . . broke into a house? Yeah. Broke into this house, we went in the back way, we picked the lock with a knife, went through, started, had our lighters out and the knife, goin' through this house didn't think anybody was home; went in this one bedroom, two old people sleepin', said, "Holy smoke, I'm gonna have a heart attack!" So I shut the door, went around the house lookin' for stuff, I found . . .

*Q:* You stayed in there? After you knew people were in there? They didn't wake up?

*A:* Nah, ah. We were real quiet. Some dude, I forget his name . . . Adam or somethin' not Adam, some other dude, I dunno, he's goin' through silverware drawer an stuff, I don't know what the hell he's looking for, but he left the drawer open; Reggie Ugger's in another room, found the old man's wallet, he comes back, we got all kinds of jewelry; I stole the pocketbook. So, Reggie, he was in one jewelry box, and he turns around and he hit another one, and it fell on the floor. We had to run out of there, and Reggie, he ran out, crashed into the silverware drawer, it hit him right here, silverware all over the place. We just kept runnin'. Got down the road a little ways, looked back, all the lights are on in the house. We got three hundred and, ah, three hundred and eighty dollars I think.

Later in the interview this subject underscored his relative lack of concern regarding the potential consequences of this and other situations:

*Q:* I was thinking about that, you said when you broke into the house that one time you found the old people asleep . . . what would you have done if they had gotten up? Do you think you would have hit them or do you think you would have run, do you think?
*A:* I don't know. I don't know if he ever came after me and tried to grab me I would hit him.
*Q:* Um, mm, but that never happened? You never did it?
*A:* No, don't have to worry about it.

This rather cavalier attitude toward potential risk and consequences is consistent with the subject's apparent lack of concern regarding the legal consequences he was currently facing in regard to another offense:

*Q:* So, really, you only broke into houses about four times altogether? One time in Yule City with Reggie, and one with Chuckie? And then the motorcycles?
*A:* Yup.
*Q:* So they sent you straight up here, and you've been here ever since.
*A:* Yup.
*Q:* And you had to go to court and everything. Or . . .
*A:* Yeah, I've been to court about twenty-five times.
*Q:* Why?
*A:* They just keep postponing it. I dunno. I gotta go Tuesday, the judge already told me I've got one-to-four. So that ain't too bad. I could've had more than that. See I really . . . I stole the motorcycle, breaking and entering, two breaking and enterings, drugs . . . so . . .
*Q:* Do you think that's reasonable?
*A:* What? One-to-four?
*Q:* Mmm.
*A:* Oh, yeah, that's easy. I'll just do my year and get out. It ain't nothin'.
*Q:* Did you ever think you'd get busted?
*A:* Nah, ah. I thought we had it made, man! Thought we'd be in Florida now. If it wasn't for Chuckie messin' up on the motorcycle, we wouldn't be here.

These subjects, as imprudent or risk oriented as they may express themselves to be, under some circumstances do clearly define certain types of criminal activity as dangerous and therefore to be avoided. The following statements, made by this same subject, illustrate this point. The first sequence occurred as the subject was explaining his current status:

*Q:* How old are you?
*A:* Sixteen. I was 15 when I did the crime, I turned 16 in here.
*Q:* So does that have something to do with the kind of sentence you got?
*A:* I dunno, I guess so. They were, ah, tryin' me as an adult.
*Q:* How do they decide that?
*A:* The case, how old you are.
*Q:* So they really thought you were armed and were gonna shoot?
*A:* Yeah.
*Q:* And, really, in all honesty, would you?
*A:* Would have shot 'em? Hell, no, man! They were cops. You shoot a cop, you go to jail for life. If he shot me first, I would've shot back. The only thing was, I didn't have no bullets, ha!

Interestingly enough, a crime conventionally viewed as less serious than burglary—forgery—was seen by this youth as being more serious. Here he describes how, after actually stealing a motorcycle (at age 15 and unlicensed) and riding it for two days, he never worried about being caught; *but*, he said, he would never forge a check or make unauthorized use of credit cards:

*Q:* Do you have your driver's license?
*A:* No. I plan on gettin' it though when I get out.
*Q:* So you didn't have a license to drive a motorcycle then?
*A:* Nope.
*Q:* Did you ever worry about that?
*A:* Why? I drove motorcycles all over Yule City and never got caught.
*Q:* When was that? Whose motorcycle?
*A:* It wasn't the one that I stole.
*Q:* How long did you have that?
*A:* Two days.
*Q:* But you never worried that they were gonna stop you and ask for a license and then find out it was stolen?
*A:* Nope. They never usually pull motorcycles over anyways.
*Q:* Do you ever do anything like, um, forge a check?
*A:* Hell no.
*Q:* Use somebody else's credit card or something like that?
*A:* No.
*Q:* Well, you say, "Hell no," like you know, like *you'd* never do that.
*A:* Nope, you can get some time for that, boy.
*Q:* Oh?
*A:* A lot, a lot of time.

*Q:* You ever think about doing that?
*A:* No!

To this youth, burglarizing a house (even knowing the owners were present), riding a stolen vehicle without a license, and doing "one-to-four" are not perceived as being particularly risky, but other behaviors (fraud, use of a firearm on a law officer) are clearly out of bounds.

The significance of this is more apparent in contrast to the attitudes of the initiator–experimenter group. The latter tend to respond with significantly greater concern to situations in which a relatively innocuous crime (such as shoplifting candy) precipitates nothing more than the sanctions of parents or, worse in the youths' eyes, personal embarrassment. Committed subjects may curtail their behavior when potential legal sanctions begin to approximate "real time" (beyond, for example, one to four years), but initiators–experimenters find embarrassment, guilt, and the mere chance of "being caught—even (or especially) by parents—a sufficient deterrent to "serious" involvement. In other words, in situations in which committed subjects give no thought to "risk," the initiators–experimenters find "serious" danger. An 18-year-old male from our purposive sample, categorized as an initiator–experimenter, gave the following response to our questions regarding whether he had ever had a chance to participate in illegal or delinquent activities but chose not to:

*A:* No. Not find . . . this was, ah, two months ago. See, you know, 'cause my friends had, you know, well, you know, one of my so-called friends you know, 'cause he had, you know, these white couple right, you know. The old guy had a lot of stereo . . . of stuff, right, but one day, you know, back when, ah, when I'm out of town, when he knows, you know, so he got . . . that he wanted to break in these people house and take their stuff, you know. I said, "No man," 'cause it's big risk.
*Q:* What's a big risk?
*A:* Going to jail for robbery, breakin' Miss Yule's house! I would say no.

Again, the 16-year-old male initiator–experimenter from our random sample, when responding to probes from the interviewer regarding why some youths, unlike himself, become involved in criminal or substance use activities, offered the following explanation:

*A:* Just the personality characteristics or traits, you know. I just feel that a certain person does things like this because they don't . . . with me, you know, it's the guilt and fear that stop me. Some people just don't have that.

The perceptions of the initiators–experimenters are perhaps best expressed by the 15-year-old female who, at the time of her initial interview, was incarcerated (for "armed robbery"). In several of her responses she articulated the "cautious" (antirisk) orientation that is characteristic of this category of subjects and the place of informal controls within this orientation. In response to our questions regarding property damage, specifically graffiti, she responded:

*Q:* How about a regular school, did you ever do it in a regular school?
*A:* Yeah.
*Q:* Did you ever get caught?
*A:* Nope.
*Q:* What about if you thought you could get thrown out of school if you got caught, would you do it then?
*A:* No.
*Q:* How come?
*A:* 'Cause it's not worth writing on the . . . writing on the wall or the desk, it's not worth getting thrown out of school.
*Q:* How about if it was just a letter, you'd have to erase it or maybe wash the desk, would you risk it then?
*A:* No, 'cause I really wouldn't want to make a fool out of myself. I just do it, so when I do it when the teacher ain't looking so I won't get caught.
*Q:* What do you think would happen to you if you got caught?
*A:* That . . . most likely you would have to just erase it. Most likely wash all the desks in the class.
*Q:* But you'd get embarrassed, huh?
*A:* Yeah.
*Q:* Tell me about that.
*A:* Why I'd get embarrassed?
*Q:* What would happen? What would that mean?
*A:* I'd have to go out of the room and get paper towels and soap and just come back and wash the desks, and, ya know, the classmates would just start making wise-cracks and stuff and then they'll end up laughing, I'd end up saying . . . exchanging with one of them and then you'll be in more, more trouble. That's why I'd rather come and do it after school [washing the desks].
*Q:* Had anything like that happened when you got busted?
*A:* Nope. I saw it happen before to this boy.
*Q:* But I mean when you got . . . when you got picked up for the . . . for the theft, did you get embarrassed by that?
*A:* Yeah! of course!
*Q:* How'd that work? What happened exactly that you got embarrassed about?
*A:* Them taking me and putting me in a police car handcuffed, taking me downtown.
*Q:* Did people you know see you?
*A:* No.

*Q:* So it was just strangers you were embarrassed about?

*A:* Yeah . . . just being there, the whole thing was embarrassing. From top to finish.

Later, in describing the one incident in which she had been "caught" shoplifting, this subject indicated her anxiety about the possibility of her mother being told and her concomitant relief at having "gotten off" without that happening:

*A:* And he took us back to this room . . . asked us our name and address and phone number and all that kind of stuff. And he said . . . we, looked nice and all this kind of stuff, and we . . . we ain't gonna do it again, 'cause we really were scared. They know we were scared, ya know. And they said, "Well, we gonna have the police drive you all home," and we said no, no, no! So they just let us walk, they let us go right. And they told us don't come back in the store if you gonna steal. If you gonna come back in here to buy, you're welcome back in here. And so we just left and was happy we got off the hook and we didn't steal no more. We just had a break.

*Q:* Is that when you stopped shoplifting?

*A:* Yeah.

*Q:* How come?

*A:* 'Cause that was scary, and I didn't want my mother to find out. No less than go to jail somewhere.

*Q:* Do you think you could have gone to jail?

*A:* Not really, but you know, they could have done something with us.

A final excerpt from this subject's interview indicates the difference between youths like her and committed youths. Here she cites not only the (potentially public) consequence of "stealing," but also having to lie to her mother, as a factor lending seriousness to the activity in question:

*Q:* Well, couldn't you use your own TV or tape deck?

*A:* Nope.

*Q:* How come?

*A:* Because my mother wouldn't let me have it, if she don't know where it came from.

*Q:* Couldn't you lie about it and say it's a friend's and it's . . . you're borrowing it or something like that?

*A:* Nope.

*Q:* How come?

*A:* 'Cause she would want to know who . . . she don't want to go from me telling her and I don't like lying to my mother.

*Q:* Uh-huh.

*A:* About nothing stupid. 'Cause once you look at stealing, it, it don't really get you nowhere but in trouble or in jail.

## Conclusion

Our interpretive investigation of the experiences of substance use and criminal or delinquent behavior that are characteristic of youths at differing stages of the sequential model suggests that questions of identity formation and risk discrimination are operative in these varying experiences. Differences in notions of worth, self, safety, and risk are at the core of the experiences of these subjects. Without looking longitudinally at these subjects, especially the initiators–experimenters, however, little more can be said about their potential for "progress" toward or away from involvement in dangerous drug use and serious crime.

## Notes

1. Very few subjects, at any level of involvement, refer to their behavior in any focal behaviors in terms of addiction and/or commitment, in and of itself.

2. It is important to recognize that a subject may (in fact, is quite likely to) display varying degrees of involvement for any given category of behavior (for example, reporting at some points patterns that are consistent with our definition of "casual" drug use, and at other points patterns consistent with our definition of "committed" use). In our typology, each subject was first categorized in terms of the highest degree of involvement reported and, hence, in some cases may have also demonstrated patterns consistent with our definitions of initiation and/or casual involvement, although they were removed from the pool of cases to be so categorized. As a result, subjects categorized as "committed" display varying patterns of adaptive or experimental involvements in other focal behaviors.

3. This is not meant to deny the importance or significance of intensive analysis of the other unique patterns of involvement. In fact, some questions relevant to the relationship of the three behaviors can only be addressed by looking comparatively at those categories characterized by the absence of one or the other of the three. Though related to the interest at hand, such analysis was not specifically done for this chapter.

4. Again, to avoid misunderstanding or misinterpretation, the greater concentration of subjects in the committed category is an artifact of our subject selection procedures rather than of actual proportions in the youth population.

# 11

# The Deterrent Effect of Adult versus Juvenile Jurisdiction

*With Margret Ksander and Bruce Berg*

Amajor strength of qualitative research is its potential for identifying unanticipated findings and new themes that emerge from the data. One such serendipitous finding was respondents' concern about going to jail. Questions aimed at uncovering why youths reduced or ceased delinquent activities were included in the interview instrument, but not specific questions about being treated as adults by the criminal justice system or being jailed. Nevertheless, several seriously delinquent youths, such as Gallo and Kevin (chapter 9), and many less delinquent youths spontaneously mentioned such concerns. Thus, in this chapter, we present themes on this subject that emerged in the interviews.[1] More intensive study of the importance of adult versus juvenile jurisdiction, however, still needs to be undertaken.

Adolescents have the highest probability of involvement in various forms of delinquency and crime. Although the data are not always consistent, research suggests that the proportion of youths who become delinquent increases from about age 12 through 15 (Conklin, 1971; Elliott and Huizinga, 1984; Gold and Reimer, 1975; Jensen, Erickson, and Gibbs, 1978; Richards, Burke, and Forster, 1979; Wolfgang, 1967). Beginning at about age 16, the proportion reporting crime either remains level or declines. The Youth-in-Transition Project, for example, longitudinally studied the high school class of 1969, interviewing the youths in 1966, when they were in the tenth grade, and reinterviewing them in five waves ending in 1974 (Bachman, O'Malley, and Johnston, 1978; Johnston and O'Malley, 1978; Johnston, O'Malley, and Eveland, 1978). Among these respondents there were important declines on an interpersonal aggression index of involvement in violence between 1966 and 1968 (that is, between ages 15 and 17) and little change thereafter.

A more recent longitudinal study, the National Youth Survey (Elliott, Knowles, and Canter, 1981; Huizinga, 1986; Huizinga and Elliott, 1981), identified these changes more clearly. Specifically, Elliott, Knowles, and Canter (1981:321) suggest that "the period of maximum involvement in delinquency, measured by frequency rates, occurred around ages 15 or 16," although drug use tended to increase with age until age 18 or later. There was considerable variation by specific offense and by cohort, but more adolescents appeared to terminate or suspend their involvement in nondrug crime than to initiate or continue those behaviors after age 16. In short, ages 15–16 appeared to be somewhat of a transition period in the general patterns of nondrug crime (Elliott and Huizinga, 1984; Huizinga, 1986).

The findings reported next identify some of the probable processes that help to bring about a decline in nondrug delinquent behavior, especially among youths (5–20 percent) who are involved in serious offenses such as burglary, major thefts, and robbery (Elliott and Huizinga, 1984; Elliott, Knowles and Canter, 1981). Our findings suggest that a deterrent process is at work. Many youths who reported relatively extensive involvement in delinquency in their early adolescent years appear to have reduced or ceased their criminal activities at approximately age 16. They reported this remission in delinquency as a part of their perceptions of differences in the criminal justice system's treatment of juvenile and adult criminals.

Here, we describe the subjects' fear of incarceration after age 16. This deterrent effect is then tied to other changes in status that occur at age 16 (for example, legal right to leave home or school, to drive a car, to hold a full-time job, and so on) and to the processes of experimentation and commitment to crime among adolescents. These findings are subsequently discussed in light of cognitive development, labeling, and deterrence theories.

## Fear of Incarceration

Several subjects who had been criminally active and who were interviewed after they turned 16 spontaneously raised the juvenile jurisdiction issue directly. As noted, no specific questions about this issue were included in the interview schedule. One 16-year-old had been engaged, between the ages of 12 and 15, in misdemeanors and felonies ranging from minor vandalism to drug wholesaling, burglary, and arson. Asked how many of his friends engaged in illegal activities, he responded: "Not that many now, because we're all 16. But everybody used to when they were 13, 14, 15. Everybody used to." When the interviewer pointed out that the subject's own criminal activities had decreased markedly in recent months, he said:

A: When you're a teenager you're rowdy. Nowadays, you aren't rowdy. You know, you just want to settle down, because you can go to jail now. [When] you are a boy, you can be put into a detention home. But you can go to jail now. Jail ain't no place to go.

Later in the interview the youth described the steps he took to control his criminal activities, such as leaving his gun at home when he was high on drugs and staying away from friends when they "get rowdy." When the interviewer asked about this change in his behavior, he explained:

A: I try to be careful as much as I can these days. 'Cause, you know, I know that I can go to jail, 'cause they changed the law. You can go to jail at 16.

The issue of going to jail rather than to a detention center came up often in the interviews. For instance, one of the youths interviewed at a detention facility had been arrested, just before his sixteenth birthday, for robbery, burglary, and possession of drugs. He saw his one- to four-year sentence to the detention facility as "easy": "I'll just do my year and get out, it ain't nothing." The friend with whom he committed the crimes was not convicted. The youth said his friend should stop his criminal activities, because "he's 16 now, he'll go to jail."

An interview with another 16-year-old who was active in crime included this exchange:

Q: When did you steal that car?
A: It was a couple of years ago. It was when I was little, I don't like stealing now. I don't want to do shit now that I'm 16.
Q: What does that mean, "now that you're 16"?
A: 'Cause you go to jail now. There's a difference now. I shouldn't tear this thing off, you know.
Q: What do you mean, "there's a difference." What makes you think there's a difference?
A: When you're . . . I don't know. I don't think nothing will happen to me anyways, the first time. You know, I haven't been busted yet.
Q: So why worry about it?
A: 'Cause it could happen.
Q: What could happen? What's your worst fear?
A: Sixteen. You go to jail now. For burglary, or whatever they can send you away for.

This youth also brought up a perception held by many respondents: that being arrested prior to age 16 is nothing to fear. In describing a friend who was arrested for stealing an automobile, he observed that "the kid got away for probation for a year," but that had he been 16, "he would be in jail." Later in the interview, when describing a fight in which he seriously injured another youth, the subject explained that the victim's parents had planned to sue him, but that they "couldn't, because I was too young."

A 15-year-old respondent in the detained sample was asked about a few of his friends who did not engage in crime:

*Q:* Why do you think they don't?
*A:* They don't want to get caught. They're too old.
*Q:* What do you mean?
*A:* Like if you're over 16 you go to jail.
*Q:* What happens if you're under 16?
*A:* Probably give you a chance or something.

In comparing the respondents' descriptions of criminal apprehension in early adolescence with that occurring after age 16, the difference is often pronounced. For instance, a 19-year-old told a story of being apprehended at age 14 for shoplifting at a downtown department store. "They took me up in the elevator and called my mother. I started crying and they let me go." A few minutes later in the interview he explained that he was no longer a shoplifter.

*Q:* What made you decide to give it up?
*A:* I turned 16 and I know this girl that got stopped. She got sent to Idaho, and then to the penitentiary. And I said, "Well, that's a girl, too, so I'm not doing it no more."

This appreciation of the change that occurs at age 16 apparently takes place quite young. The following is from an interview with a 12-year-old who had been arrested for stealing from cars. He was asked to imagine himself ten years in the future:

*A:* I don't think I would be stealing.
*Q:* Why?
*A:* . . . I won't be stealing so much because I know I would be going to jail if I get caught.
*Q:* Why? Why would you go to jail then?
*A:* 'Cause I would be over age.
*Q:* What do you mean by that?
*A:* I'd be over 16.
*Q:* Why does that make a difference?
*A:* If you [are over 15] they take you to jail.
*Q:* . . . How come? Why is it like that?
*A:* I don't know. That's the law. Don't you know that?
*Q:* How do you know that?
*A:* 'Cause. Police come to our school and a lot of stuff, and I get caught and they tell me that.
*Q:* What did they tell you?
*A:* That if you was 16, we'll book you and take you to jail.

As might have been expected, not only the youths but adults as well are aware of differences in juvenile and adult jurisdiction. A few subjects reported that adult criminals had used them or their friends for the commission of crimes on the assumption either that persons under 16 would be viewed with less suspicion, or that the arrest of a juvenile would result in less serious punishment. These respondents reported that they and their friends robbed houses, shoplifted at stores, bought drugs, and stole cars for their parents and other adults.

## Nature of the Deterrent Effect

The foregoing finding suggests that adult jurisdiction laws have a deterrent effect—namely, that youths perceive greater risk of serious punishment after age 16. On closer examination of the data, however, the relationship turns out to be more complex, and in ways that are meaningful for policy considerations. Next we consider this deterrent effect in terms of three phases in youths' lives.

### Generalized Turning Point at Age 16

Much as age 65 is meaningful to many persons because it signals a change in status, activities, and relationships with others, so too are other ages that carry both legal and other cultural significance. Age 16 was an important turning point for many of the youths in our sample: it was the age at which the adolescent was expected by adults and by other adolescents to begin the process of becoming an adult. For some subpopulations this means studying for college entrance examinations; for others it means getting a job, and for those who have had problems in school or within their families, it means considering other options. Frequently, youths in the latter group choose options that accept failure in school, such as giving up or biding time until graduation, but some youths react by "shaping up." In some cases the change can be dramatic, as with one of our subjects who had been considered a slow student until, at age 16, he began doing well in school. He explained:

A: My sister and my brother graduated when they were 16. And my younger brother is in a grade ahead of me. I'm still here. I can't stay here for the rest of my life. I had to try. So I just started working on [myself] all during the summer. I was saying what I was going to do, you know, what I had to do, 'cause I'm not going to be in school all my life. . . . I talked to a guidance teacher. He said if I wanted to I could do two years in one year. Double up. So I'm going to do that.

Put simply, young people at age 16 are suddenly treated as adults, not only by the criminal courts, but in many other areas of life as well. Of importance to many of our subjects, for instance, were their legal rights to drive, to leave home, and to drop out of school. This emerged in direct statements not only from subjects who had moved away from their parents' or guardians' homes at age 16, but also from those who probably would not do so, yet who considered it to be a serious option. For example, a 16-year-old described a fight he had with his stepsister:

> A: I told her, "My God, I'm leaving, excuse me." She says, "You can't leave." And I go, "Why can't I, I'm 16 years old" . . . My mother told her, "He's 16 years old, what are you going to do about it [if he decides to leave]?"

This same subject had realigned his relationship with his parents through their mutual understanding that at age 16 the parents had decreased dominion over him:

> A: I'm on my own basis now. My father will tell me what time to come home. If I don't come home he doesn't do anything. I mean, he can't really, I'm 16.

This youth, like other subjects, considered age 16 to be a sort of natural demarcation point, as evidenced throughout the interview. When asked how he planned to raise his own children, he explained that he wanted to "give them something I didn't have, up until a certain age, when they would be, like their sixteenth birthday, then it would be all up to them."

The subjects had plenty of opportunities to learn from other youths about laws and options related to maturation. In some instances, there was almost a family tradition regarding what one does at age 16. A 16-year-old subject noted:

> A: Every one of my brothers and sisters moved out at 16 . . . Most of my family did want to move out before they were 16, but they had to wait until they were 16, because that's what the law says. Every one of them, the minute after midnight he started moving his [belongings]. I'm serious. . . .

This subject left home before his 17th year, in his case, to join the army. In so doing, he was "joining the gang" in more ways than one. Not only did his siblings leave when they reached that age, but so did friends his age. He had been part of a street gang, which broke up because "now that they get older everybody goes places, like the army, the job corps, and things like that."

## Years of Experimentation: Ages 12–15

It is well known from previous research that many adolescents experiment with forbidden behaviors (Bachman, O'Malley, and Johnston, 1978; Elliott, Knowles, and Canter, 1981; Gold and Reimer, 1975; Johnston, O'Malley, and

Bachman, 1984). Indeed, some researchers contend that a normal function of adolescence is served by such experimentation (Hirschi, 1969; Richards, Burke, and Forster, 1979).

Two contradictory strategies are suggested by such findings. On the one hand, it might be desirable to enforce laws more strongly in order to deter a substantial number of youths who are involved in such experimentation. On the other hand, communities might wish to minimize enforcement in light of the apparent normality of such experimentation among segments of the youth population.

Our data cannot resolve this dilemma, but they do shed some light on it. Our research was not designed to provide incidence rates, but it is apparent from both the observational fieldwork and in-depth interviews that widespread experimentation was going on in Yule City. Almost all of our purposively selected and detained subjects between the ages of 12 and 15 experimented with drug use, drunkenness, shoplifting, burglary, vandalism, and fighting. Many were involved on a monthly basis with several of these. A majority of randomly selected subjects had also been involved in one or more of these behaviors but, generally, to a lesser degree. The outstanding feature of such involvement, however, was that for most subjects it was quite obviously transitory and limited. For instance, a subject might engage in shoplifting with one or two friends, do so a few times over perhaps a half-year period, but then discontinue the activity. The same holds for the use of specific drugs. Although many subjects periodically used marijuana throughout adolescence, few used prescription drugs, opiates, cocaine, or LSD more than a couple of times, although many did consider it important to "try" these drugs.

Our data suggest that many subjects, and entire peer groups, explicitly considered the ages from 12 to 15 as a period of experimentation. This comes out in a variety of discussions, as when purposively sampled subjects explain how they judge whether a person is behaving properly for his or her age, when they condemn some schoolmates as "goody-goodies," or when they compare their "rowdy" days with the calm they expect in their late adolescence. It is also shown in arguments youths present to their peers when encouraging them to participate in drug use or criminal activities. In each case, there are implicit peer group norms favoring experimentation with activities ranging from an occasional bottle of beer and keeping extra change mistakenly returned by a cashier to use of hard drugs and the commission of felony offenses.

It is especially among those who experiment with relatively serious crime and drug use that the adult jurisdiction statutes appear effective in restricting recurrent participation in such behaviors after age 16, although some youths may not be deterred and may become even more involved as young adults. Several youths volunteered that they viewed the years just prior to age 16 as the period in which to try out proscribed behaviors. As one 16-year-old who had been involved in several felonies, drug use, and drug sales put it, "When you're 15, 14, 13, is when you should do that stuff; when you turn 16 it's time to forget it." On the other hand, our subjects expressed an expectation that, if the minimum age for adult jurisdiction were lowered, the major result would be a concurrent lowering of the age at which youths become involved in crime. "All it would do, a 19-year-old suggested, "is just that it would start at a younger age."

### Disinvolvement or Commitment after Age 16

Huizinga and Elliott (1981) and Huizinga (1986) found that only a small proportion (under 5 percent) of youths nationwide report commission of a Part I offense in each of three consecutive years. A crucial question becomes: Which sorts of youths become committed to criminal activities? In the context of the present discussion the question is a more limited one, specifically: What differentiates those adolescents who reduce or eliminate serious criminal activities at approximately age 16 from those who do not? We pose this question because our data suggest that age 16 may be a point of no return for a few young people engaged in serious criminal and drug activities. This is because, as noted earlier, formal norms (such as juvenile and school statutes) and informal norms (within adolescent peer culture) tend to make age 16 a well-recognized dividing line between youthful experimentation and initiation into adulthood.

Among the 15-, 16-, and 17-year-olds in our sample, a great deal of discussion, both among the youths themselves and in the interviews, concerned the sorts of criminal involvement that would continue now that they were becoming adults. There appears to be a continuum, with, at one end, those who radically reduce or completely discontinue criminal activities around age 16, and, at the other, those who begin to commit themselves to criminal activity as a way of life or, at the least, as a regular avocation.

Many youths, however, are in the middle, a circumstance exemplified by a 19-year-old who reported that in the years since his sixteenth birthday he had frequently passed up opportunities to steal. He explained that he feared going to jail, which he saw as more likely and more serious now that he was under adult jurisdiction, and that he had made a decision to "go off felonies and stuff like that" because he did not want to be seen as a career criminal. In his case, this had not resulted in the elimination of criminal involvements but, instead, in greater caution when he did commit a crime (for example, carefully "casing" a home before attempting burglary) and an overall decrease in criminal activities. Along the same lines, a subject who was interviewed while serving a sentence in a detention facility explained why he planned to give up using and selling cocaine:

A: They say it's not too good for you, plus you can get into a lot of trouble for it. Now that I'm 16 I don't think I'd really want to get macho over coke . . . it's a bad rap. You get caught with cocaine and it's nothing like marijuana or hash; they've been around for five hundred years. But coke, you know, it's a bad thing.

## Discussion

Our findings suggest that a noticeable age differentiation in criminal processing produces a deterrent effect among segments of adolescents. This finding is commensurate with other bodies of research. Work on cognitive development by Kohlberg (1969) and others, for example, suggests that sophisticated moral thinking arises only at the end of adolescence and that such ability is quite low in preadolescents. More recent work questions some of the methodology of the previous studies but does not refute the finding that on complex adult issues that lie outside the youth's everyday world, moral development is limited (Skolnick, 1979).

If moral development is circumscribed among youths, one route to an overall reduction in criminal activity would appear to be acceptance as an unfortunate reality that a proportion of youths will commit crimes, and a concomitant recognition that (1) some of these youths can be rerouted away from criminal careers and (2) their criminality, as a group, might be reduced by emphasizing a clear upper age limit for such behaviors. In short, society might benefit by advertising its expected age of moral maturity and making that age one that is reasonable given the findings of moral development studies.

In a similar vein, sociologists and anthropologists have suggested that for many youthful offenders criminal involvement constitutes "transitional deviance"—behavior that is limited to one point in the life course—unless they are encouraged at this stage to make a commitment to a deviant career. Such encouragement may come from various sources, which this book cannot address, such as poverty, psychodynamic or other predispositions, or pathology within the family. One significant factor, however, the process of formal labeling, may be minimized by making clear distinctions between juvenile and adult offenders. Edwin Lemert (1967:94) notes:

> Most youth phase out of their predelinquency, so-called, and their law flaunting . . . maturation out of the deviance of adolescence is facilitated by a process of normalization in which troublesome behavior, even petty crimes, are dealt with by parents, neighbors, and law people as manifestations of inevitable diversity, perversity, and shortcomings of human beings—in other words, as problems of everyday living calling for tolerable solutions short of perfection. This means the avoidance wherever possible of specialized or categorical definitions which invidiously differentiate, degrade, or stigmatize persons involved in the problems.

This sort of conclusion is similar to one of the assumptions on which juvenile jurisdiction was created in the first place. A major goal at the turn of the century was to decriminalize children. As a Chicago judge put the matter at that time: "Instead of the state training its bad boys so as to make of them decent citizens, it permitted them to become the outlaws and outcasts of society; it criminalized them by the methods used in dealing with them" (Mack, 1910:293). Indeed, from early in the history of U.S. justice, this issue has been recognized. A 1923 report raised the question: "Can it be consistent with real justice, that delinquents . . . should be consigned to the infamy and severity of punishments which must inevitably tend to perfect the work of degradation, to sink them still deeper in corruption, to deprive them of their remaining sensibility to the shame of exposure, and establish them in all hardihood of daring and desperate villainy" (quoted in Fox, 1970:1189).

Also relevant are statistics that suggest the importance of symbolic means of deterrence, such as a highly visible cutoff age for juvenile status. A variety of studies (e.g., Empey, 1978) find that about 10 percent or fewer of delinquent acts are detected by the police, and that only about 2.5 percent result in court action and conviction. One implication is that effective threats of punishment may act as a more realistic deterrent than does actual punishment. Only such messages, unlike actual punishments, are likely to reach more than a small percentage of the adolescents who actually commit or contemplate crimes. As recent work in deterrence theory suggests, the actual apprehension or conviction rates are important primarily insofar as they contribute to perceived danger of punishment (Erickson and Gibbs, 1978; Erickson, Gibbs, and Jensen, 1977; Tittle, 1980; Zimring and Hawkins, 1973). As Burkett and Jensen (1975) have shown, the deterrent effects of laws and legal actions among adolescents are dependent on the degree of support they receive within peer groups. In that light, our findings indicate a specific deterrent effect among adolescents: the widespread perception among youths in a community of serious legal sanctions awaiting them at age 16. We believe that a well-advertised difference in kind and severity between juvenile and adult criminal justice agencies is as an effective deterrent to crime for an important segment of the youth population.

## Note

1. A brief report of these findings appears in *Social Problems*, December 1983.

# 12
# Summary and Conclusion

We began this study by arguing that to address delinquency from the perspectives and experiences of adolescents is to shed a different light on prevailing questions in the literature. Our intention was to provide for the reader an inside view of adolescent drug use and criminal involvement—to let the youths speak to the reader from their own points of view. Specifically, we focused on the question of the relationship between drugs, alcohol, and crime among adolescents. In this chapter we conclude with a summary of our main findings.

1. *Seriously delinquent youths are usually regular users of drugs and alcohol.*

The most delinquent youths in our study typically reported very extensive patterns of alcohol and marijuana use (near daily to multiple times per day), as well as less regular use of such other substances as speed, hallucinogens, pills, and cocaine. (Parallel findings among the nation's youth are reported in Elliott and Huizinga, 1984; Johnson and Wish, 1986; Johnson, Wish, and Huizinga, 1986; McBride and Clayton, 1985.) Such substance use was generally a major source of self-identity, commitment, and recreation. By contrast, even the most delinquent youths characterized their criminal and delinquent acts as irregular, episodic occurrences; rarely were such acts a source of self-identity or commitment. Thus, serious delinquents exhibit a life-style in which their drug and alcohol use is usually more regular than their delinquency.

Relatively few youths who reported committing serious or frequent delinquencies were not regular users of alcohol and marijuana. Most such youths were relatively young (under age 15) and appeared likely to become regular drug and alcohol users in their later teens.

2. *Youths relied on conventional wisdom in explaining how drugs and alcohol influence the criminality of others, but not themselves.*

Almost all our respondents drew on the conventional wisdom (disinhibition, addiction, economic acquisition, mental illness) to explain how drugs and alcohol influenced the criminality of *others*, typically those they did not know personally. The most criminally active youths, however, did not believe that *their* crimes were substantially influenced by their drug or alcohol use.

3. *The linkages between drugs/alcohol and criminal activities are complex and take on different meanings for youths depending on time, place, and interactions with others.*

Among seriously delinquent drug-using youths, the three focal behaviors appeared to be relatively independent events. The vast majority of their instances of drug and alcohol use occurred without crimes, and most crimes occurred without prior substance use (see Johnson et al., 1984; McBride and Clayton, 1985). When drug or alcohol use occurred prior to or about the same time as criminal events, delinquent youths reported that such substance use was among the less important of many parallel factors (peer group activity, need for goods or money, availability or access to property, and so on) influencing the crime. Delinquent youths clearly believed that their drug use was incidental to, and not an important contributing factor to, their crimes (unless obtaining drugs or alcohol was the objective of the crime). They reported committing crimes at times when they were under the influence of alcohol or drugs, but said they were never out of control. Rather, delinquent youths maintained that they chose when and how to use alcohol and drugs: under some conditions these substances were used because they enhanced an activity; at other times they were avoided because they interfered with the skillful execution of a crime.

4. *Virtually all delinquents state that they do not commit thefts and other property crimes to gain money with which to buy drugs.*

Crimes were committed to have fun, to obtain valued goods, or to get money for a variety of purposes. Most drugs (alcohol, marijuana, and pills) could be obtained within the usual adolescent budget for movies, lunch, and records. Although drugs were stolen, and stolen money was sometimes used for drugs, drugs were not a more important item in this respect than fashionable clothing, stereo equipment, jewelry, or a multitude of other consumer goods that youths defined themselves as "needing" in order to be popular teenagers.

5. *Youths who sold drugs on a relatively regular basis were among the most regular users of drugs.*

Virtually all youths who sold a substance were users of that substance, and many were daily users of marijuana and alcohol. Youths distinguished between "sellers" and "dealers." *Sellers* typically sold small amounts to close friends in order to support their own use without cash expenditure. *Dealers*, although they also sold in small amounts to close friends to support their own use without cash expenditure, engaged in many more sales, sold to a wider range of persons, and sometimes sold in public places. Dealers also obtained from adult suppliers, frequently on credit, much of the supply of marijuana and other drugs for sale and use to other youths in the community. Such dealers were at high risk of becoming victims of crimes (robbery, theft, burglary) and of assaulting others while defending themselves and their cash and drug supplies from would-be victimizers.

6. *Delinquent youths attempt to legitimate their crimes and to minimize the risk of apprehension and the personal harm they inflict on their victims.*

Intensive discussions with youths about a wide variety of criminal events provided information about the circumstances under which crimes are proposed, carried out, and result in violence. Delinquents emphasized that being caught was not their only concern; they were also concerned with not hurting individuals and, therefore, preferred crimes without personal confrontation (such as shoplifting and other thefts, vandalism, and burglary).

Much adolescent theft was opportunistic rather than clearly planned, as when youths stole a car with keys in it. When youths planned crimes, they sought out stores and individual victims who were careless with their possessions. Thus, one of the clearest findings of the study is that failure by individuals and businesses to provide basic protection for property (secure locks, mirrors, visible security personnel and security devices, enforced notice of intent to prosecute) makes them vulnerable to ordinary juvenile theft in two ways. First, their property is, in fact, unprotected and can be taken with little risk or effort. Second, youths interpret such behavior as carelessness or indifference and use it to legitimate their crime. Careless victims are perceived as responsible for their own victimization; it is not considered wrong to take advantage of such a "sucker."

Youths frequently chose to commit crimes requiring no interaction with the victim (shoplifting, car thefts, vandalism), thereby decreasing the risk of apprehension. The few youths who did commit crimes with a high probability of interacting with victims (purse snatching, robbery, and burglary) expected victims to be passive—that is, to behave "properly" and turn over their money or goods without protest. Victims were harmed mainly when they resisted during a robbery or when they interrupted a burglary. Not only did unpredictable behavior by the victim often lead to violence, but the youths believed that such victims "deserved it" or brought it on themselves.

7. *Fear of criminal sanctions as an adult has a deterrent effect among segments of adolescent delinquents.*

At approximately age 16, many of our criminally active subjects ceased or curtailed their involvement in crime because they feared being apprehended and adjudicated in adult court and, in particular, being sent to adult jail. The demarcation between juvenile and adult jurisdiction, however, was only one of several concomitants of adulthood that curtailed crime at this age. The youths considered approximately ages 12–15 as the period for experimentation with crime. Major involvements after that age were perceived to entail long-term commitments to crime and increased risk of incarceration. Thus, many youths who were quite delinquent in early adolescence voluntarily gave up such behavior as they approached adulthood.

## Conclusion

Although a number of studies have been conducted on the relationship between drugs, alcohol, and crime, few have asked these questions about "normal" adolescents, and from the perspectives of the adolescents themselves.

Through the use of a theoretical/methodological orientation that takes youths' perspectives seriously, our study empirically addressed the question of the relationship between drugs, alcohol, and crime among normal adolescents.

Over the past four years and through constant rereading of the transcripts, we have come to appreciate the extensive diversity in the lives of the 100 youths studied. Above all, we have come to appreciate the complexity of apparently simple questions about delinquency. Drug use and criminal behavior are situational; hence, involvement in such behaviors is not static. As we witness in the cases of Gallo, Kevin, Norris, and Elizabeth, delinquency is a process that involves contextual as well as experiential considerations.

Stories such as theirs and those of the other youths in this study helped move our thinking away from static causal models of the relationship between drugs, alcohol, and crime. Although we mainly addressed the question of the relationship between drugs, alcohol, and crime, our findings also underline the importance of addressing other questions regarding adolescent drug use and criminal behavior and the need to further investigate them from the perspectives of the youths. Most salient are what our data suggest about involvement and avoidance, demographic characteristics, and adolescent worlds.

Our data reveal as much about avoidance as about involvement in delinquent activities. All of the youths spoke of situations and/or lengths of time where they avoided drug use or criminal involvement. The substance and bases of youths' theories and practices of avoidance as well as involvement are valuable for those interested in asking questions about prevention of drug use and crime.

New approaches to the role of demographic variables in adolescent drug use and crime are also suggested by our findings. Paying attention to experience revealed that male and female adolescents in our study differed in type and extent of criminal involvement—particularly in the areas of theft and drug selling. How this is so needs further exploration if we wish to create modes of prevention meaningful for all youths. Similarly, new approaches to race, class, and gender as factors that structure experiences in American society are an important aspect of the study of drug use and criminal activity among adolescents. We suggest that these characteristics be taken into account not merely as variables but in terms of the kinds of experiences youths may encounter due to their place in society. Whether youths' experiences differ or are alike and how they influence their perspectives and actions regarding drug use and criminal involvement are important alternatives for looking at the relationship between demographic characteristics and delinquent behavior.

Our data also reveal that the lives of even the most delinquent youths are filled with much more than drugs and crime. The transcripts of our interviews with youths are infused with talk about their families, school, friends, worries, fears, and the future and reveal the ways in which they view and act in their worlds. Understanding these aspects of youths' lives is important to the understanding of how drug use and criminal involvement fit into their lives.

These are only some of the issues that have come up in our data. Some of these questions are elaborated upon and addressed elsewhere (Ksander, forthcoming; Stuck, 1985; Glassner and Loughlin, 1987). Others await further analysis. All point to the need for future studies that will investigate these issues.

We are convinced that it is because we *listened* to kids that we were able to learn so much about them. Too often, such important findings remain untold because those who study adolescents place themselves entirely outside adolescents' worlds.

# References

Abelson, Herbert; Cohen, R.; Schrayer, D.; and Rappeport, M. 1973. Drug experiences, attitudes and related behavior among adolescents and adults. In National Commission on Marihuana and Drug Abuse, *Drug use in America: Problem in perspective* (Vol. 1, Appendix, pp. 488–608). Washington, DC: U.S. Government Printing Office.

ADAMHA/OJJDP (Alcohol, Drug Abuse, and Mental Health Administration/Office of Juvenile Justice and Delinquency Prevention). 1984. *Research Conference on Juvenile Offenders with Serious Drug, Alcohol, and Mental Health Problems.* Washington, DC: Alcohol, Drug Abuse, and Mental Health Administration and Office of Juvenile Justice and Delinquency Prevention.

Adler, Israel, and Kandel, Denise. 1981. Cross-cultural perspectives in developmental stages in adolescent drug use. *Journal of Studies on Alcohol, 42*(9):701–715.

Adler, Patricia A. 1985. *Wheeling and dealing: An ethnography of an upper-level drug dealing and smuggling community.* New York: Columbia University Press.

Adler, Patricia A., and Adler, Peter. 1982. Relationships between dealers: The social organization of illicit drug transactions. *Sociology and Social Research, 67*(3):261–278.

Adler, Patricia A., and Adler, Peter. 1983. Shifts and oscillations in deviant careers: The case of upper-level drug dealers and smugglers. *Social Problems, 31*(2): 195–218.

Adler, Peter T., and Lotecka, Llynn. 1973. Drug use among high school students: Patterns and correlates. *International Journal of Addictions, 8*:537–548.

Agar, Michael H. 1986. *Speaking of ethnography.* Bevery Hills, CA: Sage.

Bachman, Jerald G.; O'Malley, Patrick M.; and Johnston, Jerome. 1978. *Youth in transition: VI. Adolescence to adulthood: Change and stability in the lives of young men.* Ann Arbor: Institute for Social Research, University of Michigan.

Ball, John C.; Rosen, Lawrence; Flueck, John A.; and Nurco, David. 1981. The criminality of heroin addicts when addicted and when off opiates. In James A. Inciardi (Ed.), *The drugs–crime connection* (pp. 36–65). Beverly Hills, CA: Sage.

Ball, John C.; Shaffer, John W.; and Nurco, David N. 1983. The day-to-day criminality of heroin addicts in Baltimore: A study in the continuity of offense rates. *Drug and Alcohol Dependence, 12*:119–142.

Becker, Howard S. 1963. *Outsiders.* New York: Free Press.

Becker, Howard S. 1966. Introduction in C. Shaw, *The Jack Roller* (2nd ed.). Chicago: University of Chicago Press.

Becker, Howard, and Geer, Blanche. 1960. Participant observation: The analysis of qualitative data. In R.N. Adams and J.J. Preis (Eds.), *Human organization research* (pp. 267–289). Homewood, IL: Dorsey Press.

Berkowitz, Leonard. 1978. Is criminal violence normative behavior? *Journal of Research in Crime and Delinquency, 15*:148–161.

Blos, Peter. 1967. The second individuation process of adolescence. *Psychoanalytic Study of the Child, 22*:162–186.

Blum, Richard. 1972. *The dream sellers.* San Francisco: Jossey-Bass.

Blumer, Herbert. 1969. *Symbolic interactionism: Perspective and method.* Englewood Cliffs, NJ: Prentice-Hall.

Blumstein, Alfred; Cohen, Jacqueline; Roth, Jeffrey A.; and Visher, Christy (Eds.). 1986. *Criminal careers and career criminals.* Washington, DC: National Academy Press.

Bogdan, Robert C., and Biklen, Sari K. 1982. *Qualitative research for education: An introduction to theory and methods.* Boston: Allyn and Bacon.

Bogdan, Robert C., and Taylor, Steve. 1975. *Introduction to qualitative research methods.* New York: Wiley.

Britain, C.V. 1963. Adolescent choices and parent–peer cross pressure. *American Sociological Review, 28*:385–391.

Brook, Judith S.; Lukoff, Irving F.; and Whiteman, Martin. 1977. Peer, family, and personality domains as related to adolescent drug behavior. *Psychological Reports, 41*:1095–1102.

Brook, Judith S.; Lukoff, Irving F.; and Whiteman, Martin. 1978. Family, socialization and adolescent personality and their association with adolescent use of marijuana. *Journal of Genetic Psychology, 133*:261–271.

Brook, Judith S.; Lukoff, Irving F.; and Whiteman, Martin. 1980. Initiation into adolescent marijuana use. *Journal of Genetic Psychology, 137*(1):133–142.

Brown, Bradford B. 1982. The extent and effects of peer pressure among high school students: A retrospective analysis. *Journal of Youth and Adolescence, 11*(2): 121–133.

Brunswick, Ann F. 1979. Black youths and drug-use behaviors. In George M. Beschner and Alfred S. Friedman (Eds.), *Youth drug abuse: Problems, issues, and treatment* (pp. 443–490). Lexington, MA: Lexington Books.

Brunswick, Ann F. 1980. Social meaning and developmental needs: Perspectives on black youths' drug abuse. *Youth and Society, 2*(4):449–473.

Brunswick, Ann F. 1985. Health services for adolescents with impairment, disability, or handicap: An ecological paradigm. *Journal of Adolescent Health Care, 6*(2): 141–151.

Brunswick, Ann F., and Boyle, John M. 1979. Patterns of drug initiation: Developmental and secular influences on age at initiation. *Youth and Society, 11*(2):139–162.

Brunswick, Ann F., and Merzel, Cheryl. 1986. Biopsychosocial and epidemiologic perspectives on adolescent health. In Norman Krasnegor, Josephine D. Aresteh, and Michael D. Cataldo (Eds.), *Child health behavior: A behavioral pediatrics perspective* (pp. 149–158). New York: Wiley.

Brunswick, Ann F.; Merzel, Cheryl; and Messeri, Peter. 1985. Drug use initiation among urban black youth: A seven-year follow-up of developmental and secular influences. *Youth and Society, 17*(2):189–216.

Buffalo, M.D., and Rogers, J.W. 1971. Behavioral norms, moral norms, and attachment: Problems of development and conformity. *Social Problems,* 19:101–113.

Bureau of Justice Statistics. 1983a. *Prisoners and alcohol.* Washington, DC: U.S. Department of Justice.

Bureau of Justice Statistics. 1983b. *Prisoners and drugs.* Washington, DC: U.S. Department of Justice.

Bureau of Justice Statistics. 1983c. *Prisoners in prison.* Washington, DC: U.S. Department of Justice.

Bureau of Justice Statistics. 1983d. *Report to the nation on crime and justice.* Washington, DC: U.S. Department of Justice.

Burgess, Robert G. 1984. *In the field: An introduction to field research.* London: George Allen and Unwin.

Burkett, Steven, and Jensen, Eric. 1975. Conventional ties, peer influence, and the fear of apprehension. *Sociology Quarterly,* 16:522–533.

Burns, Thomas F. 1980. Getting ready with the boys. *Journal of Drug Issues,* Spring, pp. 273–286.

Campbell, Anne. 1981. *Girl delinquents.* New York: St. Martin's Press.

Campbell, J.K. 1964. *Honour, family and patronage: A study of moral values in a Greek mountain community.* London: Oxford University Press.

Carey, James T. 1968. *The college drug scene.* Englewood Cliffs, NJ: Prentice-Hall.

Cicourel, Aaron. 1964. *Method and measurement in sociology.* New York: Free Press.

Clausen, John A. 1966. Family structure, socialization, and personality. In M.L. Hoffman and L.W. Hoffman (Eds.), *Review of child development: Research Vol. II.* New York: Russell Sage Foundation.

Cloward, Richard, and Ohlin, Lloyd E. 1960. *Delinquency and opportunity.* New York: Free Press.

Cohen, Albert. 1955. *Delinquent boys: The culture of the gang.* Glencoe, IL: Free Press.

Coleman, James S. 1961. *The adolescent society.* New York: Free Press.

Collins, Gary. 1982. *Alcohol and disinhibition.* Rockville, MD: U.S. Department of Health and Human Services.

Collins, James J., Jr. (Ed.). 1981. *Drinking and crime.* New York: Guilford Press.

Collins, James J., Jr.; Rachal, J. Valley; Hubbart, Robert; Cavanaugh, Elizabeth R.; Craddock, S. Gail; and Kristiansen, Patricia L. 1982a. *Crime and crime indicators in the treatment outcome propective study.* Research Triangle Park, NC: Research Triangle Institute.

Collins, James J., Jr.; Rachal, J. Valley; Hubbart, Robert; Cavanaugh, Elizabeth R.; Craddock, S. Gail; and Kristiansen, Patricia L. 1982b. *Criminality in a drug treatment sample: Measurement issues and initial findings.* Research Triangle Park, NC: Research Triangle Institute.

Conklin, G.E. 1971. Criminal environment and support for the law. *Law and Society Review,* 6:247–259.

Crawford, Gail; Washington, Melvin; and Senay, Edward. 1980. Socio-familial characteristics of black male heroin addicts and their non-addicted friends. *Drug and Alcohol Dependence,* 6:383–390.

Denzin, Norman K. 1978. *The research act* (2nd ed.). New York: McGraw-Hill.

Division of Alcoholism and Alcohol Abuse. 1984. *Alcohol use among secondary school students in New York State.* Albany, NY: Division of Alcoholism and Alcohol Abuse.

Division of Substance Abuse Services. 1984. *Substance use among New York State's public and private school students in grades 7–12, 1983.* Albany, NY: Division of Substance Abuse Services.

Dunford, Franklyn W., and Elliott, Delbert. 1982. *Identifying the career offender: Assessing the deterrent effect of arrests on criminal behavior and career patterns.* Boulder, CO: Behavioral Research Institute.

Dunford, Franklyn W.; Elliott, Delbert; and Huizinga, David. 1983a. *Assessing the seriousness hypothesis with self-reported data: A study of chronic offenders.* Boulder, CO: Behavioral Research Institute.

Dunford, Franklyn W.; Elliott, Delbert; and Huizinga, David. 1983b. *Characteristics of career offending: Testing four hypotheses.* Boulder, CO: Behavioral Research Institute.

Elliott, Delbert S.; Ageton, Suzanne S.; Huizinga, David; Knowles, Brian; and Canter, Rachelle J. 1983. *The prevalence and incidence of delinquent behavior: 1976–1980.* National Youth Survey Report 26. Boulder, CO: Behavioral Research Institute.

Elliott, Delbert S.; Dunford, Frank W.; and Huizinga, David. 1983. *The identification and prediction of career offenders utilizing self-reported and official data.* Boulder, CO: Behavioral Research Institute.

Elliott, Delbert S., and Huizinga, David. 1984. *The relationship between delinquent behavior and ADM [Alcohol, Drug, and Mental Health] Problems.* Boulder, CO: Behavioral Research Institute.

Elliott, Delbert S.; Huizinga, David; and Ageton, Suzanne S. 1985. *Explaining delinquency and drug use.* Beverly Hills, CA: Sage.

Elliott, Delbert S.; Knowles, Brian A.; and Canter, Rachelle J. 1981. The epidemiology of delinquent behavior among American adolescents. In *The dynamics of delinquent behavior: A national survey.* Project Report No. 14. Boulder, Co: Behavioral Research Institute.

Empey, LaMar T. 1978. *American delinquency: Its meaning and construction.* Homewood, IL: Dorsey Press.

Empey, LaMar T., and Lubeck, Steven G. 1968. Conformity and deviance in the situation of company. *American Sociological Review, 33*:760–774.

Erickson, Maynard, and Empey, LaMar T. 1963. Court records, undetected delinquency and decision making. *Journal of Criminal Law, Criminology, and Political Science, 54*:456–469.

Erickson, Maynard, and Gibbs, Jack. 1978. Objective and perceptual properties of legal punishment and the deterrence doctrine. *Social Problems, 18*:253–264.

Erickson, Maynard; Gibbs, Jack; and Jensen, Gary. 1977. The deterrence doctrine and the perceived certainty of legal punishments. *American Sociological Review, 56*:305–317.

Erlanger, Howard S. 1979. Estrangement, machismo and gang violence. *Social science Quarterly, 60*(2):235–246.

Farrington, David P.; Berkowitz, Leonard O.; and West, David J. 1982. Differences between individual and group fights. *British Journal of Social Psychology, 21*:323–333.

Federal Bureau of Investigation. 1982. *Crime in the United States   1982.* Uniform Crime Reports. Washington, DC: U.S. Department of Justice.

Feldman, Harvey M. 1974. *Street status and the drug researcher: Issues in participant observation.* Washington, DC: Drug Abuse Council.

Feldman, Harvey M. 1980. Background and purpose of the ethnographers' policymakers' symposium. In Carl Akins and George Beschner (Eds.), *Ethnography: A research tool for policymakers in the drug and alcohol fields.* Rockville, MD: Department of Health and Human Services.

Feldman, Harvey W.; Agar, Michael H.; and Beschner, George M. 1979. *Angel dust: An ethnographic study of PCP users.* Lexington, MA: Lexington Books.

Fox, Stanford J. 1970. Juvenile justice reform: A historical perspective. *Stanford Law Review,* 22:1187–1239.

Frazier, Charles E. 1978. The use of life histories in testing theories of criminal behavior. *Qualitative Sociology,* 1:122–142.

Freud, Anna, 1958. Adolescent. *Psychoanalytic Study of the Child,* 13:178–255.

Friedenberg, Edgar Z. 1963. *Coming of age in America: Growth and acquiescence.* New York: Random House.

Gandossy, Robert P.; Williams, Jay R.; Cohen, Jo; and Harwood, Hendrick J. 1980. *Drugs and crime: A survey and analysis of the literature.* Washington, DC: National Institute of Justice.

Glaser, Barney, and Strauss, Anselm. 1967. *The discovery of grounded theory.* Chicago: Aldine.

Glaser, Daniel. 1975. *Strategic criminal justice planning.* Center for Studies of Crime and Delinquency. Rockville, MD: National Institute of Mental Health.

Glassner, Barry, and Loughlin, Julia. 1987. *Drugs in adolescent worlds.* New York: St. Martin's.

Gold, Martin. 1970. *Delinquent behavior in an American city.* Belmont, CA: Brooks/ Cole.

Gold, Martin, 1977. Scholastic experiences, self-esteem, and delinquent behavior: A theory for alternative schools. *Crime and Delinquency,* 24(3):290–308.

Gold, Martin, and Petronio, Richard J. 1980. Delinquent behavior in adolescence. In J. Abelson (Ed.), *Handbook of adolescent psychology* (pp. 495–535). New York: Wiley.

Gold, Martin, and Reimer, David J. 1975. Changing pattterns of delinquent behavior among Americans 13 through 16 years old: 1967–72. *Crime and Delinquency Literature,* 7:483–517.

Gold, Martin, and Williams, Jay R. 1969. The effect of getting caught. Apprehension of the juvenile offender as a cause of subsequent delinquencies. *Prospectus,* 3:1–12.

Goldstein, Paul J. 1985. The drugs/violence nexus: A tripartite conceptual framework. *Journal of Drug Issues,* Fall, pp. 493–506.

Goode, Erich. 1970. *The marijuana smokers.* New York: Basic Books.

Goode, Erich. 1971. Empirical data on the escalation process. In National Commission on Marihuana and Drug Abuse, *Marihuana: A signal of misunderstanding* (Vol. 1, Appendix, pp. 340–367). Washington, DC: U.S. Government Printing Offfice.

Goode, Erich. 1972. *Drugs in American society* (2nd ed.). New York: Knopf.

Gropper, Bernard. 1985. *Probing the links between drugs and crime.* Washington, DC: National Institute of Justice.

Gould, Leroy C.; Walker, Andres C.; Crane, Lansing E.; and Litz, Charles W. 1974. *Connections: Notes from the heroin world.* New Haven, CT: Yale University Press.

Hamparian, Donna Martin; Schuster, Richard; Dinitz, Simon; and Conrad, John P. 1978. *The violent few: A study of dangerous juvenile offenders.* Lexington, MA: Lexington Books.

Harlan, John P., and McDowell, Charles P. 1980. Vindictive vandalism and the schools: Some theoretical considerations. *Journal of Police Science and Administration,* 8(4):399–405.

Haskell, M., and Yablonsky, Louis. 1974. *Juvenile delinquency.* Chicago: Rand McNally.

Hendin, Herbert; Pollinger, Ann; and Ulman, Richard. 1982. The functions of marijuana abuse for adolescents. *American Journal of Drug and Alcohol Abuse,* 8:441–456.

Hirschi, Travis, 1969. *Causes of delinquency.* Berkeley: University of California Press.

Holsti, C.R. 1960. *Content analysis for the social services and humanities.* Reading, MA: Addison-Wesley.

Horowitz, Ruth, and Schwartz, Gary. 1974. Honor, normative ambiguity and gang violence. *American Sociological Review, 30* (April):238–251.

Huba, George J.; Wingard, James A.; and Bentler, Peter M. 1980. Longitudinal analysis in beginning adolescent substance use: An application of setwise canonical correlation methods. *Multivariate Behavioral Research, 15:*259–279.

Huizinga, David H. 1982. Unpublished tables on nondrug crime rates among drug users and types of delinquents among the nation's youth in 1976–1980. New York: Interdisciplinary Research Center.

Huizinga, David H. 1984. Unpublished tables on nondrug crime rates among drug users, drug sellers, and types of delinquents among the nation's youth in 1979. New York: Interdisciplinary Research Center.

Huizinga, David H. 1986. The relationship between delinquent and drug use behaviors in a national sample of youths. In Bruce D. Johnson and Eric Wish (Eds.), *Crime rates among drug abusing offenders* (pp. 145–194). New York: Interdisciplinary Research Center.

Huizinga, David, and Dunford, Franklyn W. 1985. *The delinquent behaviors of arrested individuals.* Paper prepared for the 1985 annual meeting of the Academy of Criminal Justice Sciences, Las Vegas, Nevada, April. Boulder, CO: Behavioral Research Institute.

Huizinga, David, and Elliott, Delbert S. 1981. *A longtiudinal study of drug use and delinquency in a national sample of youth: An assessment of causal order.* Project Report No. 16. Boulder, CO: Behavioral Research Institute.

Inciardi, James A. 1979. Heroin use and street crime. *Crime and Delinquency,* 25:335–346.

Inciardi, James A. 1980. Youth, drugs, and street crime. In Frank Scarpitti and Susan K. Datesman (Eds.), *Drugs and the youth culture* (pp. 175–204). Beverly Hills, CA: Sage.

Inciardi, James A. 1981. *The drugs–crime connection.* Beverly Hills, CA: Sage.

Inciardi, James A. 1984. *Criminal justice.* Orlando, FL: Academic Press.

Jensen, Gary R.; Erickson, Maynard; and Gibbs, Jack. 1978. Perceived risk of punishment and self-reported delinquency. *Social Forces,* 57:57–78.

Jensen, Gary R., and Rojek, Dean G. 1980. *Delinquency: A sociological view.* Lexington, MA: D.C. Heath.

Jessor, Richard; Graves, Theodore D.; Hanson, Robert C.; and Jessor, Shirley L. 1968. *Society, personality, and deviant behavior—A study of a tri-ethnic community.* New York: Holt, Rinehart and Winston.

Jessor, Richard; Graves, Theodore D.; Hanson, Robert C.; and Jessor, Shirley L. 1976. Predicting time of onset of marijuana use: A developmental study of high school youth. *Journal of Consulting and Clinical Psychology, 44*:125–134.

Jessor, Richard, and Jessor, Shirley. 1977. *Problem behavior and psychosocial development—A longitudinal study of youth.* New York: Academic Press.

Jessor, Richard; Jessor, Shirley; and Finney, J.A. 1973. A social psychology of marijuana use: Longitudinal studies of high school and college youth. *Journal of Personality and Social Psychology, 26*:1–15.

Johnson, Bruce D. 1973. *Marihuana users and drug subcultures.* New York: Wiley.

Johnson, Bruce D. 1980. Towards a theory of drug subcultures. In Dan Lettieri et al. (Eds.), *Theories on drug abuse: Selected contemporary perspectives* (pp. 110–119). Research Monograph 30. Rockville, MD: National Institute on Drug Abuse.

Johnson, Bruce D. 1981. *Variable field codebook for coding transcripts and field notes.* New York: Interdisciplinary Research Center (Appendix B).

Johnson, Bruce D.; Goldstein, Paul; Preble, Edward; Schmeidler, James; Lipton, Douglas S.; Spunt, Barry; and Miller, Thomas. 1983. *Final report: The economic behavior of street opiate users.* Prepared for the National Institute on Drug Abuse and National Institute of Justice. New York: Narcotic and Drug Research, Inc.

Johnson, Bruce D.; Goldstein, Paul; Preble, Edward; Schmeidler, James; Lipton, Douglas S.; Spunt, Barry; and Miller, Thomas. 1985. *Taking care of business: The economics of crime by heroin abusers.* Lexington, MA: Lexington Books.

Johnson, Bruce D., and Wish, Eric (Eds.). 1986. *Crime rates among drug abusing offenders.* New York: Interdisciplinary Research Center.

Johnson, Bruce D., and Wish, Eric D. 1987. *Criminal events among seriously criminal drug abusers.* New York: Interdisciplinary Research Center.

Johnson, Bruce D.; Wish, Eric; and Huizinga, David. 1986. The concentration of delinquent offending: The contribution of serious drug involvement to high rate delinquency. In Bruce D. Johnson and Eric Wish (Eds.), *Crime rates among drug abusing offenders* (pp. 106–143). New York: Interdisciplinary Research Center.

Johnson, Bruce D.; Wish, Eric; Huizinga, David; and Schmeidler, James. 1984. Drug involved delinquencies: Drug and alcohol use near the time of the crime. Paper presented at a meeting of the American Criminology Society, Cincinnati, Ohio, November.

Johnson, Bruce D.; Wish, Eric; Strug, David; and Chaiken, Marcia. 1983. Violence among heroin abusers. Paper presented at a meeting of the American Sociological Association, Detroit, Michigan, September.

Johnston, Lloyd; Bachman, Jerald G.; and O'Malley, Patrick M. 1982. *Student drug use, attitudes, and beliefs: 1975–1982.* Rockville, MD: National Institute on Drug Abuse.

Johnston, Lloyd, and O'Malley, Patrick. 1978. A cross-cohort comparison of the drugs–delinquency connection. Paper presented at the Symposium on Cohort Studies, Uppsala, Sweden.

Johnston, Lloyd; O'Malley, Patrick; and Bachman, Gerald G. 1984. *Highlights from "Drugs and American high school students: 1975–1983."* Rockville, MD: National Institute on Drug Abuse.

Johnston, Lloyd; O'Malley, Patrick; and Eveland, Leslie K. 1976. Nonaddictive drug use and delinquency: A longitudinal analysis. In Robert Shellow (Ed.), *Drug use and crime: Report of the Panel on Drug Use and Criminal Behavior* (pp. 325–350). Washington, DC: National Technical Information Service.

Johnston, Lloyd; O'Malley, Patrick; and Eveland, Leslie K. 1978. Nonaddictive drug use and delinquency: A longitudinal analysis. In Denise B. Kandel (Ed.), *Longitudinal research on drug use: Empirical findings and methodological issues* (pp. 137–156). New York: Wiley.

Kandel, Denise B. 1976a. Adolescent involvement in illicit drug use: A multiple classification analysis. *Social Forces, 55*:438–458.

Kandel, Denise B. 1976b. Stages in adolescent involvement in drug use. *Science, 190*:912–914.

Kandel, Denise B. (Ed.). 1978. *Longitudinal research on drug use: Empirical findings and methodological issues.* Washington, DC: Hemisphere.

Kandel, Denise B. 1980. Drug use by youth: An overview. In Dan J. Lettieri and Jacqueline P. Ludford (Eds.), *Drug abuse and the American adolescent* (pp. 1–21). Research Monograph 38. Rockville, MD: National Institute on Drug Abuse.

Kandel, Denise B.; Kessler, Ronald; and Margulies, Rebecca Z. 1978. Antecedents of adolescent initiation into stages of drug use: A developmental analysis. *Journal of Youth and Adolescence, 7*(1):13–40.

Kandel, Denise B., and Logan, John A. 1983. Periods of risk for initiation, stabilization and decline in drug use from adolescence to early adulthood. Paper presented at the annual meeting of the Society for the Study of Social Problems, New York, August.

Kandel, Denise B.; Margulies, Rebecca Z.; and Davies, Mark. 1978. Analytical strategies for studying transitions into developmental stages. *Sociology of Education, 51* (July):162–176.

Kandel, Denise B., and Yamaguchi, Kazuo. 1984. *Developmental patterns of the use of legal, illegal, and medically prescribed psychotropic drugs from adolescence to young adulthood.* Paper presented at Workshop on Etiology of Drug Abuse Implications for Prevention. Rockville, MD: National Institute on Drug Abuse.

Kaplan, John. 1973. *Criminal justice.* Mineola, NY: Foundation Press.

King, Charles T. 1975. The ego and the integration of violence in homicidal youth. *American Journal of Orthopsychiatry, 45*(1):134–145.

Kirk, Jerome, and Miller, Marc L. 1986. *Reliability and validity in qualitative research.* Beverly Hills, CA: Sage.

Kitsuse, John I., and Cicourel, Aaron V. 1963. A note on the uses of official statistics. *Social Problems, 11*:131–139.

Klemke, Lloyd W. 1978. Does apprehension amplify or terminate shoplifting activity? *Law and Society, 12*(3):391–401.

Kohlberg, Laurence. 1969. Stage and sequence: The cognitive-developmental approach. In David A. Goslin (Ed.), *Handbook of socialization theory and research* (pp. 347–480). Chicago: Rand McNally.

Krippendorff, Klaus. 1980. *Content analysis.* Beverly Hills, CA: Sage.

Ksander, Margret M. forthcoming. *Practical theories of deviance: Adolescent motive talk.* Unpublished dissertation, Syracuse University.

Larson, Lyle E. 1974. An examination of the salience hierarchy during adolescence: The influence of the family. *Adolescence, 9*:317–332.

Lemert, Edwin. 1967. The juvenile court: Quest and realities. In President's Commission on Law Enforcement and the Administration of Justice, *Task force report on juvenile justice and youth crime* (pp. 91–106). Washington, DC: U.S. Government Printing Office.

Levine, Edward M., and Kozak, Conrad. 1979. Drug and alcohol use, delinquency, and vandalism among upper middle class pre- and post-adolescents. *Journal of Youth and Adolescence,* 8(1):91–101.

Levinson, David. 1983. Alcohol use and aggression in American subcultures. In Robin Room and Gary Collins (Eds.), *Alcohol and disinhibition: Nature and meaning of the link* (pp. 331–337). Research Monograph 12. Rockville, MD: National Institute on Alcohol Abuse and Alcoholism.

Lindelius, Rolf, and Salvin, I. 1975. Alcoholism and crime. *Journal of Studies on Alcohol,* 36:1452–1457.

Lofland, John. 1969. *Deviance and Identity.* Englewood Cliffs, NJ: Prentice-Hall.

Lyerly, Robert R., and Skipper, James K., Jr. 1981. Differential rates of rural–urban delinquency. *Criminology,* 19(3):385–399.

MacAndrew, Craig, and Edgerton, Robert B. 1969. *Drunken comportment: A social explanation.* Chicago: Aldine.

Mack, Julien. 1910. The juvenile court as a legal institution. In Hart Hastings (Ed.), *Preventive treatment of neglected children.* New York: Charities Publication Committee.

Marsh, Peter. 1978. *Aggro: The illusion of violence.* London: Dent and Son.

Matza, David. 1969. *Becoming deviant.* Englewood Cliffs, NJ: Prentice-Hall.

McBride, Duane C., and Clayton, Richard R. 1985. Methodological issues in the etiology of drug abuse. *Journal of Drug Issues,* Fall, pp. 509–529.

Mead, Margaret. 1970. *Culture and commitment.* New York: Doubleday.

Melvinhill, Donald J.; Tummit, Melvin M.; and Curtis, Lynn A. 1969. *Crimes of violence: A staff report.* Submitted to the National Commission on the Causes and Prevention of Violence. Washington, DC: U.S. Government Printing Office.

Miller, Judith D.; Cisin, Ira H.; Gardner-Keaton, Hillary; Harrell, Adele V.; Wirtz, Phillip W.; Abelson, Herbert I.; and Fishburne, Patricia M. 1983. *National survey on drug abuse: Main findings 1982.* Rockville, MD: National Institute on Drug Abuse.

Mitchell, J. Clyde. 1983. Case study and situational analysis. *The Sociological Review,* 31(2):187–211.

Montmarquette, Claude, and Nerlove, Marc. 1985. Deterrence and delinquency: An analysis of individual data. *Journal of Quantitative Criminology,* 1(1):37–58.

Morgan, Patricia. 1983. Alcohol, disinhibition, and domination: A conceptual analysis. In Robin Room and Gary Collins (Eds.), *Alcohol and disinhibition: Nature and meaning of the link* (pp. 405–430). Research Monograph 12. Rockville, MD: National Institute on Alcohol Abuse and Alcoholism.

Nash, Jeffrey E., and Spradley, James P. 1976. *Sociology: A descriptive approach.* Chicago: Rand McNally.

Nurco, David; Ball, John C.; Shaffer, John; and Hanlon, Thomas. 1985. The criminality of heroin addicts. *Journal of Nervous and Mental Disease,* 173(2):94–102.

Nurco, David N.; Cisin, Ira H.; and Balter, Mitchell B. 1981a. Addict careers: I. A new typology. *International Journal of the Addictions,* 16(8):1305–1325.

Nurco, David N.; Cisin, Ira H.; and Balter, Mitchell B. 1981b. Addict careers: II. The first ten years. *International Journal of the Addictions,* 16(8):1327–1356.

Nurco, David N.; Cisin, Ira H.; and Balter, Mitchell B. 1981c. Addict careers: III. Trends across time. *International Journal of the Addictions,* 16(8):1357–1372.

Office of Drug Abuse Services. 1978. *Substance use among New York State public and parochial school students in grades 7 through 12.* Albany, NY: Office of Drug Abuse Services (now Divison of Substance Abuse Services).

O'Malley, Patrick; Bachman, Jerald; and Johnston, Lloyd. 1977. *Youth in transition: Final report. Five years beyond high school: Causes and consequences of educational attainment.* Ann Arbor, MI: Institute for Social Research.

O'Malley, Patrick; Bachman, Jerald; and Johnston, Lloyd. 1984. Period, age, and cohort effects on substance use among American youth. *American Journal of Public Health,* 74:682–688.

Packard, Herbert L. 1968. *The limits of the criminal sanction.* Stanford, CA: Stanford University Press.

Pernanen, Kai. 1976. Alcohol and crimes of violence. In Ben Kissin and Henry Begleiter (Eds.), *The biology of alcoholism:* IV. *Social aspects of alcoholism.* New York: Plenum.

Pernanen, Kai. 1981. Theoretical aspects of the relationship between alcohol use and crime. In James W. Collins, Jr. (Ed.), *Drinking and crime* (pp. 1–69). New York: Guilford Press.

Polk, Kenneth; Frease, Dean; and Richmond, Lynn F. 1974. Social class, school experiences, and delinquency. *Criminology, 12*(1):84–96.

Potvin, Raymond H., and Lee, Che-Fu. 1980. Multistage path models of adolescent alcohol and drug use. *Journal of Studies on Alcohol, 41*(5):531–542.

Rawlings, M. Lawrence. 1973. Self control and interpersonal violence: A study of Scottish adolescent male severe offenders. *Criminology, 11*(1):23–48.

Richards, Pamela; Burke, Richard A.; and Forster, Brenda. 1979. *Crime as play: Delinquency in a middle class suburb.* Cambridge, MA: Ballinger.

Richardson, S. 1965. *Interviewing: Its form and function.* New York: Free Press.

Robins, Lee. 1966. *Deviant children grown up: A sociological and psychiatric study of sociopathic personality.* Baltimore, MD: Williams and Wilkins.

Robins, Lee N., and Wish, Eric. 1977. Development of childhood deviance: A study of 223 urban black men from birth to 18. *Social Forces, 56*(2):448–473.

Room, Robin, and Collins, Gary (Eds.). 1983. *Alcohol and disinhibition: Nature and meaning of the link.* Research Monograph 12. Rockville, MD: National Institute on Alcohol Abuse and Alcoholism.

Sanchez, Jose, and Johnson, Bruce D. 1986. Crime rates among drug using inmates at the women's house of detention (Riker's Island). In Bruce D. Johnson and Eric Wish (Eds.), *Crime rates among drug abusing offenders* (pp. 55–80). New York: Interdisciplinary Research Center.

Schatzman, Leonard, and Strauss, Anselm. 1973. *Field research.* Englewood Cliffs, NJ: Prentice-Hall.

Schwartz, Howard, and Jacobs, Jerry. 1979. *Qualitative sociology.* New York: Free Press.

Shannon, Lyle W. 1982. *Assessing the relationship of adult criminal careers to juvenile careers: A summary.* Washington, DC: National Institute for Juvenile Justice and Delinquency Prevention.

Shaw, Clifford R. 1930. *The jack roller.* Chicago: University of Chicago Press. 2nd Edition 1966.

Short, James F., and Strodtbeck, Fred L. 1965. *Group process and gang delinquency.* Chicago: University of Chicago Press.

Single, Eric, and Kandel, Denise. 1978. The role of buying and selling in illicit drug use. In Arnold Trebach (Ed.), *Drugs, crime, and politics* (pp. 118–128). New York: Praeger.

Skolnick, Arlene. 1979. Children's rights, children's development. In LaMar Empey (Ed.), *The future of childhood and juvenile justice* (pp. 138–174). Charlottesville: University Press of Virginia.

Smith, Charles P.; Alexander, Paul S.; Haltyn, Thomas V.; and Roberts, Chester. 1980. *A national assessment of serious juvenile crime and the juvenile justice system: The need for a rational response: II. Definitions, characteristics of incidents and individuals, and relationship to substance abuse.* Reports of the National Juvenile Justice Assessment Centers. Washington, DC: National Institute of Justice.

Spradley, James. 1979. *The ethnographic interview.* New York: Holt, Rinehart and Winston.

Strasburg, Paul A. 1978. *Violent delinquents.* A Report to the Ford Foundation by the Vera Institute of Justice. New York: Simon and Schuster.

Stuck, Mary F. 1985. *Adolescents, drugs, and sports involvement: A qualitative study.* Unpublished dissertation, Syracuse University.

Suchman, E. 1968. The hang-loose ethic and the spirit of drug use. *Journal of Health and Social Behavior* 9:146–155.

Sutherland, Edwin. 1947. *Principles of criminology* (4th ed.). Philadelphia: Lippincott.

Sykes, Gresham M., and Matza, David. 1957. Techniques of neutralization: A theory of delinquency. *American Journal of Sociology,* 22:664–670.

Tinklenberg, Jared R. 1973. Drugs and crime. In National Commission on Marijuana and Drug Abuse, *Drug use in America: Problem in perspective* (Vol. I, Appendix, pp. 242–299). Washington, DC: U.S. Government Printing Office.

Tinklenberg, Jared R.; Murphy, Peggy; Murphy, Patricia L.; and Pfefferbaum, Adolph. 1981. Drugs and criminal assaults by adolescents: A replication study. *Journal of Psychoactive Drugs, 13*(3):277–287.

Tinklenberg, Jared R., and Ochberg, Frank M. 1981. Patterns of adolescent violence: A California sample. In Jared R. Tinklenberg and Frank M. Ochberg (Eds.), *Biobehavioral aspects of aggression* (pp. 121–140). New York: Alan R. Liss.

Tinklenberg, Jared R.; Roth, Walton T.; Kipell, Bert S.; and Murphy, Patricia. 1976. Cannabis and alcohol effects on assaultiveness in adolescent delinquents. In R.L. Dornbush, M. Fink, and A.M. Freedman (Eds.), *Chronic cannabis use* (pp. 85–94). Annals of the New York Academy of Sciences (Vol. 282). New York: New York Academy of Sciences.

Tittle, Charles. 1980. *Sanctions and social deviance.* New York: Praeger.

Toby, Jackson. 1983a. School violence. In Michael Tonry and Norvil Morris (Eds.), *Crime and justice—An annual review of research* (pp. 1–47). Chicago: University of Chicago Press.

Toby, Jackson. 1983b. *Violence in schools.* NIJ Research in Brief. Washington, DC: National Institute of Justice.

Toch, Hans. 1969. *Violent men.* Chicago: Aldine.

Tracy, Paul A.; Wolfgang, Marvin; and Figlio, Robert. 1985. *Delinquency in two birth cohorts: Executive summary.* Washington, DC: National Institute for Juvenile Justice and Deliquency Prevention.

Truzzi, Marcello (Ed.). 1974. *Verstehen: Subjective understanding in the social sciences.* Reading, MA: Addison-Wesley.

Tudor, Cynthia G.; Petersen, David M.; and Elifson, Kirk W. 1980. An examination of the relationship between peer and parental influences and adolescent drug use. *Adolescence, 15*(60):783–797.

Waldorf, Dan; Murphy, Sheigla; Reinarman, Craig; and Joyce, Briget. 1977. *Doing coke: An ethnography of cocaine snorters.* Washington, DC: Drug Abuse Council.

Webb, Eugene J.; Campbell, Donald T.; Schwartz, Richard D.; and Sechrest, Lew. 1966. *Unobtrusive measures.* Chicago: Rand McNally.

Weiner, Neil. 1984. Recidivism among violent delinquents: A failure rate regression analysis of birth cohort information. Paper presented at the American Society of Criminology, Cincinnati, Ohio, November.

Weis, Joseph G., and Sederstrom, John. 1981. *The prevention of serious delinquency: What to do?* U.S. National Institute for Juvenile Justice and Delinquency Prevention. Washington, DC: U.S. Government Printing Office.

Weissman, James C. 1979. Drug control principles: Instrumentalism and symbolism. *Journal of Psychoactive Drugs, 11*(1):203–210.

Wish, Eric, and Johnson, Bruce D. 1986. *The impact of substance abuse on criminal careers.* In Alfred Blumstein, Jacqueline Cohen, Jeffrey A. Roth, and Christy A. Visher, *Criminal careers and "career criminals"* Vol. 2, (pp. 52–88). Washington, DC: National Academy Press.

Wolfgang, Marvin E. 1967. The culture of youth. In President's Commission on Law Enforcement, *Task force report: Juvenile delinquency and youth crime* (p. 147). Washington, DC: U.S. Government Printing Office.

Wolfgang, Marvin E. 1983. The violent juvenile: A Philadelphia profile. In Kenneth R. Feinberg (Ed.), *Violent Crime in America* (pp. 17–23). Washington, DC: National Policy Exchange.

Wolfgang, Marvin E.; Figlio, Robert M.; and Sellin, Thorsten. 1972. *Delinquency in a birth cohort.* Chicago: University of Chicago Press.

Yablonsky, Louis. 1959. The delinquent gang as a near-group. *Social Problems, 7*(2):108–117.

Zimring, Franklin E., and Hawkins, Gordon J. 1973. *Deterrence: The legal threat in crime control.* Chicago: University of Chicago Press.

# Index

Abelson, Herbert, 8, 9

Acid, selling of, 52

ADAMHA/OJJDP (Alcohol, Drug Abuse, and Mental Health Administration/Office of Juvenile Justice and Delinquency Prevention), 100

Addiction, 191, 199–200

Adler, Israel, 187, 189, 190

Adler, Patricia A., 9, 39–40, 47

Adler, Peter T., 9, 39–40, 148

Agar, Michael H., 24

Age: ages 15–16 as a transition period in nondrug delinquency, 209–210; critical age of 13, 120; disinvolvement with delinquency or commitment after age 16, 216–217; experimental ages 12–15, 214–216; significance of age 16, 213–214

Ageton, Suzanne S., 12, 17, 58

Aggression: alcohol/drugs and increased, 32; ritualized aggression among youths, 88

Alcohol abuse: assaultive crimes and, 10–11; disinhibition and, 33

Alcohol–crime association, adolescents' perspectives on: alcohol use is incidental to crime, 35, 219–220; consumption of alcohol before a crime, 36–37; life is more fun with the use of alcohol, 34–35; noninvolved youths and, 28–29, 37; psychological effects of, 32–34; relatively experienced youths and, 29–30, 37; seriously involved youths and, 30, 37; violence and, 32, 87–88, 97–99

Alcohol use: in the Elizabeth case, 137–138; as an entry drug, 189; in the Gallo case, 160, 161–162, 173; relationship of drug/alcohol users and seriously delinquent youths, 219; as a secondary drug, 190

Alexander, Paul S., 21, 142

Amphetamines in the Gallo case, 163, 171, 172, 173

Arson, 116–117; in the Gallo case, 168

Automobiles, theft of, 105, 106–107

Bachman, Jerald G., 12, 15, 17, 120, 209, 214, 215

Ball, John C., 10

Balter, Mitchell B., 10

Becker, Howard S., 4, 5–6, 24, 187–188

Bentler, Peter M., 119

Berkowitz, Leonard, 88, 89, 99

Biklen, Sari K., 7, 24

Blos, Peter, 119

Blum, Richard, 9, 39, 40

Blumer, Herbert, 4

Blumstein, Alfred, 11

Bogdan, Robert C., 4, 5, 7, 24

Boyle, John M., 119

Britain, C.V., 119

Brook, Judith S., 119

Brown, Bradford B., 146, 184

Brunswick, Ann F., 11, 119, 185

Buffalo, M.D., 187

Bureau of Justice Statistics, 8

Burgess, Robert G., 4

Burke, Richard A., 146, 209, 215

Burkett, Steven, 218

Burns, Thomas F., 10
Buyers of drugs: types of, 53–54, 58; as victims, 110

Campbell, Anne, 88, 99
Campbell, Donald T., 24
Campbell, J.K., 88
Canter, Rachelle J., 17, 209, 210, 214
Carey, James T., 7, 40
Case studies: background of, 119–121, 145–146; comparison of Gallo and Kevin cases, 183–186; value of, 142. *See also under* Elizabeth, case study of; Gallo, case study of; Kevin, case study of; Norris, case study of
Cash, theft of, 72–75
Cavanaugh, Elizabeth R., 10
Chaiken, Marcia, 110
Cicourel, Aaron, 24, 88
Cisin, Ira H., 10
Clausen, John A., 119
Clayton, Richard R., 9, 39, 58, 219, 220
Cloward, Richard, 146
Cocaine: experimenting with, 191–192; in the Gallo case, 167, 175; selling of, 52
Cohen, Albert, 146
Cohen, Jacqueline, 11
Cohen, Jo, 27
Cohen, R., 8, 9
Coleman, James S., 119
Collins, Gary, 10, 33, 87, 88, 97
Collins, James J., Jr., 10, 87, 97
Conklin, G.E., 209
Conrad, John P., 87
Consumer goods, theft of, 62–64
Corporations as victims of crime, 110, 111
Craddock, S. Gail, 10
Crawford, Gail, 10
Crime: considered unsafe by committed-experimenters, 201–204; effects of adult jurisdiction on, 216–217; type of deterrents to initiator-experimenters, 204–207. *See also* Alcohol-crime association, adolescents' perspectives on; Delinquency; Drug-crime association, adolescents' perspectives on
Criminal justice sanctions as a deterrent to delinquency, 12–13, 221–222. *See also* Deterrent(s)
Curtis, Lynn A., 87

Davies, Mark, 119
Delinquency: ages 15–16 as a transition period in nondrug, 209–210; critical age of 13 and, 120; disinvolvement with, or commitment after age 16, 216–217; experimental ages 12–15 and, 214–216; influence of peers on, 127–130; and other crimes committed by Elizabeth, 139–141; and other crimes committed by Gallo, 159–171; and other crimes committed by Norris, 123–125; prior to drug use, 120; relationship of drug/alcohol users and seriously delinquent youths, 219
Denial of: injury, 100, 103; the victim, 103, 115, 116
Denzin, Norman K., 7
Detention center(s): Kevin at a, 148; lack of fear of, 211
Deterrent(s): ages 15–16 as a transition period in nondrug delinquency, 209–210; criminal justice sanctions as a, to delinquency, 12–13; effects of adult jurisdiction on, 216–217; experimental ages 12–15 and, 214–216; fear of incarceration, 210–213; to initiator-experimenters, 204–207; moral development as a, 217; significance of age 16, 213–214
Dinitz, Simon, 87
Disinhibition, 10–11; alcohol and, 33; drugs and, 178; violence and role of, 97–99
Drug-crime association, adolescents' perspectives on, 8–9; committed-experimenters and, 201–204; consumption of drugs before a crime, 36–37; drug use is incidental to crime, 35, 219–220; in the Gallo case, 177–178, 180; heavy drug users and violence, 90, 99; initiators-experimenters and, 204–207; lack of concern regarding risks involved with, 202–207; life is more fun with the use of drugs, 34–35; motivation for crime did not include drug use, 35–36; noninvolved youths and, 28–29, 37; psychological effects of, 32–34;

relatively experienced youths and, 29–30, 37; seriously involved youths and, 30–32, 37; theft and, 31–32, 84; violence and, 32, 87–88, 97–99

Drug dealers: adolescents as, 49–50; adults as, 47–49; big-time, 48; characteristics of adolescent, 41–46; involvement of, with other crime, 45–46, 58; legal/parental authority and views of, 57, 59; Mafia as, 48–49; marijuana and, 44–45; relationship of adolescents with, 53; sellers versus, 40, 41–42, 58, 172, 220–221; as users of drugs, 39–40, 44–45, 58, 59, 220–221; as victims, 110

Drug dealing, difference between selling and, 40, 41–42, 58, 172, 220–221

Drug distribution violence, 91

Drug Freedom, 148–149, 185

Drug safety, lack concern for, 194

Drug selling: acid, 52; areas of specialization in, 51; cocaine and, 52; difference between dealing and, 40, 41–42, 58, 172, 220–221; effect of seasons on, 56–57; to family members, 53; to friends, 53; hashish and, 52; locations for, 55–56, 58, 59; marijuana and, 52; method of communication in a drug transaction, 54; prescription-type drugs and, 52; reasons for, 42–44, 58; rush and, 52; sources for drugs, 47; speed and, 52; supply and demand and, 50–52; types of buyers, 53–54, 58

Drug use: accessibililty/availability of drugs and, 190; alcohol as an entry drug, 189; alcohol as a secondary drug, 190; assaultive crimes and, 10–11; casual stage of, 188; characteristics of illicit drug users, 121; developmental stages in adolescent involvement with, 120; delinquent behavior prior to, 120; disinhibition and, 178; in the Elizabeth case, 138–139; in the Gallo case, 159–160, 161, 162–164, 166–167, 169–170, 171–181; influence of peers on,

120–121, 128–130, 147; in the Kevin case, 147, 148; marijuana as an entry drug, 189; marijuana as a primary commitment drug, 190; in the Norris case, 128–131; property crimes linked to, 9–10; relationship of drug/alcohol users and seriously delinquent youths, 219; routine stage of, 188; safe versus unsafe drugs, 190; secondary drugs, 190; stages of involvement, 188

Drug use, committed-experimenters and: chance versus choice of, 193–194; entry drugs for, 189–190; fear of heroin and PCP, 192–193; lack of concern for drug safety, 194; primary drug for, 190; reasons for experimenting, 194; what is "serious" criminal/delinquent behavior to, 201; willingness to experiment, 191–192

Drug use, initiators-experimenters and: addiction and, 191, 199–200; effects of drugs on, 195; entry drugs for, 189, 190–191; reaction to alcohol, 196, 197; reaction to cigarette smoking, 196; reaction to drugs in general, 197; reaction to marijuana, 195–196; reasons for not continuing with drugs, 194–196; safe and unsafe drugs and, 197–199; what is "serious" criminal/delinquent behavior to, 201, 204–207

Dunford, Franklyn W., 21, 58, 59, 87, 90, 146

Edgerton, Robert B., 10, 100

Elifson, Kirk W., 148

Elizabeth, case study of, 3; alcohol and, 137–138; background of, 133; behavior of, in school, 136; delinquency and other crimes committed by, 139–141; drugs and, 138–139; future plans of, 141–142; peer influence on, 135–137; prognosis for, 142, 143; relationship with family, 133–135; relationship with sister, 136–137

Elliott, Delbert S., 11, 12, 17, 20, 21, 22, 27, 39, 58, 59, 87, 90, 119, 120, 121, 133, 145, 146, 177, 187, 209, 210, 214, 216, 219

Empey, LaMar T., 87, 188, 218
Erickson, Maynard, 88, 146, 209, 218
Erlanger, Howard S., 88, 99
Ethnic antagonism, 92–93
Eveland, Leslie K., 12, 27, 209

Family members: Elizabeth's relationship with, 133–137; Gallo's relationship with, 156–158, 159–161, 163, 169–170; selling drugs to, 53; theft of, 110–111
Farrington, David P., 88, 89, 99
Fear: of incarceration, 210–213; tactics, 6
Federal Bureau of Investigation, 15
Feldman, Harvey M., 6, 24
Fighting, violence and, 99
Figlio, Robert, 11, 87
Finney, J.A., 119, 120
Flueck, John A., 10
Forster, Brenda, 146, 209, 215
Fox, Stanford J., 218
Frazier, Charles E., 24
Frease, Dean, 87
Freud, Anna, 119
Friends: selling drugs to, 53; theft of, 110–111
Fun, random targets and crime committed for, 116–117

Gallo, case study of, 1; alcohol and, 160, 161–162, 173; amphetamines and, 163, 171, 172, 173; arson and, 168; assault of a policeman, 165, 168–169; background of, 153; behavior of, in school, 163, 168, 171; cocaine and, 167, 175; contacts for, 47–48; "cool" image of, 153–155; crime and drug relationship for, 177–178, 180; crime committed during a drug deal, 46, 91, 166, 170; development of delinquent career, 159–171; drug dealing and selling by, 55, 166, 172–173; as an expert, 155; future plans for, 182–183; hashish and, 161, 163; importance of drugs for, 174–176; introduced to a source of supply, 50; LSD and, 163–164; marijuana and, 159–160, 161, 162–163, 173–174; mentorship

and, 157, 159, 163, 169–170; mushrooms and, 169; opium and, 169–170; PCP and, 164, 172, 173; peer influence on, 161–162; Quaaludes and, 167–168, 169, 172, 173; reasons for using drugs, 178–181; relationship with brothers, 157–158, 159–161, 163, 169–170; relationship with family, 156–159; responsibility for family and, 158–159; self-perceptions, 153–159; supply specificity and, 51; thefts committed by, 164–166, 170
Gandossy, Robert P., 27
Gang violence, 91–92
Geer, Blanche, 24
Gibbs, Jack, 146, 209, 218
Glaser, Barney, 7, 24, 87
Glassner, Barry, 34, 223
Gold, Martin, 11, 12, 13, 87, 107, 146, 209, 214
Goldstein, Paul J., 10, 110
Goode, Erich, 9, 39, 187
Graves, Theodore D., 119

Haltyn, Thomas V., 21, 142
Hamparian, Donna Martin, 87
Hanlon, Thomas, 10
Hanson, Robert C., 119
Harlan, John P., 103, 107
Harwood, Hendrick J., 27
Hashish: in the Gallo case, 161, 163; in the Norris case, 129–130; selling of, 52
Haskell, M., 187
Hawkins, Gordon J., 13, 218
Hendin, Herbert, 120
Heroin, fear of, 192–193
Hirschi, Travis, 148, 184, 215
Holsti, C.R., 24
Homosexual approach, protection against, 95
Honor: protecting someone else's, 96–97; testing and protecting one's, 95–96; violence and, 88–89, 99
Horowitz, Ruth, 88, 99
Huba, George J., 119
Hubbart, Robert, 10
Huizinga, David H., 9, 10, 11, 12, 17, 20, 21, 22, 27, 39, 45, 58, 87, 88, 90, 99, 119, 120, 121, 133,

145, 146, 177, 187, 209, 210, 216, 219, 220

Incarceration, fear of, 210–213
Inciardi, James A., 10, 27, 84
Injury, denial of, 100, 103
Insanity, drug-crime relationship and, 29
Interactionism, 4–5

Jacobs, Jerry, 5, 24
Jensen, Gary R., 103, 146, 188, 209, 218
Jessor, Richard, 11, 12, 119, 120, 186
Jessor, Shirley L., 11, 12, 119, 120, 186
Johnson, Bruce D., 9, 10, 20, 21, 22, 24, 27, 29, 39, 45, 47, 58, 84, 87, 88, 90, 99, 110, 187, 219, 220
Johnston, Lloyd, 12, 15, 17, 27, 120, 209, 214
Joyce, Briget, 9, 39, 47

Kandel, Denise B., 9, 11, 12, 39, 119, 120, 121, 146, 186, 187, 189, 190
Kaplan, John, 13
Kessler, Ronald, 119
Kevin, case study of, 2; backkground of, 146–147; behavior of, in school, 147; change of values for, 150, 151–152; at a detention home, 148; at Drug Freedom, 148–149; drugs used by, 148; influence of peers on, 147; overdose and suicidal feelings of, 149; reasons for using drugs and getting into trouble, 149; at Rehab House, 149–150; relationship between drugs and theft, 31; relationship with parents, 147–148, 149, 152; type of victim he would choose, 109–110; at a youth camp, 148
King, Charles T., 87
Kipell, Bert S., 8
Kirk, Jerome, 24
Kitsuse, John I., 88
Klemke, Lloyd W., 61
Knowles, Brian, 17, 209, 210, 214
Kohlberg, Laurence, 217

Kozak, Conrad, 184
Krippendorff, Klaus, 24
Kristiansen, Patricia L., 10
Ksander, Margret M., 223

Larson, Lyle E., 119
Lee, Che-Fu, 119
Lemert, Edwin, 217
Levine, Edward M., 184
Levinson, David, 10
Lindelius, Rolf, 97
Lipton, Douglas S., 110
Listening, research method, 7–8
Lofland, John, 88, 99
Logan, John A., 12
Lotecka, Lynn, 148
Loughlin, Julia, 34, 223
LSD: in the Gallo case, 163–164; as a secondary drug, 190
Lubeck, Steven G., 188
Lukkoff, Irving F., 119
Lyerly, Robert R., 146

MacAndrew, Craig, 10, 100
Mack, Julien, 218
Mafia, drug dealing and the, 48–49
Margulies, Rebecca Z., 119
Marijuana: in the Gallo case, 159–160, 161, 162–163, 173–174; influence of peers and the use of, 120–121, 128–129; in the Norris case, 128–129; as a primary commitment drug, 190; selling of, 52; use of, 44–45; use of, preceded other drugs, 189
Marsh, Peter, 88, 99
Matza, David, 4, 5–6, 100, 103, 115, 146
McBride, Duane C., 219
McDowell, Charles P., 103, 107
Mead, Margaret, 119
Media, crimes committed by Norris and the influence of the, 125
Melvinhill, Donald J., 87
Mental instability, drug-crime relationship and, 29
Mentorship, in the Gallo case, 157, 159, 163, 169–170
Merzel, Cheryl, 119, 185
Messeri, Peter, 119
Miller, Marc L., 24
Miller, Thomas, 110

Mitchell, J. Clyde, 119
Montmarquette, Claude, 12
Moral development as a deterrent to crime, 217
Morgan, Patricia, 10
Murphy, Patricia L., 8
Murphy, Peggy, 8
Murphy, Sheigla, 9, 39, 47
Mushrooms: in the Gallo case, 169; in the Norris case, 130

Nash, Jeffrey E., 6
National Youth Survey, 17, 21, 29, 87, 88, 121, 133, 209
Nerlove, Marc, 12
New York State: Division of Alcoholism and Alcohol Abuse, 17; Division of Substance Abuse Services, 17, 20; Office of Drug Abuse Services, 17
Norris, case study of, 2; background of, 121–122; behavior of, in school, 122–123; delinquency and other crimes committed by, 123–125; future plans of, 132–133; influence of the media on, 125; neighborhood of, 122; peer influence on, 127–132; prognosis for, 142, 143; reasons for using drugs and alcohol, 128; relationship with parents, 123–124, 125–127
Nurco, David N., 10

Ochberg, Frank M., 8
Ohlin, Lloyd E., 146
O'Malley, Patrick M., 12, 15, 17, 27, 120, 209, 214
Opium in the Gallo case, 169–170

Packard, Herbert L., 13
Parents, relationship with: in the Elizabeth case, 133–135; in the Gallo case, 156–159; in the Kevin case, 147–148, 149, 152; in the Norris case, 123–124, 125–127
PCP, 6; fear of, 192–193; in the Gallo case, 164, 172, 173
Peers: drug use influenced by, 120–121, 128–130, 147; influence of, in the Elizabeth case, 135–137; influence of, in the Gallo case,

161–162; influence of, in the Kevin case, 147; influence of, in the Norris case, 127–132
Pernanen, Kai, 87
Perspectives, use of, 4–6
Peterson, David M., 148
Petronio, Richard J., 11, 12
Pfefferbaum, Adolph, 8
Polk, Kenneth, 87
Pollinger, Ann, 120
Potvin, Raymond H., 119
Preble, Edward, 110
Precocity, 11
Prescription-type drugs: in Norris case, 129; selling of, 52
Protection against homosexual approach, violence and, 95
Protection of property, violence and, 94–95, 170
Protectionism, violence and, 99
Purse snatching, 112, 113

Quaaludes in the Gallo case, 167–168, 169, 172, 173

Rachal, J. Valley, 10
Random targets and crime committed for fun, 116–117
Rappeport, M., 8, 9
Rawlings, M. Lawrence, 88, 89
Rehab House, 149–150, 185
Reinarman, Craig, 9, 39, 47
Reimer, David J., 12, 13, 87, 146, 209, 214
Research methods: advantages and limitations of methodology, 25; assessing the data, 24–25; characteristics of respondents, 19–23; drug user categories, 21; fieldwork and sample selection, 18–19; how criminal involvement was determined, 21; interview schedule, 23–24; of listening, 7–8; questions asked, 8–13
Research site, selection of, 15–17
Retribution for insults, 108–109
Revenge, 93
Richards, Pamela, 146, 209, 215
Richardson, S., 24
Richmond, Lynn F., 87
Roberts, Chester, 21, 142
Robins, Lee N., 11, 142, 187

Rogers, J.W., 187
Rojek, Dean G., 103, 188
Room, Robin, 10, 33, 87, 88, 97
Rosen, Lawrence, 10
Roth, Jeffrey A., 11
Roth, Walton T., 8
Rush: selling of, 52; use of, 193–194

Salvin I., 97
Sanchez, Jose, 84
Schatzman, Leonard, 4, 24
Schmeidler, James, 21, 87, 99, 110, 220
School: behavior of Elizabeth in, 136; behavior of Gallo in, 163, 168, 171; behavior of Kevin in, 147; behavior of Norris in, 122–123
Schools and personnel, vindictive vandalism and, 107–108
Schrayer, D., 8, 9
Schuster, Richard, 87
Schwartz, Gary, 88, 99
Schwartz, Howard, 5, 24
Schwartz, Richard D., 24
Sechrest, Lew, 24
Sederstrom, John, 146, 184
Sellin, Thorsten, 11, 87
Senay, Edward, 10
Shaffer, John W., 10
Shannon, Lyle W., 142
Shared perspective, 5
Shoplifting: in the Elizabeth case, 139–140; in the Gallo case, 164
Short, James F., 88, 99, 187
Single, Eric, 9, 39
Skipper, James K., Jr., 146
Skolnick, Arlene, 217
Smith, Charles P., 21, 142
Speed: definition of, 192; experimenting with, 191–192; selling of, 52
Spradley, James, 6, 24
Spunt, Barry, 110
Stash, theft of, 45–46
Strausburg, Paul A., 87
Strauss, Anselm, 4, 7, 24
Strodtbeck, Fred L., 88, 99, 187
Strug, David, 110
Stuck, Mary F., 223
Suchman, E., 119
Sutherland, Edwin, 146
Sykes, Gresham M., 100, 103, 115, 146

Taylor, Steve, 4, 5, 24
Theft: to acquire consumer goods,, 62–64; of automobiles, 105, 106–107; avoidance of helpless victims, 112; careless victims right for, 104–107; of cash, 72–75; of drug dealers and buyers, 110; drug use and, 31–32, 84; equated with borrowing, 106–107; of friends and family, 110–111; gender and, 83–84; inappropriate victims for, 110–112; motives for, 30, 62; planned, 66–68; purse snatching, 112, 113; reasons for, 220; routine, 65–66; as shopping for goods, 64; as sport, 81–83; of stash, 45–46; unplanned, 68–72; as work/business, 75–81
Tinklenberg, Jared R., 8
Tittle, Charles, 218
Toby, Jackson, 107
Toch, Hans, 88, 99
Tracy, Paul A., 11
Truzzi, Marcello, 4
Tudor, Cynthia G., 148
Tummit, Melvin M., 87

Ulman, Richard, 120

Valium, 189
Vandalism: random, 115–116; vindictive, 107–108
Verstehen, 4
Victims, adolescents' views of, 221; avoidance of helpless victims, 112; careless victims right for theft, 104–107; corporations as, 110, 111; crime without a victim, 115–117; denial of, 103, 115, 116; deserving, 107–110; drug dealers and buyers as victims, 110; empathy for, 111–112; inappropriate, 110–112; negation or escalation of harm to victim, 113–115; random targets and crime committed for fun, 116–117
Violence: alcohol/drugs and increased, 32, 87 –88, 97–99; characteristics of subjects most involved in, 89–91; denial of injury and, 100; disinhibition and, 97–99; drug distribution and, 91; ethnic antagonism

Violence *(continued)*
  and, 92–93; fighting and, 99;
  gang, 91–92; heavy drug users and,
  90, 99; honor and, 88–89, 95–97,
  99; how and why, occurs, 91–97;
  justifications for, 103; protection
  against homosexual approach and,
  95; protection of property and,
  94–95, 170; protectionism and, 99;
  retribution for insults, 108–109;
  revenge and, 93; ritualized aggression among youths and, 88;
  serious, committed by subjects,
  91–94, 100; types of youths who
  commit felony assaults, 88; vindictive vandalism and, 107–108
Visher, Christy, 11

Waldorf, Dan, 9, 39, 47
Washington, Melvin, 10

Webb, Eugene J., 24
Weiner, Neil, 11
Weis, Joseph G., 146, 184
Weissman, James C., 10
West, David J., 88, 89, 99
Whiteman, Martin, 119
Williams, Jay R., 12, 27
Wingard, James A., 119
Wish, Eric, 10, 11, 20, 21, 22, 27,
  29, 39, 45, 58, 87, 88, 90, 99,
  110, 142, 187, 219, 220
Wolfgang, Marvin E., 11, 12, 21, 87,
  209

Yablonsky, Louis, 88, 146, 187
Yamaguchi, Kazuo, 146
Youth-in-Transition Project, 209

Zimring, Franklin E., 13, 218

# About the Authors

**Cheryl Carpenter** is a Ph.D. candidate in the Department of Sociology at Syracuse University.

**Barry Glassner** is Chair, Department of Sociology, and professor of sociology at the University of Connecticut at Storrs. He was formerly a professor at Syracuse University. He has coauthored several books, including *A Rationalist Methodology for the Social Sciences, Drugs in Adolescent Worlds, Discourse in the Social Sciences*, and *Essential Interactionism*, and he has written numerous articles. He received a Ph.D. in sociology from Washington University.

**Bruce D. Johnson** is the principal investigator of two NIDA-funded projects, the "Economic Behavior of Street Opiate Users" and "Behavioral Sciences Training Program in Drug Abuse Research." He also directed a seven-year Interdisciplinary Research Center for the Study of the Relations of Drugs and Alcohol to Crime, of which this book is one primary product. He has authored *Marijuana Users and Drug Subcultures, Drug Use and Abuse among U.S. Minorities, Minorities and Drugs, Taking Care of Business: The Economics of Crime by Heroin Abusers*, and numerous articles, agency publications, and presentations on drug use, abuse, and criminality. His current research interests focus upon the linkages of cocaine and crack to criminality. He received his Ph.D. in sociology from Columbia University.

**Julia Loughlin** is an associate professor in the Department of Sociology at Syracuse University. She has written articles for *Knowledge*, the *Journal of Medical Education*, and *Clinical Research*, and she coauthored *Research on Human Subjects: Problems of Social Control in Medical Experimentation and Drugs in Adolescent Worlds*. Her Ph.D. in sociology is from Columbia University.